ISBN 81 7062 168 2
ISSN 0970-2512
Apr-Jun 2009, Vol. 24 (2)

INDIAN DEFENCE REVIEW

Foremost since 1986

www.indiandefencereview.com

Cover photograph : INS Shishumar leaving Goa harbour for a sortie. Photograph by Capt S K Sharma, IN

EVERY JANUARY, APRIL, JULY & OCTOBER FROM NEW DELHI

idr@indiandefencereview.com
lancer@lancerpublishers.com

Conte

The Chinese are coming!

A China tourism hoarding outside Kathmandu airport with the message, 'Welcome to Nepal-Gateway to China'.

IDR Net Edition: www.indiandefencereview.com

Online Military Bookshop: www.lancerpublishers.com

Contributors may please send thier articles, not exceeding 3500 words, in a disk with a hard copy, with suitable illustrations to Editor, Indian Defence Review.

The views expressed are the contributors' own and do not necessarily represent the opinions or policies of the Indian Defence Review.

Publisher: Capt Bharat Verma, Indian Defence Review, Lancer Publishers & Distributors, New Delhi.

Advertising: For information and rates, please contact Anuradda Verma, Director Coordination or the Publisher.

How to reach us: Indian Defence Review, 2/42 (B) Sarvapriya Vihar, New Delhi-110016.
+91 11 41759461, 26854691 • Telefax +91 11 26960404 • idr@indiandefencereview.com • www.indiandefencereview.com
Printed at Sona Printers Pvt. Ltd., New Delhi.

Price: Rs 300

Develop Cutting Edge Defence Industries

TO DEVELOP CUTTING EDGE DEFENCE industries, New Delhi must eschew the inherent divisive tendencies. Instead of consolidating Aero India 2009 as the foremost Asian aerospace show, we reduced its functional importance by taking away two aspects integral to it. The Ministry of Civil Aviation held a separate international civil air power show at Hyderabad and Bangalore, which ended with the first international space exhibition that practically had no visitors. The uncalled for turf war between different ministries created unwanted segmentation and compartmentalization between space, civil and military air power assets that are technically inter-linked. Besides diluting the holistic structure of Aero India, conduct of three different exhibitions trebled the cost to the Indian taxpayer and the foreign vendor!

It was pompous of the Defence Minister in Aero India 2005 to announce that "the defence sector has been opened up for private investment and it is not that we are dying for investment. It is for the interested companies to make necessary investment."

To be a dominant Asian power, India requires to consolidate the genius of the private sector with existing national assets to build state-of-the-art defence industries. This unity of purpose will enable New Delhi to defend its expanding economic interests in a globalized environment and permit it to speak from a position of strength in the existing hostile neighborhood.

However, to achieve the twin goals of becoming an economic powerhouse and the ability to militarily defend its democratic values, it is essential that we exploit the favorable international environment for deep military technology transfers. This alone can modernize the defence industries. Therefore cutting edge thinking at the political level is essential too.

With increasing fundamentalist upsurge, majority of the Islamic countries continue to regress and therefore remain technology-deficit. China at best is a 'reverse- engineering' genius. None of these countries, in any case, will be eager to improve India's military might! Technology transfer from Russia is possible, but only to a point. Of course, most of the technology available is archaic.

The West has the latest technologies and weapon platforms that India needs to equip its Armed Forces to face the combined threat posed by authoritarian regimes on its land borders. While communist China is denied acquisition of advanced sensitive military technologies by the Western alliance, there exists a unique opening for New Delhi to access the same. This can help create a formidable defence industrial hub in Asia, if the opportunity is seized.

On two counts, the threat perception dictates that India rapidly modernize its Armed Forces as well as its internal security apparatus. First, public confirmation by Islamabad that the China-Pakistan axis threatens India jointly dictates swift modernization of the armed forces. Second, the inevitable Talibanization of Pakistan and Bangladesh creeping towards our borders, threatens to destroy the multi-cultural social fabric of India. It is imperative that the threat from the Taliban is contained and destroyed within Pakistan. Therefore, to neutralize these two threats, the military requires extraordinary offensive capabilities, which are available with the West alone.

To develop India into a major low-cost high-end R&D base and defence industries hub in Asia, New Delhi should generate intelligent policy shifts to create a business friendly environment that attracts frontier technologies. It was pompous of the Defence Minister in Aero India 2005 to announce that "the defence sector has been opened up for private investment and it is not that we are dying for investment. It is for the interested companies to make necessary investment." Such diplomatic gaffe out of lack of confidence results in dampening the confidence and enthusiasm of the foreign investor.

To attract FDI, the foreign investor's stake should be raised from 26 percent to 49 percent. To instill confidence in the foreign entrepreneur, increase his share to 51 percent where cutting edge technology is brought in.

Instead of re-inventing the wheel, we need to leapfrog the technological gap by accepting deep transfers of technology against the offset clause. This in turn will subsequently ensure that we have world-class equipment to export.

To attract FDI, the foreign investor's stake should be raised from 26 percent to 49 percent. To instill confidence in the foreign entrepreneur, increase his share to 51 percent where cutting edge technology is brought in.

FDI is Primarily influenced by a stable and favorable investment climate, economic freedom and a fair market access. Therefore for New Delhi to expect that the foreign investor will invest his resources where he exercises no significant control, cannot access other markets within the country or for exports, and is restrained by strict capacity controls instead of scales of economy is unrealistic. Indian bureaucratese and government over regulations are perceived to pose the biggest risk to his investment. This perception needs to be corrected through intensive dialogue.

The Defence Minister should announce a slew of measures to deregulate the defence industry sector during 2009 – incorporate the genius of the private sector to compete with the sluggish public sector, increase the legitimate stakes of the foreign investor in the economic pie as an incentive, and announce India's readiness to join the 'global factory' concept with the West.

A technologically advanced and vibrant defence industry is critical for India's security and its global aspirations. Therefore, it is time the MoD fine-tunes its policies by bringing them at par with the existing international business norms, instead of living in a mental ghetto.

Bharat Verma

BHARAT VERMA
bharat.verma@indiandefencereview.com

Indian Intelligence

BY ANAND K VERMA

INDIAN INTELLIGENCE IS FREQUENTLY in the news, often for the wrong reasons. It is a favourite kicking target for a large number of those who compulsively articulate, like the media, political leaders, academics, etc. Why should it be so when its stellar contributions to national security have quite often been praised by different Prime Ministers at different times in India's history? A public acknowledgement of the services rendered is also indicated by the Padma awards, bestowed on intelligence personnel from time to time.

But there is no denying that the system suffers from many fault lines, some systemic, some a legacy of the past but most due to reluctance, express or implicit at various levels in the power structure of the country, to bring about a change. It is the cumulative mindset, operating at the cutting level in the country which is mostly responsible for this dismal state of affairs. Also, the mindset does not or perhaps cannot change in a few short decades. National security has never been a hot issue with the people at large as evident from several public polls conducted in the country. Removal of the fault lines, therefore, remains a low priority. The episodic prominence the subject receives now and then has proved incapable of influencing the frozen channels in the subconscious.

Investigations into Mumbai 26/11 events reveal that intercepts of Voice over Internet Protocol conversations between the terrorists in Mumbai and their handlers in Pakistan had to come from foreign agencies. States share intelligence in absolute self interest and not for considerations of ethics, morality or law.

For any State, Intelligence is a prime necessity, not only to know about adversaries but also about friends, so as to remain forewarned about their intentions and capabilities and to prevent surprises. It is a multi-dimensional complex activity but its basics remain the same – collection, analysis, counter intelligence and covert actions. A fair idea about the functioning of Indian intelligence can be made by examining how well it is equipped for handling these four sectors.

Collection is a three pronged exercise, each arm performing a distinct role. Published information provides the bulk of intelligence, close to 80 percent. Well researched articles and books and field journalists not only prove invaluable source of key facts, they also provide reliable insights into any situation a country maybe interested in. Advent of computers now makes recording, indexing and retrieval of such information a lot easier, but if the organization is not computer savvy, a good part of such information would fail to get stored. One suspects that such skills are still to be universally acquired and mastered in the world of Indian intelligence. If this is correct, it bespeaks of a handicap at the starting level itself.

Technological and scientific means invariably produce intelligence of high accuracy. The gadgetry required for technical collections is very expensive and the state of art equipment is not available in the market. Investigations into Mumbai 26/11 events reveal that intercepts of Voice over Internet Protocol conversations between the terrorists in Mumbai and their handlers in Pakistan had to come from foreign agencies. States share intelligence in absolute self interest and not for considerations of ethics, morality or law. Imagine, if foreigners had not been the victims of 26/11 carnage, the requisite information in all probability would have remained hidden from Indian authorities. Selective concealment is an acceptable reality of the intelligence world. At no stage in the past did India's collaborating partners disclose to India anything about Pakistan's ongoing nuclear weapon development programme and China's stellar role in it, when it was widely known that this programme directly targetted India.

Anand K Verma
former Chief of RAW and author of Reassessing Pakistan
verma_anandkumar@yahoo.com

The solution lies in having an in-house research and development capability with an extremely high powered technical staff, second to none, that can work on dedicated technical requirements of the intelligence. It calls for a very high level of funding, something which is not very kindly looked upon by the fund managers of the country. The alternative is to tie up with governmental and non-governmental hi-tech institutions to look for answers.

The key to the highest grade of intelligence is held by human sources to raise whom a great deal of focussed attention, ingenuity, daredevilry and deep pockets are necessary. It is not a job of a run of the mill kind which can be performed by anyone.

The key to the highest grade of intelligence is held by human sources to raise whom a great deal of focussed attention, ingenuity, daredevilry and deep pockets are necessary. It is not a a run of the mill kind of job which can be performed by anyone. A successful operator, capable of recruiting high net worth human agents, has to belong to a rare breed. Identifying such potentially gifted operators and enrolling these into intelligence then becomes a matter of incentives and competitive remunerations.

This area has been a long standing weakness of Indian intelligence. The problem dates back to the dawn of Indian independence when many of the legacies of the British colonial rule were uncritically accepted and passed on down the line. The British had created a steel framework to rule the country and a police system which, among other things, kept watch on nascent political trends. The steel frame attracted gifted individuals, scholars and thinkers because of the extraordinarily high compensation package. The prime tool made available to the police was repression. There was no comparable incentive for a bright Indian to join its ranks, except that of getting employed. The steel frame had lorded over British India. The legacies continued after the British left. Even today the rule exists that ensures that no member of any other service can overtake his IAS colleague of the same seniority in emoluments or rank even if he is a genius. Then why should the Indian intelligence attract the best when it is required to exist at an inferior level? In point of fact it does not. The results that get produced, therefore, are matching the caliber that is to be found in such establishments today.

This problem can be fixed only by the political managers of the country. India now finds itself in a very complex national security environment, requiring intelligence to become the first line of defence. Men who work in it must have the capacity to develop the highest levels of professional values and solid leadership qualities.

Centuries ago a Chinese sage, Sun Tzu, admonished: "Nothing should be as favourably regarded as Intelligence; nothing should be as generously regarded as intelligence; nothing should be as confidential as the work of intelligence". To produce intelligence of this order, service in intelligence must be made as attractive as the British had made their premier colonial service in India. intelligence organizations of other countries run their establishments on this paradigm. They often are the best paid organizations in their own country. The CIA is reputed to attract the highest number of PhDs from the best schools into its ranks, as compared to other US organizations. The terms and conditions of service, apart from the opportunities of work, serve as a magnet to pull the talent of supreme quality among whom will be engineers, management specialists, scholars, bankers, scientists, economists, sociologists and academics. In India, unfortunately, it is only the second grade that thinks of gravitating towards intelligence. In recent times, even this category is not offering to look at intelligence as a career. A revolving door policy as in the US should also not be ruled out to draw in expertise and eminence.

Another negative factor is that intelligence in India has no locus in law, especially for those who work in foreign intelligence. India's intelligence agencies have not been created by Acts of the Parliament. The entire range of foreign operations is covered by just executive instructions. An instruction to operate in a foreign country ipso facto implies a requirement to break the local laws but no legal authority exists for issuing such instructions or indemnifying the would be violator under the laws of the home country. This is a very serious lacuna which does not seem to have caught the attention of anyone in authority. As the law stands today all those who issue such executive instructions and those who carry out these instructions in a foreign country to spy and steal secrets can be held accountable under the Indian laws. Foreign Intelligence is the only organization directed by the government to violate the local laws of the country of operation, but the government does so without enjoying any legal authority to do so. This state of affairs is reflective of the apathy in which Intelligence is held in India.

Analysis comes in the picture to make a sense from collected raw intelligence in juxta position with publicly available data. It interprets the pooled information and comes up with likely scenarios of what may happen. This exercise has to be meaningful because Government's policy decisions could be based on them. In fast moving contexts like an ongoing terrorist engagement, speed of the analysis becomes a key determinant to catch the action. However, the process as it takes place has serious flaws.

These arise from a mistaken apprehension that intelligence will seek to overtake the role of policy making or even replace it. In fact intelligence has no commanding part in the making of policy. On the other hand the policy maker has to set the agenda for intelligence to work on so that intelligence becomes custom produced. However, intelligence support to policy makers becomes more meaningful if it is allowed participation in policy debates, told about gaps in knowledge and encouraged to disclose constraints on intelligence capabilities to close these gaps, and focus its analysis on policy issues and options under scrutiny. If such opportunities are missing, intelligence works in the dark, benefiting no one.

India now finds itself in a very complex national security environment, requiring intelligence to become the first line of defence.

Years ago in an article by me the role of the analyst was described in the following words: "A good intelligence analyst is an asset to the national security apparatus. In the intelligence organizations in India, analysts work for several years at the same desk and are therefore able to develop a much better insight and expertise in their fields than those serving other wings of the government. Although not infallible, sound analysis can often point to the likely course of events. It takes into account all the information available, secret or published, mentions what remains unknown if it is relevant to the issue under study, describes the reality of the facts stated, indicating guardedly of how they were obtained, and transparently and cogently explains the logic of the conclusions and estimates it projects. The analyst's expertise serves as the backdrop to the inferences drawn – the deeper his experience, the more value he can get out of the data assembled to make his submissions of likely scenarios of the future. When the analyst is tasked in the context of national security by the policy maker, his study is lifted out of the academic realm and becomes a basis for choosing a course of policy".

Indian Intelligence can boast of having in its ranks many excellent analysts with deep expertise and insights but it is not certain if full use has been made of them. There is hardly any culture in the country requiring policy papers to be prepared on national security issues, with participation from intelligence, diplomats, military specialists, scientists etc., detailing likely scenarios and examining the pros and cons of each. Kargil and Mumbai 26/11 demonstrated the pitfalls of absence of coordinated analysis. Where coordination is called for between the centre and the states to deal with an internal security problem in a cohesive manner, the Indian Constitution can become sometimes the stumbling block as powers stand delegated to the states, some of whom may disagree with the Centre's approach. In the face of such differences the tasks of Intelligence become even more difficult. Dealing with Naxalism is an issue which proves this assumption.

The quality of Indian Intelligence analysis has been applauded by foreign intelligence partners. Senator Claiborne Pell, former Chairman of the US Senate Foreign Relations Committee, is on record, stating that Indian analysis of developments in Afghanistan in the late 1980s was the only accurate indication available to the West, of what was happening there.

In the Indian system the operations officer and the analyst often double up for each other. In small outfits this may not be a serious handicap but as organizations grow larger, the two streams of intelligence should have their own dedicated cadres for best results.

Counter intelligence prime functions are identifying operations and agents of foreign intelligence organizations, and protecting the secrets of the State from penetration through use

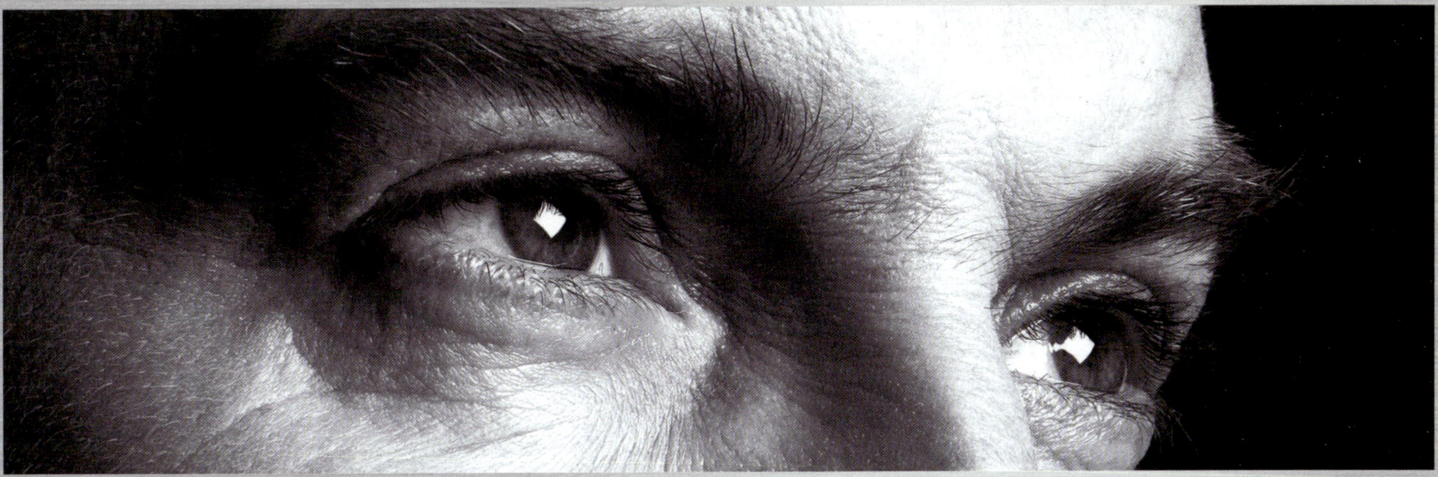

of human agents and technical means like bugs, monitoring, surveillance from space, interception of communication channels, etc. Lack of national awareness generally for the needs of security makes the task of counter intelligence more difficult. Dangers arise equally from hostile and friendly agencies, driven by the operational necessity of discovering protected information.

Results from counter intelligence have been a mixed bag of successes and shame. Over the years counter intelligence has been able to unmask several of the Indian agents of all the major intelligence organizations of the world. The shame lies in the fact that it could not prevent foreign penetration even into their senior ranks. Actual truth may hurt even moere. There is a general belief in the country that the influence of foreign intelligence organizations has reached deep into the civil society. Suspicion was cast once even on a Prime Minister. Due to various reasons exposures of highly placed Indian moles has always proved to be a daunting task.

The quality of Indian Intelligence analysis has been applauded by foreign intelligence partners. Senator Claiborne Pell, former Chairman of the US Senate Foreign Relations Committee, is on record, stating that Indian analysis of developments in Afghanistan in the late 1980s was the only accurate indication available to the West, of what was happening there.

The field of counter intelligence has exponentially grown with the advent of international terrorism. This phenomenon poses a multi-dimensional threat of mass destruction through acquisition of a nuclear device, mass disruption of communication systems through cyber attacks, ideological brain washing through selective interpretations of religious doctrines, and jehadi military style attacks at random on people and key sites. Countering such terrorism has to be a composite exercise requiring participation, apart from intelligence, of other organs of the state such as armed forces, state police, crisis management groups, paramilitary directorates and science and technical communities among others. Countering ideological indoctrination in a sustained manner is perhaps yet to kick start in the country. It is not that the dangers are not realized but extraneous factors like vote bank politics relegate the issue to the lowest priority.

Since terrorist organizations which work on the cell system are extremely difficult to penetrate, good preventive intelligence may not be easily forthcoming, despite the best efforts of the intelligence agencies. Because of large numbers of what can constitute a target it may also not be possible to provide effective perimeter security to every single target. If terror attacks like Mumbai 26/11 continue, sooner or later the authorities will have to decide and declare the policy steps which should compel their sponsors to weigh the costs involved. A new counter terrorism architecture in the country, aiming at better analysis, coordination and prevention, can at best remain a good defensive exercise, but the need of the hour may turn out to be offensive rather than defensive tactics.

In offensive counter terrorism, the intelligence and armed forces will have distinctive and definitive roles. They may have to work together on the lines of the CIA and US military command that have been jointly handling Iraq and Afghanistan.

Nations are no longer squeamish about employment of covert techniques though specific operations may continue to be shrouded by the mystique of deniability. Nations seem willing to use any tool of statecraft to strengthen national security though the arm chair liberal or the abstract human rights activist may raise objection on grounds of ethics and morality. The Indian state in the past was not hesitant in using such instruments. This is widely known. But one cannot switch to covert actions overnight. Long preparations are necessary. If "all options" are being kept open to deal with the vicious terrorist threat from across the borders, it will be proper to give a green signal to the intelligence now to make its covert plans. Pakistan is proving to be an enduring threat. A redefinition of national interests will bring out that India needs to move out of its-self created soft image and to entrust the Intelligence with a new range of responsibilities to become more secure.

Even otherwise, Intelligence needs to develop new perspectives as globalization advances, defining a new permissiveness in the political environment, creating opportunities for newer forms of economic penetration and triggering fast technological changes which render borders meaningless. After the demise of the Soviet Union the world has been left uni-polar but the equation of balance of power remains far from settled. In Asia, the rivalry between three rising entities, China, Japan and India, each of whom will be competitively looking for new markets and new sources of

TO SUPPORT INDIA'S FRONTLINE
YOU NEED TO UNDERSTAND INDIA'S BACKGROUND.
For over 60 years BAE Systems, the world's number one land systems company, has been in partnership with India, supporting them as a leading defence force. Whether it's Howitzers on land, Hawks in the air, Harriers at sea, or the technology behind them, BAE Systems has played a key role with India's armed forces. But it's not just about hardware. Partnership is about sharing technology, working with Indian industry and investing in training. And when you can deliver all of these capabilities, that's a real advantage.
BAE SYSTEMS
REAL PARTNERSHIP. REAL ADVANTAGE.
www.baesystems.com/india

resources, can become acute. The national security architecture worldwide remains shifting in a kaleidoscopic pattern, recreating newer axes of conflict and conciliationall the time. Add to them the hunger for land and water, symbolized by refugee flows and mass migrations, and differing international concerns for climatic changes and ecology. Correct analysis and assessment of trends over a vast spectrum has become a national necessity to keep the country's interests safe and secure. Knowledge now is the new coefficient of power and Indian Intelligence must keep step with such knowledge.

The current systems are unlikely to match the challenges that have emerged. Drastic reforms are necessary to unshackle Intelligence from its rigid bureaucratic mould and to invest it with a dynamism and innovative spirit which should be the hallmark of an unconventional organization. The very first step of reform should begin by giving Indian Intelligence the backing of legislative enactments. The laws should provide a degree of autonomy which frees intelligence from all bureaucratic restraints and controls relating to financial management, administrative functions, pay scales, recruitment, posting and promotions, hire and fire policies and enforcement of discipline. The laws should spell out the charter and authorize the Central Government to fix broad targets within the charter. This will prevent misuse of the institutions by those in authority. The laws should hold intelligence accountable to the Cabinet or its committee for security but also create a parliamentary committee for oversight. Detailed rules can be worked out to determine the parameters of oversight and areas of intelligence work over which it will be exercised, in consultation with the parliament. The laws should give the right to the Government to authorize any kind of covert action and keep all such activities outside the ambit of oversight. The process of oversight and accountability can be expected to keep intelligence on its toes. However, even after such reforms, errors due to human frailties and intellectual stubbornness will not all disappear, but their numbers can be expected to be far less.

> In offensive counter terrorism, the intelligence and armed forces will have distinctive and definitive roles. They may have to work together on the lines of the CIA and US military command that have been jointly handling Iraq and Afghanistan.

There is a new area of activity which Intelligence must consider if it has not already done so. Outsourcing, which globalization has promoted, has a good potential for intelligence work. The Japanese corporate world and intelligence have cooperated with each other over the past several years with both reaping good dividends out of such collaboration. The US is believed to have taken major steps in this direction. According to one estimate the US Intelligence community invests 70% of its budget on its joint ventures with the American Industrial Complex. The Indian corporations are also traversing the multinational route. One may expect that overtures to them will be rewarding to intelligence.

One last word. Is there any way that can measure the depth of devotion and commitment of Intelligence to the national cause? The following anecdote can be a revealing guide. At the height of the Afghan resistance to Soviet Union in 1989, the situation in Kabul became so dangerous that the US, British and other Western countries withdrew their Ambassadors and staff from the country. Our foreign office and Ambassador wanted to follow suit, Intelligence included. Intelligence refused. While others came back to Delhi, Intelligence remained at Kabul to continue to fly the Indian flag over the Embassy in Kabul.

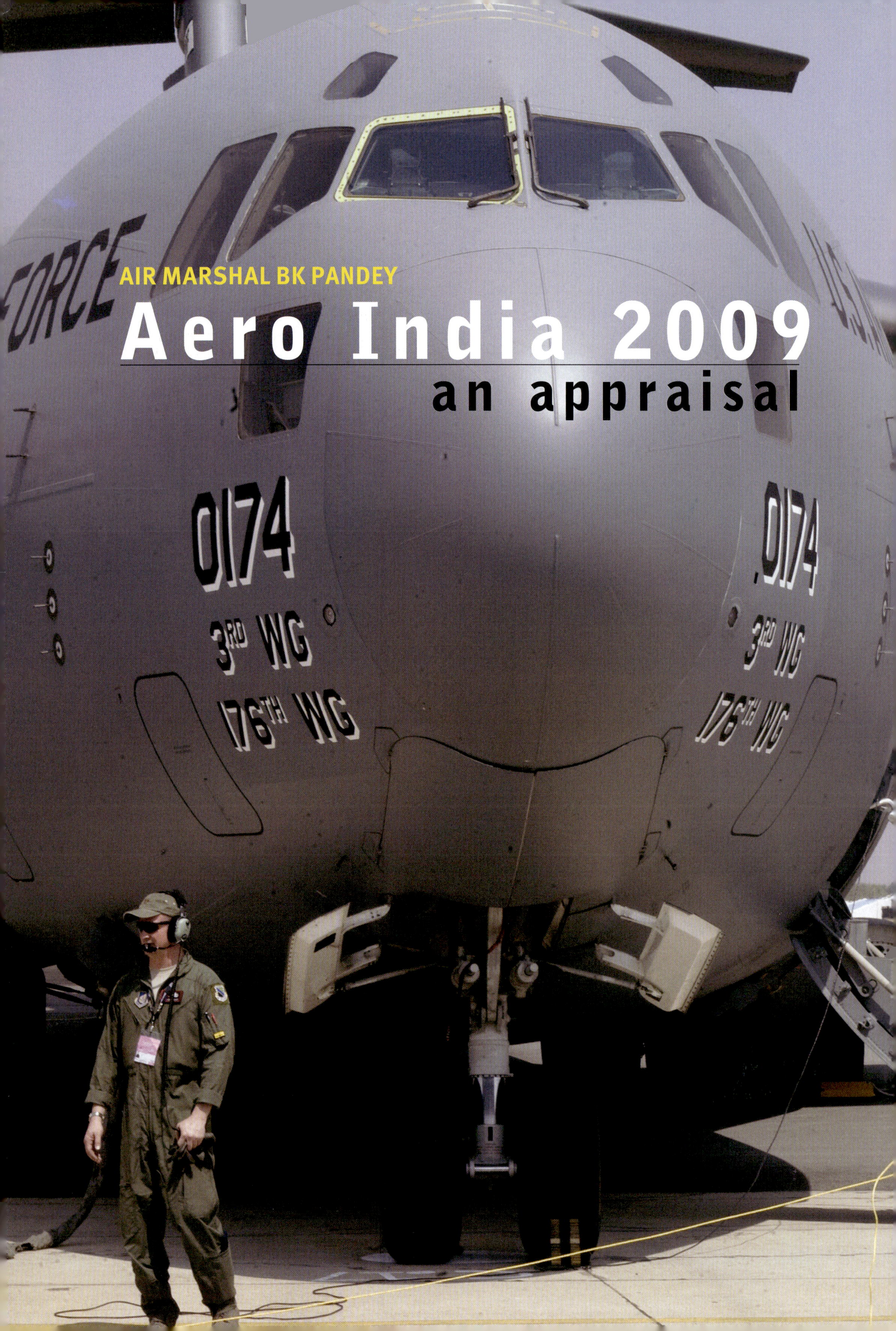

AIR MARSHAL BK PANDEY

Aero India 2009

an appraisal

Aero India 2009, a prestigious international air show opened on February 11 at Air Force Station, Yelahanka in the northern suburbs of Bangalore. The five-day event was kicked off by the Defence Minister of India, AK Antony accompanied by a retinue of VIPs, military and civilian, witnessed by surging crowds of lesser mortals. The inaugural ceremony was accompanied by the usual unsubdued enthusiasm and fanfare even as the world struggled to come to terms with the global economic convulsions that have engulfed practically all nations big and small, albeit to varying degrees. Dispelling apprehensions about the ominous shadows on Aero India 2009 cast by the deepening economic distress especially amongst the leading developed economies that dominate the global aerospace industry, in all, 592 companies including 303 from abroad were present at the air show. In comparison with Aero India 2007, the number of participants had in fact increased by nearly 100, no mean achievement in the context of the discouraging economic environment.

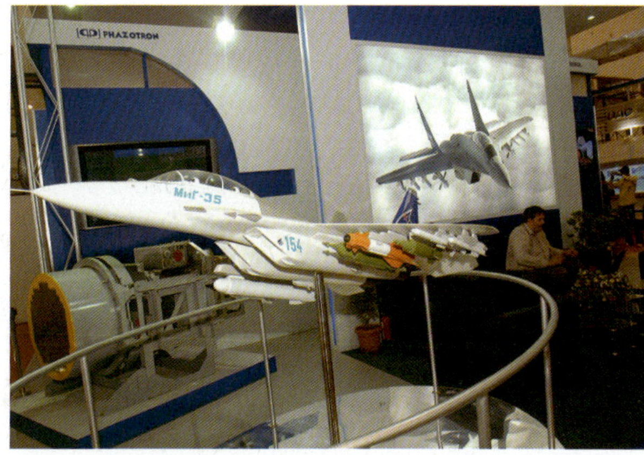

Historical Perspective

Aero India was held for the first time in 1996, eighty seven years after the first such event in the world that was organized in Paris only with domestic participants. The timing of Aero India 2009 is of particular significance as although in existence only for 13 years, in a sense, it marks a centenary of air shows as it comes precisely 100 years after the pioneering French exposition! However, the Indian effort has a long way to go before it can hope to come anywhere close to the Paris Air Show, which is acknowledged as the largest exposition in the world in the regime of the global aerospace industry. The Paris Air Show has enjoyed international status for the last six decades.

Air Marshal BK Pandey is former AOC-in-C Training Command, IAF
bejoy.pandey@gmail.com

Other important international events of this nature are routinely held usually every two years in different parts of the world, namely Farnborough, Berlin, Moscow, Dubai, Singapore and Zhuhai (Guangdong Province, China). The expositions in Moscow and Zhuhai are recent entrants on the international scene and are unique as these provide opportunities to obtain insight into the

new capabilities and potential of the resurgent aerospace industry in Russia and China that for decades have been shrouded in mystery behind impenetrable curtains of different types.

Implications for the Domestic Aerospace Industry

The strategic objectives of Aero India transcend mere festivity and entertainment for the general public provided by an impressive line up of a variety of military and civil aircraft. Excitement amongst the spectators is heightened by the breathtaking aerial displays by the latest generation of combat platforms from the leading manufacturers of the world. On a more serious point, India being one of the largest importer of weapon systems in the world, an exposition such as Aero India 2009 provided the opportunity to the global aerospace industry to showcase the latest technological advancements and future trends in the regime of military and civil aviation, aerial weapons and other related systems or equipment. Israel, which has overtaken Russia as a supplier of high technology military hardware was present in strength with a variety of products on offer that included UAVs, new air defence systems and the Conformal Airborne Warning and

Control System configured around a Gulfstream 550 platform. Vying for a slice of the pie were practically all the big names in the aerospace industry in the US, Europe, Russia and South America.

Although there is no information available on any major deal concluded during the air show, it did provide a convenient platform for interaction between the aerospace industry and potential markets for exchange of information and ideas. It also provided the opportunity for the initiation of dialogue that in due course could lead to collaborative arrangements and joint ventures. Whatever be the technological status, no country today attempts to develop or manufacture a new generation aircraft without collaboration or joint venture. As these have now become a pre-requisite for any country venturing into design, development and manufacture of aircraft, there would have been opportunities galore at Aero India for even small and medium Indian aerospace companies in the private sector. This was manifest in the fact that there were nearly as many Indian companies participating in the air

show as from abroad. And a majority of the Indian companies present were from the private sector. The exercise has also been of immense benefit to the Indian aerospace industry in the public sector and the government owned Research & Development Organizations.

The fortunes of the private Indian aerospace companies have in addition received a major fillip by certain favorable changes in the Defence Procurement Procedure (DPP). The newly introduced "Offset Clause" makes it mandatory for a foreign contractor to plough back 30 to 50 per cent of the value of contract of Rs 300 crore or higher into the Indian aerospace industry. However, fulfilling the requirement of the Offset Clause in some cases could become a difficult proposition especially in the case of mega deals like the $10 billion (Rs 50000 crore) contract for the 126 Medium Multi-Role Combat Aircraft (MMRCA) for the Indian Air Force (IAF). This contract has the potential to create $5 billion (Rs 25000 crore) worth of business for the Indian aerospace industry, a veritable windfall for a sector that is just learning to walk. On its part, the domestic aerospace industry would need to rise to the occasion to exploit the enormous potential that lies embedded in procurement of defence equipment from foreign sources. Seemingly a tall order, nevertheless quite achievable if the private sector has a level playing field. As per the Minister of Defence,

plans for modernization of the armed forces will continue, notwithstanding the recession in the economy. That certainly would be music to the ears of the Indian aerospace industry.

MMRCA FOR THE IAF

No proposal for acquisition of combat aircraft has generated as much hype, interest and excitement in the global aerospace industry as the $10 billion MMRCA tender which has been underway since the early 21st century. There are six aircraft in the race, two from the US, three from Europe and one from Russia. Four of the six types, i.e. the Boeing F/A 18 Super Hornet, the Lockheed Martin F16 IN Super Viper, the Eurofighter Typhoon and the Russian MiG 35 were present at the air show and the visitors were duly impressed with the highly

impressive flying displays. The two other contenders, the Dasault Rafale and the SAAB Gripen were conspicuous by their absence. The true capability of all the contenders would be assessed in the grueling flight evaluation expected to commence in the near future.

As the process of selection has so far reached only the technical evaluation stage, it is difficult to speculate on the likely winner of the contract as also the time frame for induction of the selected aircraft. Going by the track record of decision making by the Indian establishment in respect of procurement of military aircraft and weapon systems from non-Russian sources, it appears that the MMRCA is unlikely to be a reality in a respectable time frame. Despite the urgency, it took more than two decades to induct the Advanced Jet

Trainer (AJT), the Hawk 132 into the IAF. In the event of inordinate delay in the induction of the MMRCA, the fleet could well be outdated by the time it is operational in the IAF. There are therefore reasons to hasten the decision making process that are as compelling if not more as the crippling erosion of combat potential that is staring the IAF in the face. The Indian Light Combat Aircraft (LCA) Tejas, which displayed some signs of maturity at the air show, is still unlikely to fill the gap in the combat potential of the IAF in the near future.

Flight evaluation of the six types of aircraft in the race for the MMRCA which is yet to begin, would be the most crucial phase in the selection process. However, as the aircraft belong approximately to the same generation, these are likely to differ only marginally in terms of overall capability. Setting aside the fundamental issue of whether the IAF needs a twin-engine aircraft or a single-engine aircraft, the final decision is likely to hinge on the total financial outlay. This would consist of the initial Acquisition Cost and subsequent Life Cycle Cost. The latter has been introduced into the DPP in the recent past to identify the product that in addition to the right operational attributes would provide the best value for money over its total life. But the critical factor that could tilt the

balance in favor of any one of the contenders is the political leverage the vendor nation can exercise.

In the recent years, there has been considerable strengthening of Indo-US relations, a process clearly demonstrated by the manner in which the Indo-US civilian nuclear deal was pushed through by the Bush administration and continues to receive support from the Obama administration. In the emerging new world order, the US aims at forging a strategic partnership with India, a critical element of which is 'interoperability' between the armed forces of the two nations. Induction of military hardware of US origin into the Indian armed forces would facilitate interoperability and

considerably facilitate matters for the US military should joint operations be necessary in the region. The change in US perception of India is reflected in the progressively increasing participation in Aero India in recent times. In 2005, the marketable products displayed by US aerospace majors were largely confined to the civil segment of the industry with minimal presence of military aircraft. In Aero India 2007, there was a noticeable increase in US participation, both civil and military. However, in Aero India 2009, the US aerospace industry clearly dominated the scene with military aircraft and was

duly supported by the presence of high ranking diplomats, government officials and the US India Business Council (USIIBC).

There are however two imponderables. First is the level of offset which some of the companies may find difficult to cope with. Bell Helicopter has already withdrawn from the tender for 197 Light Utility Helicopter ostensibly for this reason. However, as witnessed during the air show, US companies are signing up for joint ventures with Indian companies in a wide range of disciplines to generate adequate business potential in India

should any major deal requiring high offsets materialize. Second is the long standing dispute over the End User Monitoring Certificate required under the US legal system which the Indian government finds difficult to accept. If the ongoing dispute over this issue is not resolved soon enough, efforts by the US companies to exploit the lucrative Indian market could well suffer a set back.

The two aircraft of US origin on offer, the Boeing F/A 18 Super Hornet and the Lockheed Martin F16 IN Super Viper are proven combat machines and hence are unlikely to offer any surprises to the user. There is also a strong possibility of access to next generation technology should India settle for the American offer. Boeing and Lockheed Martin have already clinched important deals worth around $4 billion (Rs 20000 crore) for the Boeing Business Jets for VIP communication, the Boeing P 8I for the Indian Navy and the C 130J Super Hercules for the IAF dedicated to special operations. Also on offer at the air show were the Boeing C 17, Strategic Airlift Aircraft and the twin-rotor Chinook heavy lift helicopter, both of interest to the IAF. In the prevailing geopolitical environment, American aerospace majors are therefore likely to benefit from the growing Indo-US strategic partnership.

The Russian offer of the MiG 35 is backed by nearly three decades of strategic alliance with the erstwhile Soviet Union and later with Russia, cemented by procurement of huge quantities of military hardware for the Indian armed forces. As the indigenous aerospace industry as well as the IAF have the wherewithal to manufacture, operate and maintain aircraft of Russian origin, the MiG 35 would have the advantage of logic. Besides, India is already part of a programme with Russia for the joint production of the fifth generation fighter aircraft for which sizeable funds have already been committed. Also, the Indian Navy has recently acquired a number of the MiG 29K for the refurbished aircraft carrier Gorshkov. Also, despite recent differences over cost escalation of military hardware already contracted for, relations at the macro level between Russia and India continue to project a reasonably healthy appearance. The one single factor that could however militate against the offer of the MiG 35 is the issue of Life Cycle Cost in respect of which, the Russian offer may not prove to be competitive against contemporary equipment of western origin.

N15NS

Smoking

The three European aircraft competing for the MMRCA contract are undoubtedly state-of-the-art fourth generation machines, but are likely to be less price-competitive with regard to the initial procurement cost. However, on the positive side, these aircraft are likely to offer better Life Cycle Cost. There would also be the need to create the required infrastructure from scratch and absorb sophisticated western technology transferred under the terms of the agreement. While the IAF and the HAL could well adapt to these new inductions without difficulty, perhaps the most critical requirement on the part of the European governments involved would be to find ways to enhance political traction in support of their offer. The French government appears somewhat proactive in this regard reiterating in a media interaction during the air show French support for India's bid for a seat in the UN Security Council. France has already extended uninhibited cooperation in the field of nuclear energy. After Boeing declined assistance, EADS fielding the Eurofighter Typhoon, has come forward with proposals to salvage the Indian LCA programme by way of consultancy services to resolve a number of outstanding technical problems plaguing the project, assist in the development of a carrier version and help speed up the process of the Operational Clearance programme. They are also in dialogue to provide a new engine from Eurojet, the EJ 200 to replace the GE 404 currently employed. Although not directly linked to the MMRCA contract, these moves by the EADS could exert a positive influence.

Military Diplomacy

Aero India 2009 provided an opportunity to the IAF to project its image through display of its front line combat aircraft as also force multipliers, such as In-flight Refuelling Aircraft in action, the renowned formation aerobatic team Surya Kiran and the helicopter display team Sarang. But quite apart from aerial display, the event provided a venue for informal contact amongst foreign military delegations invited to the show and exchange ideas on technological developments and new security challenges that the world is confronted with. It is understood that Aero India 2009 had the privilege to host for the first time ever, a high level delegation from the PLAAF led by the Deputy Chief. If an invitation can be extended to the Chinese Air Force, it is difficult to understand why the Pakistani Air Force is not extended this privilege.

Military to military interaction can sometimes offer an effective and convenient start point for the launch of confidence building measures between usually not-so-friendly nations. It may also pay dividends to educate not only friendly but even hostile nations about the span and depth of the aerospace industry that could help mellow hostility to some extent and have a sobering effect. Aero India is thus clearly much more than a mere air show!

The Subverted Indo-Bangladesh Border

BY VK SHASHIKUMAR

OPERATION ZERO LINE INVESTIGATES the gateway of terror in the East - the 4,095 km (2,979 km land border and 1,116 km riverine border) long India-Bangladesh border, half of which is along West Bengal. Assam, Meghalaya and Tripura are the other states which encircle Bangladesh. The India-Bangladesh border is porous. It runs through rivers, ponds, agricultural fields, villages and even houses where the entrance is in India and the backdoor in Bangladesh. It is perhaps the most complex land border anywhere in the world. That is why for nearly three decades this long stretch of the border was the hub for illegal migration, human trafficking, smuggling of narcotics, guns and ammunition and essential supplies.

A BSF post

All of the above continues unabated. But a new dimension has been added to the existing security threats. And that is infiltration by terrorists. The Border Security Force has identified 46 places along this border that is prone to infiltration. Fencing of this long border has already begun at several points along the border. Some sections have already been completed. Millions of Bangladeshis have entered India through this porous border and acquired Indian citizenship. Official figures stand at 1.2 million. But the latest Census figures of 2001 show that the demography of the six border districts of West Bengal have dramatically changed because of illegal migration.

To show how porous the border is and how easy it is for terrorists to infiltrate, I travelled along the South Bengal frontier from South Dinajpur till the Sundarbans. I crossed from India into Bangladesh at the Indian border town of Hilli to its namesake in Bangladesh and came back in via the same route. Here we also caught on camera stunning visuals of smuggling and Bangladeshis waiting to cross over. Further down in Malda at the dead of the night I experienced first hand how despite the 24 hours vigil by the Border Security

The author receiving the *Ramnath Goenka Excellence in Journalism Award* from the Chief Justice of India.

VK Shashikumar is a senior editor with CNN-IBN.
shashikumar.vk8@gmail.com

Photographs by **Debashish Nandy**

A BSF jawan standing at the three layered border fence.

Force (BSF), it is possible for terrorists to cross over. I visited border villages in Malda and Murshidabad sectors which are right on the Zero Line and found out how easy it is for Bangladeshi illegal migrants, smugglers and terrorists to enter Indian Territory.

On paper, a long zigzag border separates India and Bangladesh. On the ground, little does. If the frontier along Malda is ideal for infiltrators to step across the zero line, at the border town of Hilli, a wall meant to divide two countries is now a channel for smuggling. There are border villages hugging the zero line where all anyone has to do to enter India is just walk across. The porous Indo-Bangladesh border presents a clear and present danger to India's national security.

Smugglers on the Wall

At the border town of Hilli in South Dinajpur crossing the border simply means stretching a leg from a sturdy branch of tree to a wall. This is how easy it is to cross the border. Everyday, from the first daylight till sun down, a frenetic smuggling run takes place on a patch of a wall on the India-Bangladesh border. Nobody knows who built this wall in West Bengal's border town of Hilli. The local administration says it was built during the pre-partition days. After all, Hilli was once a town with a railway line running right through its middle. In 1947 the areas west of the railway line became Indian Territory and the areas on the East retained the name of the town but became part of another country. But far from dividing two countries it's a wall that unites smugglers, illegal infiltrators and in recent times terrorists. On the Indian side of the wall the houses are just an arm's length away. On the Bangladeshi side are the Hilli railway station and the railway line, which is the lifeline of smuggling and illegal activities and is used by the illegal infiltrators, terror agents and terrorists for their movement.

> The ease with which smugglers can bring in arms and ammunition and terror infiltrators to cross over into India is, perhaps, not adequately understood in the corridors of power in New Delhi.

I walked from the main square of the Hilli square in the Indian part of the town down the road, turned left into a packed residential locality, walked down the twisting and turning alleyways and reached the border wall standing on the zero line. On one side of the wall separated by a narrow lane are houses on the Indian side overlooking the railway line and across the wall, in the Bangladeshi side, I saw hordes of boys waiting to carry away smuggled goods. On the wall scores of teenage boys waited for their Indian counterparts to hand over sacks of rice, cooking oil, medicinal drugs, phensydyl cough syrup bottles and almost everything that has a demand in Bangladesh. Since the wall technically is on Bangladeshi territory it's virtually impossible to stop smuggling activities because it is considered to be a legitimate means of livelihood for a large proportion of the population on both sides of the border.

At one point the border wall curves left towards Bangladesh along a narrow alley-way and just at the turn is a small, sunken border pillar, the only marker of sovereignty in this small patch of a fuzzy borderland. Along with an Indian local I nonchalantly turned the corner and within seconds, just two steps and I had walked into Bangladeshi territory. For a while nobody noticed me and then I started attracting attention because an outsider is easy to spot in the milieu. But suspicious gazes gave way to a sudden flurry of activity. My local companion informed me that this was a sign of a train about to pull into the Hilli Station on the Bangladeshi side of the wall.

Every train that stops at Hilli station carries away smuggled Indian goods and also brings potential infiltrators and illegal migrants. My presence initially inhibited the smugglers on the wall. But they continued to stand fearlessly on the wall waiting to receive packages and sacks from their Indian agents. Soon noticing the Bangladeshi boys frozen on the wall and watching my movements, a man walked out of a house from the Indian side. "This is a daily occurrence. It goes down at night." I realized that he might be involved in smuggling activities and was indirectly suggesting that I should go away so that the boys on the wall could go back to business-as-usual.

Almost everyone in Hilli is involved in smuggling. Women couriers wrap small packages around their saris. Their destination: houses within touching distance of the border wall. These houses are crammed around narrow lanes and close to the border wall. For these Bangladeshi boys on the border wall, the last point between India and Bangladesh, it's simply a hop, skip and jump into Bangladesh. They carry sacks of phensydyl, drugs, rice in broad daylight, in clear knowledge of everyone in this town. "I am going to take rice from here. I carry around 200 kg in installments, a sack-load of 50 kg in each trip. If the Bangladeshi Rifles catch us they just verbally abuse and let us go and the process goes on," said a smuggler on the wall.

A video shot by an intelligence agency and in the author's possession shows groups of Bangladeshi smugglers on one side of the railway track waiting to dodge the Bangladeshi Rifles border guard. But what's more worrying in the video are images of Bangladeshi infiltrators waiting to cross over into India. And guess what's even more worrying? These visuals show Bangladesh Rifles soldiers not making any attempt to stop smuggling or infiltration.

Smuggling is the main economic activity along the India-Bangladesh border. The ease with which smugglers can bring in arms and ammunition and terror infiltrators to cross over into India is, perhaps, not adequately understood in the corridors of power in New Delhi. On the Zero Line, right on the International Border, Bangladeshis and Indians live in close proximity; a situation that virtually makes the border and all security arrangements to make it inviolate absolutely meaningless. This is easily exploited by terror infiltrators and anti-national operatives and insurgents based in Bangladesh.

Hilli is only one of several vulnerable spots along the 4095-kilometre Indo-Bangladesh border. Through Israeli manufactured thermal imaging devices I witnessed Bangladeshi infiltrators trying to sneak into India in the dead of night. Staking out border locations in the Malda sector along with highly motivated BSF troops I was experienced first hand and understood the reasons why terrorists from Al-Qaeda backed outfits like the Lashkar-e-Tayebba, Jaish-e-Mohammad and Harkat-ul-Jehadi-Islam prefer to enter India from Bangladesh.

Terror Trail in the East

The India-Bangladesh border is now the hub for terrorist infiltrators. After almost every recent terror attack the Government claimed that the terrorists had infiltrated into India from Bangladesh – men like Safiqul, alias Dipak, a suspected Lashkar-e-Tayebba terrorist. Safiqul used to regularly enter and leave India from Bangladesh, until he was arrested by the crime branch of the West Bengal police in Harishchandrapur in Malda last month, from the house of an ex-army driver. According to Siddhinath Gupta, DIG, CID (Operations), "...he (Safiqul) has confessed before the police that he had brought two LeT militants from Bangladesh in to J&K. Apart from that he was given the task of opening a shop in front of Siliguri cantonment and inform the Bangladeshi handler about the movement of the Army."

> Further that night along with the BSF I planned a series of simulation exercises to find out for myself how infiltration happens along the Indo-Bangladesh border. The reality on the ground is astounding.

I decided to trace the trail of terror along the border, and find out just how easy it is for infiltrators to enter India. I visited the stretch along the border in Malda, which Safiqul allegedly used. At the border, I found an improvised border fence, not much of a deterrent for a determined infiltrator. Sometimes I would come across small border pillars, but at the dead of the night, these pillars have little meaning or significance for border dwellers on both sides. "The infiltrators are not using any other border region as much as they use the India-Bangladesh border. This is why the BSF is very concerned about this region and has tightened the security here," said Nilkanta Tada, BSF soldier.

BSF soldiers like Rai Singh work nearly 14 hours a day. Longer, when they are on night patrol. But despite their vigil, day after day, night after night, people make their way across this porous border. Each soldier has to guard a stretch of around 500 meters to 1 kilometer, armed with a gun and a torch. After sun down infiltrators are always waiting to make their move. "Yes they do. They watch our movements and when we cross a point or turn our back they cross over. Sometimes they also cause diversions to distract us and take advantage of the ensuing chaos..." Singh's voice fades away as he walks into the darkness along the small patch of India's border in the Malda sector that he was tasked to guard on the day I met him.

2859 km of the 4095 km long border have been fenced with barbed wire and concrete by India, under an over Rs 600 crore rupee project. But as this author found out, migrants and infiltrators still make it across.

Further that night along with the BSF I planned a series of simulation exercises to find out for myself how infiltration happens along the Indo-Bangladesh border. The reality on the ground is astounding. Along the vast, dark, unfenced areas of the border visibility is less than 15 feet. On a cloudy night or foggy night the visibility drops to 5 feet. Consider a small nugget of information that you might have read earlier in this piece; a BSF soldier is detailed to guard a stretch of 500 meters, sometimes even 1 km stretch in some areas. In the simulation exercises where I played the role of an illegal migrant, I would be merely 15 feet away from a BSF *naka* point or check post, but they could not see me. But I knew, like all the human traffickers and the guides who direct illegal migrants and subversive operatives, where the BSF soldiers were positioned by monitoring their patrolling movements. So if I were an illegal migrant, or even a terrorist, I could have easily evaded the check post and made my way into India.

A BSF post at a riverine stretch of the border

The BSF's vigil along the eastern border has been scaled up significantly. Recognizing the BSF's operational handicaps, the government has started a modernization drive. Some units have been given these night vision devices, to enable them to see in the dark. However, even with the help of scarce night vision devices distributed across units guarding vulnerable stretches of the border, the operational difficulties in fog and darkness disables the objective of effective domination of the border. Recently, the BSF Director General, Mahendra Kumawat, stated that on the eastern frontier fencing is 75 per cent complete with 2,859 km of the sanctioned 3, 783 km fenced. The BSF will set up 300 additional Border Observation Posts (BOPs) on the eastern frontier in the next five years. These would include floating BOPs to monitor and interdict movements on the riverine border that stretches to about 1,160 km. At present there are two F/BOPs deployed in the Ichamati River along the riverine border in the Sundarbans area of West Bengal. The BSF's water wing is being modernized to take up the enormous challenges of coastal security in the Sundarbans.

Night visibility along the eastern borders is a key issue. In the pitch darkness of the night it is easy for determined terrorists to sneak across to India. The BSF's vigil along the eastern border has been scaled up significantly. But even then the task of border management continues to be challenging. This border continues to remain an easy passageway for terror.

The Infiltrators

Off camera senior BSF officers admit that some corrupt soldiers do accept inducements from infiltrators. But along the eastern border, overworked and stretched thin, 45,000 troops of the BSF soldiers are still India's unsung heroes. The three-layered fence to secure India's eastern border hasn't been able to deter illegal migrants and all variety of smugglers. I have video evidence of narcotics smuggling across the fence. Small consignments of narcotics are hidden in dense vegetation along the fence. A group of smugglers keep watch on border patrols and communicate with each other through mobile phones. Once an all clear signal is given, a smuggler rushes out of his hiding place, picks up a bundle and throws it over the three-layered fence, much like a expert basket ball player. Slam, dunk! The people who throw such consignments with practiced ease are called 'throwers' in the eastern borderland areas and, predictably, are much in demand. Soon across the fence on the Bangladeshi side, shadowy figures emerge; one of them scoots to the consignment, picks it up and vanishes into the undergrowth.

Narcotics are rampantly smuggled across the India-Bangladesh border. The three-layered fence is meant to accomplish the nettlesome task of preventing smugglers, migrants, traffickers and gun-runners from entering India from Bangladesh. As mentioned earlier, 2859 km of the 4095 km long border have been fenced with barbed wire and concrete by India, under an over Rs 600 crore rupee project. But as this author found out, migrants and infiltrators still make it across.

I met Kohinoor Asrafi, a suspected terrorist infiltrator, at the 57 Battalion HQ, BSF in the Malda sector. Interrogators from various agencies found out that he was fluent in Hindi and Bengali. He was caught by the BSF with a diary full of contacts in Pakistan, Delhi and Patna. The 2002 diary begins with the handwritten lines, 'Ya Allah! Destroy these people'. But Asrafi claimed innocence and said the diary was an old one and simply had personal details. I was allowed to interact with Asrafi. "A coolie demanded Rs 800 to get me across and Rs 400 for returning. I came here with the help of a *dalal* (human trafficker). He warned me if I tell anyone he will get me caught."

Others like Safia cross over in search of a better life. Safia, who lives in Jessore district in Bangladesh, claims she entered India legally from the Petrapol border crossing, to get treatment for appendicitis.

"Q: How much did operation cost?

A: Rs 15,000/-?

Q: How much did you bring from Bangladesh?

A: Rs. 200/-

Q: How did you get so much money?

A: I begged at Hazir Ali Dargah in Kolkata."

Once in Kolkata, Safia decided to stay back and do household work as a domestic help. "I earned Rs 4,500 because I needed the money to cross the border." She was caught by the BSF while trying to illegally cross back into Bangladesh with her eight year old son. Safia says she was trying to fetch her daughter from Bangladesh, but was abandoned by a trafficker when they were spotted by the BSF.

"He ran away to Bangladesh. I could not. I fell down and could not get up.

Q: How many people from your village have crossed over?

A: None from my place ...from other villages.

Q: Why do people cross over?

A: Bangladesh is a poor country. We cross over to earn money."

Large stretches of the infiltration-prone region continue to be unfenced, like the border areas of Barasat, just two hours away from Kolkata, where Indians and Bangladeshis live in close proximity. "I have my relatives there. My son has been settled in Bangladesh for a long time, he has also married there. We meet either when he comes here by road or when we go to Bangladesh with our passports and visas. Lots of people here have relatives in Bangladesh," said Mosiur Rehman Sheikh. In some stretches along the north 24 Parganas district of West Bengal, the border appears to be better guarded.

A small border pillar on a village pathway demarcating the border. The border here runs through the village and houses.

Illegal migration along this stretch is an open secret. I met an illegal Bangladeshi migrant who has acquired all necessary

Anexample of the unique India-Bangladesh border. BSF Jawan on the edge a village track which is in India. Behind him is Ichamati river and across the river is India. But just across the track, the man with the bicycle is in Bangladesh.

documentation to prove his Indian citizenship. I video-recorded his interview along with pictures of his Indian voter identity card. This is what he had to say: "There are millions of Bangladeshi migrants who have settled down in India by procuring Indian citizenship documents, primarily ration cards and voter identity cards. There are travel agents in the Bangladeshi border towns that employ human traffickers. They have contacts with political agents in West Bengal. It's an elaborate network. So the moment a Bangladeshi migrant crosses over he or she knows where to go, whom to meet. They establish contact with representatives of the local politicians. The local politicians in turn have another set of people who interact with the bureaucracy and the police. So it's a well oiled machinery that facilitates the entry of illegal migrants. Once through the right channels an illegal migrant is introduced to the local politicians and government officers and he or she has paid the requisite speed money, everything gets done. Ration card, enrolment in the voters list, followed by voters identity card, driving license, all documents to prove Indian citizenship, genuine documents, are created. This entire process takes three to six months."

> The porosity of the eastern frontier is so mind boggling that it should be made mandatory for bureaucrats, policy makers and politicians in key ministries dealing with security issues to visit these locations to appreciate and familiarize themselves with ground realities.

Over 30 years the Left Front government has allowed Bangladeshi migrants to cross over into West Bengal to bloat their vote bank. I met many Bangladeshis who are now Indian by documentation and all of them revealed that they have made it into the voters list, and cast their ballots in elections. Here are some more quotable quotes of illegal Bangladeshi migrants. All these quotes are on record in video taped interviews.

Illegal Migrant 1, Name Withheld

"We paid the *dalals* (human traffickers). The amount varies depending on the security environment extant on that day when the illegal crossing over has been for. It varies from Rs 200 to Rs 400/-. There are human traffickers on both sides who have pro-active contact with the BSF and the BDR personnel. Only the *dalals* (human traffickers) know which border guards of the BSF and BDR are vulnerable to allurements. This feedback is given to them by their counterparts who live in Indian border villages and, therefore, are in daily contact with the personnel."

Illegal Migrant 2, Name Withheld

"I came to India with the help of *dalals*

A border pillar demarcating India and Bangladesh.

(human traffickers) who bribed both the BSF and the BDR. Representatives of powerful politicians assist in arranging genuine Indian documentation in exchange for money. My voter identity card was issued based on the basis of my mother's voter identity card because she moved to India before I did.

West Bengal police intelligence and central intelligence agencies in the state have information on politicians who back illegal immigration. With the turn of the century and in the years that followed, a pan-Indian terror network operationalized by Al Qaeda backed terror groups in Pakistan and supported by their Indian collaborators came into existence. The trail of investigations into several terror attacks in the country has led straight to the porous India-Bangladesh border. So is it any surprise, therefore, that it was only in 2003 that the West Bengal government admitted in the floor of the state assembly that its eastern frontiers were indeed vulnerable to terrorist incursions.

The state government, various political parties, the local administration, local police and lower judiciary and most importantly the border-dwellers are the most important stakeholders in ensuring the uniquely porous India-Bangladesh border is inviolate. It's only with this kind of support that the BSF can effectively carry out its task of managing and securing the borders. Unfortunately, the most important stakeholders in border management find the BSF's role contrarian. The civil society in the border areas find smuggling lucrative and so are severely opposed to the BSF's presence. Is it any surprise, therefore, that the terrorists follow the same routes that illegal migrants take into India?

Border Crossings

The India-Bangladesh border is unique for several reasons. One such unique characteristic is the close proximity of Indian and Bangladeshi border villages. In the border villages there are houses where the front door is in India and rear opens on the Bangladeshi side. Such instances are the norm and not an exception. During my month long travel along the south Bengal frontier I effortlessly crossed over from India into Bangladesh and vice versa with ease. By doing this I wanted to demonstrate how easy it is for illegal migrants and terrorists to infiltrate.

I met Aslam, a Bangladeshi in the Indian village of Haripukur. He had sauntered across the border to meet his friends and relatives. I told him I wanted to visit his village and he readily agreed to escort me. He took me through the winding lanes of Haripukur and soon we reached a narrow and precarious path behind a mud house. On one side was the mud wall of the house and on the other a pond. I watched my steps as I followed Aslam, ten feet away he stopped at a concrete pillar. I smiled at him. It was the border pillar marking the sovereign domains of two countries. His hands carved a line in the air as he traced the alignment of border. From the pillar I took one step and I was in another country, in Bangladesh. The porosity of the eastern frontier is so mind boggling that it should be made mandatory for bureaucrats, policy makers and politicians in key ministries dealing with security issues to visit these locations to appreciate and familiarize themselves with ground realities.

Unless, a massive border development programme is undertaken with a missionary zeal, India's border dwellers will find it difficult to give up smuggling as a vocation. After all hunger and survival are primeval in nature and overshadows concepts such as national security and national interest.

Later along with Aslam I crossed over back into India. People along bordering villages do this on a regular basis every single day. They simply walk

An Indian villager, gated out by the border fence, stepping into Indian territory

ON THE SPOT REPORT

Solitary jawan patrolling the charland

across from Bangladesh into India. The villages are just next to each other. The houses are cheek by jowl. The people live in such close proximity that it become difficult for BSF to distinguish between Bangladeshis and Indians. Now consider how easy it is for a terrorist to walk in and to take shelter in a house in a border village. Locals revealed that this is what illegal migrants do. They cross over, take shelter in a safe house, stay there for a period of time to get their Indian citizenship documentation, basically a ration card and carry on to Kolkata and then to various parts of the country. This is how, for instance, visible Bangladeshi presence has grown in Indian cities - the rickshaw-wallahs in Noida, domestic workers in Jaipur and Delhi.

The Panchayat members confessed that Left parties and the state government help Bangladeshi migrants to get Indian citizenship documents. In return, the migrants vote for the CPI (M) in state and national elections.

Here are snippets of my recorded conversations with Aslam, who told me that he spends most of his time in the Indian border village of Haripukur.

"Q: Where do you stay?

A: In Raibagh, in Bangladesh.

Q: So you live nearby enabling you to easily cross over to India?

A: Yes we can, so can our relatives."

In border villages like Haripukur there are village houses on the zero line, hugging each other. This is a common feature of the South Dinajpur stretch of the India-Bangladesh border. This is a border area where fencing cannot be done unless the border populations are moved back from the zero line and buffer zone of at least a kilometer is created. But villagers are against any such move. "It would be a great inconvenience for us since all our properties and lands are here. Our earnings come from our lands, so how can we shift back?" said Sheikh Younis, a resident of Haripukur village.

Terrorists don't need an elaborate plan to infiltrate. They just have to reach a border village on the Bangladeshi side which is contiguous with a border village on the Indian side, like the village of Haripukur that stands between two countries. And walk in like I did along with local facilitators. Haripukur exemplifies the problem of effectively dominating the India-Bangladesh border. Most houses built along the zero line alignment have doors built on rear walls for easy accessibility from Bangladesh and vice versa. Here it's impossible for an outsider to figure out where the border begins and where it ends. At times even BSF patrols are confused and have to tread cautiously. As I walked on the border tracks I could understand and visualize the operational problems that the BSF faces in ensuring that no illegal migration takes place through such border villages.

I came across a house on the zero line, in the Indian side, stocked with phensydyl bottles. This cough syrup is consumed as an intoxicant in Bangladesh because of its strict prohibition laws. By now that stock would have already found its way to Bangladesh in small consignments and a fresh stock dispatched from Kolkata would have replaced it. Clearly, the proximity of Indian and Bangladeshi village houses is a boon for smugglers and infiltrators. The livelihoods of the border villagers depend on smuggling and they are incapable at the moment to comprehend the security implications of their activities. Besides, the local administration is so deeply involved in these activities. Again, therefore, is it any surprise that local civil administration and the police don't find it essential to inform and educate the border dwellers on national security concerns. Is it any surprise, therefore, that there is no incentivized reward system for locals to cooperate with the BSF in sharing real time human intelligence?

A BSF watch tower overlooking the charland

"Smuggling is the only means for us to earn our livelihoods." I heard this over and over again. It's an incontrovertible truth because there is no employment option in most border areas. The truth is smuggling continues unabated even in areas where the fencing is complete. The fence does not take into account either human depravity or the extra-ordinarily varied geography of the border, which cuts through Indian and Bangladeshi towns, villages, houses, agriculture fields, ponds, rivers, vast scrubland and miles of char-lands created by the meandering Ganges. Unless, a massive border development programme is undertaken with a missionary zeal, India's border dwellers will find it difficult to give up smuggling as a vocation. After all hunger and survival are primeval in nature and overshadows concepts such as national security and national interest.

As we walk around Haripukur village I realized the truism that one can't argue with geography, it simply is what it is. On the zero line I came across a Masjid, its rear wall in India, the rest of the structure in Bangladesh! Walking further I reached a narrow strip of land through the middle of a pond. I found out that the locals were aware of the border alignment. As I walked on the narrow strip of land, voices behind me cautioned not to cross the half way mark because I could unintentionally step into Bangladesh and if anything happened they wouldn't be able to help! An elderly Bangladeshi gentleman walked upto me at the halfway point to chat. He said for the border villagers, united by poverty and deprivation, nationality and sovereignty are alien concepts to them. He said the people from both sides cross over regularly, all the time. So, when New Delhi says that the border has been sealed, the reality is that you can break this seal by just walking across.

The Politics of Infiltration

Kanchakarpur is a border village a couple of hours away from Kolkata. Members of the village panchayat meet almost every day of the week, and one of their most prominent concerns are Bangladeshi infiltrators. "About six months back, an immigrant came to India with guns in a sack of sugar. Such small incidents happen, like a man was arrested by the police, an infiltrator, who was let off soon after once he had bribed the police. The infiltrators can even choose to swim across some of the water bodies which separate the two countries," said Shishir Dutta, member of Kanchakarpur Panchayat.

The Panchayat members confessed that Left parties and the state government help Bangladeshi migrants to get Indian citizenship documents. In return, the migrants vote for the CPI (M) in state

Cattle on the charland

ON THE SPOT REPORT

and national elections. "There are some people who have houses both in India and Bangladesh, who have managed to procure ration cards, etc., by paying bribes to the right people, and again there are Indians who haven't got any of these, and are facing problems as they do not have the money to bribe the officials," revealed Rashid Ali, member, Kanchakarpur Panchayat

In Panpakuria, angry villagers displayed their APL cards, or Above Poverty Line ration cards given to them by the government. The villagers say they are desperately poor, and need BPL or Below Poverty Line cards, but they don't get them. "Bangladeshi migrants or those associated with them get it easily. Because we are not with CPI (M) we don't get it," said Samsunara, a villager. "Cadres of Left parties are helping the migrants infiltrate and settle down by providing them with ration cards, BPL cards and monetary help. CPI (M) helps the immigrants," said Ranjana Biswas, a community activist.

It is safe to conclude that almost everyone from these internment camps migrated to West Bengal.

Along the border districts of West Bengal the presence of Bangladeshi immigrants is unmistakable. Prof Sunanda Sanyal of Ganamukti Parishad, a civil society organization, said, "It was easier in earlier times, in 1971 for example, when you could tell people from Bangladesh and India apart. Now this is no longer the case as Bangladeshis easily mix with the people here after infiltrating through the porous border. Even if you check their dialect it is no longer possible to tell them apart." "The sinister part was that a minister of the Left Front used to encourage them, and as he was in charge of food, he issued ration cards to them, which helped them get on the voter's list," said Debabrata Bandhopadhyay.

Large numbers of Bangladeshi refugees came to India after partition. By 1948, over 12 lakh people had crossed over to West Bengal, Assam and Tripura. Sixty years after Independence that number has gone up to 20 million, according to the Home Ministry. "First type of migrants – those who come for money – are not a threat to national security. But there's another category called

The Lawangola post on the charland guarding a vulnerable cattle smuggling point

Bihari migrants. This section of people are a real threat to national security, as people who fought against India and Bangladesh, and whom Pakistan refused to take in due to demographic reasons settled in India with an anti-Indian attitude which has persisted into the second or even third generation immigrants. They are a threat to our security," explained Bandhopadhyay.

Over the last six decades the demographic profile of West Bengal's border districts has changed dramatically.

Darjeeling:	Hindus (240%)	Muslim (1235%)
Maldah:	Hindus (174%)	Muslim (372 %)
Murshidabad:	Hindus (175%)	Muslim (294 %)
Nadia:	Hindus (285%)	Muslim (357 %)

Source: 2001 Census Report

From 1951 to 2001, there has been a rapid growth of Muslim enclaves along the entire stretch

A cattle smuggler shot dead by the BSF border guards. He is seen lying on the fence he had cut. A red fence cutter can also be seen.

of the Bengal-Bangladesh border. This has happened despite the increase in BSF deployment along the border over the last three decades. As long as Bangladeshi migrants are seen as politically expedient, India's eastern frontier will continue to remain one of its biggest national security threats. "The Bihari Muslim population in East Pakistan (Bangladesh) who supported Pakistan, fought alongside Pakistan, was interned at three concentration camps near Dhaka. There were more than a million interns, but that number has dwindled to about a lakh or so from 1971-2008. The one million should have increased to two million or so by now if one goes by the rate of population growth in the region. It is safe to conclude that almost everyone from these internment camps migrated to West Bengal. One route where Bengali was not spoken was Chicken's Neck at North Dinajpur, where Bengali, Hindi as well as Urdu are spoken. And once they gain entry into India, the rest of India is also open to them. Another more sophisticated route was Jalandi-Karimpur region, the Nadia-Murshidabad border to South 24 Parganas, straight to Kolkata at Kidderpore where a large section of the population speak Urdu or Watgunj, Metiabruz area of Kolkata. It was in this area where Wajid Ali Shah, the 10th and last nawab of the princely kingdom of Awadh (Oudh) in present day Uttar Pradesh in India, settled after his kingdom was peacefully annexed by the colonial British administration in 1856. So the Bihari Muslims of Bangladesh who have settled in the urdu speaking belt of Kolkata are a real threat to national security, as people who fought against India and Bangladesh, and whom Pakistan refused to take in due to demographic reasons settled in India with an anti-Indian attitude which has persisted into the second or even third generation immigrants. They are a threat to our security," said Bandhopadhyay.

In Tripura the border pillars separating India and Bangladesh are mute spectators to the infiltration across the 850 kilometre long border in the state. Many illegal migrants make their way to Agartala, the capital of Tripura. "It's true that lots of Bangladeshis come through the border but it's not possible by looking at the person to tell he is just a worker or a terrorist," said a villager in a border village. Infiltration is an almost routine affair along unfenced portions of the border. A fact acknowledged and accepted by local politicians like Sudip Roy Burman, a member of Tripura's legislative assembly from Agartala: "There is no doubt that hundreds of Bangladeshis cross the border each and every day. One wonders how that happens resulting in hundreds of Bangladeshis name in the electoral role, in spite of the fact that their names do exist in Bangladesh's electoral list also."

The Sundarbans, a maze of mangrove forests, river channels and river islands is very vulnerable to terrorist incursion. In fact, from the Bangladeshi side of the Sundarbans, a speed boat at 40 knots can reach the heart of Kolkata city within two and a half hours.

In Tripura's borderland new fences are being built. But many villages are still dangerously close to the boundary, their proximity open to exploitation by terror groups. In fact, hundreds of Bangladeshis cross over as daily wage workers and at the end of the day, they go back to their villages in Bangladesh. "They cross over from the border. They come after breakfast, ply their rickshaws, have lunch here and go back before nightfall and we locals starve," said a rickshaw puller in Agartala. More than 10,000 families have been displaced to make way for the border fence, and another 5,000 families face eviction. Citizen's groups are fighting for proper rehabilitation and compensation of the affected families.

Cattle Smuggling and Terrorism

Let's come straight to the point. The cattle-smugglers of West Bengal, their knowledge of the border areas, the gaps and the vulnerable areas through which infiltration could happen, their contacts with cattle traders and truckers in the hinterland of India and their contacts with cattle

The Ichamati River

ON THE SPOT REPORT

merchants in Bangladesh, all of this combines to form a massive cross-country network. Can't terrorists use this network to get in and out of the border? Yes, they can. If this perspective indeed generates a serious security scenario, then it's important to understand Cattle Smuggling and its link to terrorism.

Few days after I reached the border areas in the Murshidabad sector in West Bengal, I was told there was intelligence about a group of cattle smugglers who planned to take hundreds of cattle across the border. One facet that is not known is that after 6 pm the deployment in the eastern frontier switches into a combat-ready mode. Every day in many sections of the border cattle smugglers attack border guards. Lonely alert soldiers manning 500 metre stretch each are vulnerable to a sudden attack in pitch darkness. Soldiers are attacked with knives and sickles and other sharp weapons. I received information that a group of cattle smugglers has struck again, breaching an improvised fence to take cattle from India into Bangladesh. When I reached the spot, I met G. Srinivas, a BSF solider: "This place has a makeshift border fence of barbed wire and bamboo to stop people from crossing over. At 5:30 pm some cattle crossed over from here. When cattle smugglers operate there are 5-6 men to every animal. They are received by Bangladeshis on the other side. They keep in touch via mobile phones." I asked, "How do they get the cattle across?"

A floating border observation post

"They inject them with some chemical, which makes the animals restless and they start running. They do this when there is a gap in our patrols and crash through the fence so at least 5-6 of them manage to get across," he answered. The Border Security Force estimates the volume of trade at around thirty to forty thousand crore rupees. Bangladesh's economy of leather exports and bone china is also made from smuggled cattle regularized as 'animals of unknown origin' once it reaches Bangladesh.

In the final analysis the BSF soldiers show exemplary commitment in manning the border knowing fully well the operational constraints imposed by extra-constitutional political and administrative vicissitudes. The BSF has operational leeway within a 15 km band from the zero line. It has powers to detain, interrogate infiltrators and intruders to prepare a case history. But eventually it's local police who have to register a FIR, take custody of the accused and take the case through the judicial process. This is where the entire security architecture collapses because of massive corruption in the West Bengal police. Adding to that is the political interference in policing matters. Off the record I was told of several instances where the local police allegedly set free infiltrators after BSF handed them over.

At several BSF camps along the border, I came across cattle seized by BSF soldiers, seized after encounters with smugglers. In fact, I closely monitored one encounter through the night listening to gun fire and wireless conversations as the BSF soldiers tried to prevent a massive cattle run. I was told that a group of 25 smugglers had set off hundreds of cows and buffaloes to crash into the improvised fence and dash to Bangladesh. Next morning I was told that a cattle smuggler had been shot dead as he tried to slash the neck of a BSF soldier with a sickle. I went to the spot. The cattle smuggler, a 20 year old youth from a village close to the border, was lying face up on a roll of barbed wire that he had managed to snipe. A cutter and a sickle were on the ground next to him. The BSF soldiers deployed on location said that some cattle smugglers had managed to rush the cattle through. In fact, this is a daily occurrence in this part of the border in West Bengal. Everyday cattle smugglers attack these forward points to push in cattle by dismantling the temporary fence towards Bangladesh, which is hardly 200 yards from the fence.

Preventing cattle smuggling in the 'char-land' area, a riverine border region in Nadia district in West Bengal is a challenging task for the BSF. These vast tracts of land along the Ganga, made dry when the river changed its course, are where hundreds of cattle smugglers operate, illegally transporting livestock from India into Bangladesh. Tackling cattle smuggling in the 'char-land' during the monsoon when the river is in full spate is extremely risky. Cattle smugglers take advantage of this and push the cattle into the river allowing the natural current to take it to Bangladesh. "It's very dangerous. It becomes very difficult to stay in control. There are 4-6 people in our boats whereas if a boat has 50 animals, it also has at least 100 smugglers. They sometimes attack us as well and we are forced to open fire," said Raghavin Prasad Mishra, BSF, Platoon Commander at the Lawangola post.

In some parts of the char-land the borderlanders have set up villages, like the 60 square kilometre char-land called 'Nirmal-Char'. Most border villagers are subsistence farmers and so they take to cattle smuggling to supplement their income. I spot a farmer on the charland and catch up with him. His cattle are clearly exhausted from a long journey, but Saifuddin Sheikh, like most border villagers, denies that there is any smuggling in the area.

"A: Earlier people used to cross over from both sides openly.

Q: But there are reports of infiltration from Bangladesh especially at night?

A: No, that is not the case. It's not easy anymore.

Q: Do you know cattle smuggling is done from here?

A: No, it does not happen anymore.

We have to submit our photo ID. We have to submit a photo ID of our cattle also before going," said Mushtaqin. The borderlanders share a tense relationship with the BSF. "People probably crossover from Lalgola region (Murshidabad sector), but it is we here who suffer. We have to submit our photo ID at the BSF post before proceeding to the char-land. We can only do this between 6 am and 11 am, after which entry is not allowed into the char-land," said Marjina Bibi. The BSF says that if cattle can be smuggled so easily, nothing prevents prevent terror groups from using the porous border. "Cattle smuggling is a problem, (it) is a challenge. Lakhs of cattle do come, they come from hinterlands, these are the problems we will be bringing to the notice of government and we have brought to the notice of the government. It is no crime, no offence to bring cattle from lets say Rajasthan or Madhya Pradesh. Only when it reaches the border and from the border as you know, there are a number of ways (of crossing over)," said Kumawat, BSF DG. With the eastern border becoming an infiltration zone for Pakistan and Bangladesh based terrorists, cattle smuggling could soon be used a cover by more dangerous criminals.

The Vulnerable Sunderbans

Petrapole in Barasat in West Bengal is one the state's three integrated check points with Bangladesh. It's also the busiest, with 400 trucks and over a thousand people crossing this point every day. India and Bangladesh do business worth 3.6 billion dollars ever year. And there is an additional 2.7 billion dollars in illegal trade. A newly-revived train service has increased contact between the two countries. Hilli in South Dinajpur is another integrated checkpoint high on people to people contact and trade. Despite a heavy border security presence, however, this land port is routinely exploited by illegal infiltrators and militants. Government regulations stipulate that the customs are the only authorized agency to deal with trade. So the Border Security Force is not authorized to check any of the trucks or consignments coming into, or leaving India, a rule that's crippling security at this checkpoint. Ashok Banerjee, district magistrate, Balurghat categorically confirmed that the final authority when it came to trade matters, even if its security related, was the customs.

> As I stepped out of his house I discovered that I had actually stepped out of Bangladesh and when I entered the cattle shed adjacent to his house I realized was in India. I had just experienced what it was like living in a house through which an international border went through!

But on the spot assessment revealed the truth; all the customs authorities do is give a cursory glance lifting tarpaulins and peeking at the goods. Nobody knows for sure what lies beneath. Trucks can bring in contraband, arms and ammunition from Bangladesh through this ICP. The BSF and the intelligence agencies say customs authorities don't check the goods thoroughly enough. As many as 740 licenses have been issued for trade along this point, increasing the chances of smuggling and infiltration. Customs authorities insist that the checkpoint has a problem. "The number (of licenses issued) needs to be verified. But this is indeed a problem. There are many licenses. We have to check for smuggling," said Banerjee.

The loopholes in West Bengal's border security extend beyond land as well. The Sundarbans, a maze of mangrove forests, river channels and river islands is very vulnerable to terrorist incursion. In fact, from the Bangladeshi side of the Sundarbans, a speed boat at 40 knots can reach the heart of Kolkata city within two and a half hours. India shares 70 kms of its riverine border with Bangladesh in this region, which runs through the middle of the Ichamati River. I travelled along this riverine border on a BSF speedboat. With Bangladesh and India separated by a river the only deterrence for the terrorists was the BSF speedboat patrols and vigil maintained on BSF posts on the Indian side of the river bank. Except for the presence of the BSF, coastal security in the Sundarbans is almost non-existent. The West Bengal police are yet to set up coastal police stations or recruit, train and equip the coastal police. The West Bengal government has sanctioned five coastal police stations in the Sunderbans region. But till those police stations come up this entire area is open to infiltrators from the sea.

> ... eventually it's local police who have to register a FIR, take custody of the accused and take the case through the judicial process. This is where the entire security architecture collapses because of massive corruption in the West Bengal police.

On a map the border is a straight line, but on the ground things aren't so simple. The border winds through both land and water here, making it difficult to tell whether one is in India or Bangladesh. I visited the 'First Main Pillar' which marks the beginning of the land border. Here I walked along narrow strip of land which was Indian Territory. On one side was the Ichamati River and across the river, too, was Indian Territory. But the moment I moved leftwards away from the narrow strip on the river bank I was technically walking into Bangladeshi territory. So complex is the border geography that it makes border management an enormously challenging task.

The border-dwellers are caught between a border they feel has been imposed on them. I visited a village in this region where the zero line runs right through its middle, dividing families and neighborhoods. At Rabibur Rehman's house I experienced the confusion that prevails in the border areas. As I stepped out of his house I discovered that I had actually stepped out of Bangladesh and when I entered the cattle shed adjacent to his house I realized was in India. I had just experienced what it was like living in a house through which an international border went through! This kind of unique boundary is not seen anywhere in the world.

The uniqueness of the India-Bangladesh border was further reaffirmed when I reached one of the two floating border observation posts maintained by the BSF. Anchored near the mouth of the Ichamati estuary, around 20 soldiers work here, patrolling the border. "The usual schedule is 15 days but if some other B.O.P. is under maintenance or anything it maybe further extended," said Hetram of the BSF Marine Wing. Across the riverine border which stretches almost 70 kms along the India Bangladesh border, the BSF use such floating B.O.Ps to monitor movement along the riverine border.

The BSF knows that terrorist infiltration through the sea is a clear and present danger. The riverine border areas along the Sundarbans are difficult to patrol. Inspector Vikash, a Company Commander informed me that "after 26/11 we received information that the next infiltration might be in this Sunderbans region. This is vast and riverine region and we are guarding our border up to the estuary point and for such a large area a good and effective border domination plan is required. The possibility cannot be ruled out but we are doing our duty and have effectively dominated the border."

Conclusion

Villages in No Man's Land

In the Nadia sector I travelled to Indian villages beyond the border fence. A combination of riverine and land terrain has created unusual situations along the India-Bangladesh border. The complexity of the geography of this place blurs the traditional concept of sovereignty and makes it difficult to manage the border only through the lens of security. At the Hatkhola village in West Bengal's Nadia district, many Indian citizens are effectively stranded in no-man's land because it lies beyond border fence. The village lies right on the edge of the border, with the zero line running through the middle of a water canal. According to a 1974 bilateral treaty, India cannot build defensive works within 150 metres of the frontier. The border fence has cut off thousands of Indians from the rest of India. At 6 am every morning, villagers from Hatkhola have to show their ID cards to pass through the border gates into their own country.

At one such border gate I watched Ziad Ali Sheikh, resident of Hatkhola Gram, pass through the gate after his credentials and ID card was checked by the BSF border guards.

"Q: You cross over everyday using the card. Who gave you this card?

A: This card has been issued by the Hatkhola Gram Panchayet.

Q: This jacket can be bought anywhere. It's available on the open market you could have bought it from anywhere?

A: No we have to show our voter ID card to the panchayet, then only this photo is attached and the card given to us."

Ziad Ali Sheikh uses an ID card issued by the local panchayat. The card jacket, bearing the Ashoka Chakra, can be bought from a local market for 15 rupees. Villagers in Hathkola admit that Bangladeshis who are willing to pay can easily buy Indian ration cards or voter cards. "The people do not understand. That's why they can cross over to work here or they help people to cross over in exchange of money. The people need to understand the adverse effect of crossing over and steps should be taken," said another resident of Hatkhola, Anup Kumar Dhar.

Soon after our conversation ended, I saw Ziad walking from the border gate towards the nearest village market, some 10 kilometers away. He turned back and told me "I have to get back within the next 12 hours." Thousands of Indian citizens – Hindus and Muslims – leave India and return to their homes beyond the border fence every day. The zigzag India-Bangladesh border has led to many anomalies along its route. The checks seem foolproof, yet there are ways to beat the system. "The problem is that in the present scenario if you consider the manpower of BSF here you would be able to understand that infiltrating and smuggling goods, even arms, RDX, etc are also possible and easy," said Ashadul, another Hatkhola villager.

A report in the The Hindu newspaper quoted Saheb Ali Sardar, a Hatkhola panchayat member as follows: "The administration and political parties turn a blind eye to it because objecting would result in losing votes. The elections are coming and we need the vote of the people. We cannot jeopardize our party's chances of winning by tipping off the authorities about the smugglers. That would risk angering those engaged in such illegal activities."

The threat is clear and evident. Across India's border with Bangladesh, a gateway of terror lies exposed. These glaring gaps in security could one day be exploited by groups bent on wreaking terror, unless action is taken soon.

Nepal
the ticking time-bomb

BY RSN SINGH

NEPAL IS AT A CRITICAL CROSSROAD; in fact the rebirth of the country as a new nation-state is in question. To assess the evolving situation, I recently undertook an extensive tour of the country. During the tour, I had wide interaction with various segments and classes of Nepal including some important personalities and political leaders across the political divide.

Overall Situation

From my observations and interactions, I aver that Nepal is struggling for a new identity and soul, as never before in the last two centuries. There is confusion, uncertainty, despair, apprehension and despondency amongst all segments of the Nepalese society. There is near paralysis of administration. Law and order, which was very respectable under the monarchy has totally degenerated, particularly in the Terai belt. There is abnormal increase in murders, kidnappings and extortions, and other criminal activities. Road-blocks (*bandhs*) for days together have become an endemic feature. This is adopted not as a last resort tactic, but the first one. This is something the society has learnt from the Maoists. Electricity supply in important places like Kathmandu, Janakpur and Pokhra is limited to four or five hours a day. Many people especially in the Terai region questioned the very concept of Nepal as a nation-state. Even in the hills of eastern Nepal, the Limbuans (martial class like Limbu, Rai, Magar), are questioning their association with Nepal. The Tharus and the Muslims have been demanding special status and exclusion from the Madhesh identity, something which the other Madheshis and their leaders feel, has been engineered by the Maoists to drive a wedge in the Madheshi unity. Many hill people (*paharis*) have been compelled to leave Terai and flee to the hills after selling off their properties cheap. The Maoists have lost much of their influence in the Terai region, and have been supplanted by a plethora of Madheshi organization, some of which are no less criminal in their intent and activities. Elsewhere too, the Maoists influence has considerably waned, but there does not appear to be strong alternatives in the minds of the people particularly in the hill region.

There is a distinct fault line operating the East-West Highway, threatening to vertically split Nepal.

> The only beacon of hope seems to be the President of Nepal Dr Ram Baran Yadav, who is increasingly being seen as a Gandhian and a statesman; the President, a qualified heart specialist, has been repeatedly stressing on the unity of the people of Nepal, which is being extremely well received by the people due to their growing exasperation with internecine violence and mutually ruinous hatred.

The author with the President of Nepal Dr. Ram Baran Yadav

RSN Singh, is the author of the books *Asian Strategic and Military Perspective* and *Military Factor in Pakistan*
aruna_rsn2000@yahoo.co.in

The ultimate instrument of security, i.e. the Nepal Army is being humiliated and marginalized by the Maoists in the government. The Maoists have not renounced violence. It is only the Maoists, who appear to be working with a clear purpose and objective, the other political forces are either weak or in disarray. There is an unprecedented interaction at all levels between Nepal and China. The Maoists have subverted the very idea of a Constituent Assembly by declaring policies that legally can only be adopted once the new constitution comes in force. There is a sense of disquiet amongst a large segment of the people, most political parties and the Nepal Army about the agenda and working pattern of the Maoist leaders at the helm of the government. A faint trigger may just explode Nepal.

New Moorings

The moot question, as also echoed by Kamal Thapa, King Gyanendra's home minister, is – what is going to be the new philosophical mooring of the new state? To effect a paradigm shift in the type of polity and political dispensation, the most rudimentary imperative is that the protagonists must shun violence, which the Maoists have not done. They insist on calling their militant cadres, 'Peoples Liberation Army' (PLA), on the Chinese lines. As per the *Himalayan Times,* 21 March 2009, published from Kathmandu, "former General Secretary of CPN-UML Madhav Kumar Nepal recently stated that it was a great mistake of political parties to bring the Maoists to the government while they still had a parallel army and they were still carrying arms." He further said: "there is a risk that the nation could face chaos due to wrong doing of the Maoist led government... We cannot expect respect, honour and political culture from the Maoists as they are guided by weapon-oriented ideology." The Maoist leadership on so many occasions has threatened to re-launch their armed struggle if their key demands are not met. As per Mr Harihar Dahal, member of the Interim Constitution Drafting Committee, the Maoists were adamant that the word 'democratic' should not figure and the country should be just called 'Peoples Republic'. After much of persuasion and cajoling, they conceded to include the word 'democratic'.

Even the declaration of Nepal as a secular country by the Maoist leadership does not enjoy public approval. In Madhesh as well as in the hills, the overwhelming refrain was that if a referendum were to be held, 90 percent of Nepal would vote in favor of a Hindu state. The latest move by the government to accord special status to Muslims is being seen as contrary to the basic tenets of secularism. Many in Nepal feel that the Maoist leadership has not declared Nepal a secular state out of any love for secularism, but, because they feel that religion can pose the biggest antidote to their radical left politics. One of the reasons that the Maoists created mid-western Nepal as their initial stronghold was because they felt that the ethnic groups in that region were less influenced by Hindu religious moorings.

The other issue of Nepal being a federal state is also mired in controversy. Mr Ram Chandra Jha, a UML leader and Local Development Minister, told me that there was a proposal by the Maoists to have two parliaments, one for Madhesh and other for hill region. He said that he opposed the move as it would not be a 'federation', but confederation as such. I added that the move would ultimately result in the vertical split of the country. There is another proposal to divide Nepal into 13 to 14 regions based on ethnicity. Mr Jha and some other political leaders questioned the efficacy of this proposal, as they maintained that Nepal had more than 200 ethnic groups, however in no district of Nepal, any particular ethnic group was in majority.

> There is a distinct fault line operating the East-West Highway, threatening to vertically split Nepal. The ultimate instrument of security i.e. the Nepal Army is being humiliated and marginalized by the Maoists in the government. The Maoists have not renounced violence. It is only the Maoists, who appear to be working with a clear purpose and objective, the other political forces are either weak or in disarray.

Dwindling Nationalism

In the Madhesh region acute anger against Kathmandu was palpable. People brazenly questioned their nationality. They argued that there was not a single good reason for them to be part of Nepal. They maintained that they have been neglected, rather ignored, by both Nepal and India, despite constituting 50 percent of the population. Most influential positions in governance, they said, have been traditionally enjoyed by the hill people. Most blamed the *pahari* dominated dispensation of destroying the ecology and environment of the region. They complain that the entire ecology of the region was destroyed during the construction of the East-West highway and nothing has been done to restore it. A few decades back, the Terai region was characterized by dense forests, which have disappeared with the connivance of government officials (predominantly *paharis*), causing much devastation and floods in Terai and the contiguous areas in India.

The Terai people accuse India of looking at Nepal through the prism of the Gurkha soldier, Gurkha sentry (*darban*), and Gurkha servant. Leave alone Indian citizens, even the Indian diplomats, they felt had little knowledge and awareness about them. The only ambassador, who made an attempt to address their concerns, was Mr Shyam Sharan. They averred that their past, present and future is intertwined with the contiguous states and regions of India, as their economic and social well-being was not dictated by northern Nepal, but India and the Indian people with whom they have familial ties. The hunt for bride and bridegrooms invariably extends into the Indian territory. They were generally of the strong contention that legally and historically they were part of India. Some of them invoked history to argue their case.

The lack of hostile neighbours and the Kathmandu centric orientation of the country have also contributed to the lack of nationalism. One political leader quipped that there is no one in Nepal who is ready to die for his country.

One scholar pointed out that the entire region of Madhesh was given on lease to one Mukunda Sen by the Mughal emperor Shah Alam-II for 13000/- Rupees. Mukunda Sen divided the Terai region between his two sons, who were known as Palpa Raja and Makwan Raja (Gandaki to Kosi). After Prithvai Narayan Shah, annexed these regions, he continued to pay tribute to the East India Company something which continued till the rule of Jung Bahadur Rana (hereditary prime minister). The lease extended upto Lehariasarai and Darbhanga in Bihar. After the battle of Sagauli in 1816, the East India Company took back Terai, but after two years gave it back on lease. The East India Company forces had reached upto Hetauda and were threatening to capture Kathmandu. However, the British thought it wise to enter into a treaty as their principal security concern lay in Afghanistan. The King of Nepal's position was that of a subordinate. The British never called the Nepal King as 'His Majesty'. Pleased with the contribution of Gurkha soldiers of the Nepal army in defeating the Indian war of Independence–1857, the British revoked the lease of Terai and permanantly awarded certain areas in the region refered to as Naya Nepal.

The Madheshis find it amusing and discriminatory that they are referred to as 'people of Indian origin' by the hill people. Their contention is that many hill tribes including the Shah family and the Ranas are basically Indians, who migrated to Nepal at some point of history.

The lack of development, continued self-destruction of economic assets, and total external

Recruitment rally being conducted by the Indian Army at Pokhra.
The rally was not conducted in preceding two years due to law and order situation.

dependence, have made the people of Nepal cynical and despondent about their country. They feel economically extremely vulnerable and apprehensive about Nepal being a totally consumer country. It produces only seven percent of its consumer needs. Nepal, today basically subsists on remittances, which last year amounted to Rs. 1 trillion. People in the Terai said that there is relative peace in the region because most of the Madhesh population between 18 to 35 years of age was outside the country, especially in Southeast Asia and the Gulf. As per a banker, remittances coming in Janakpur, amounted to Rs.10 crore a month. They apprehend that if there were to be reverse inflow of Nepalese labour due to global recession, there will be chaos in Terai.

The assertion of ethnicity is not only confined to the Terai, but the hill region as well. The Limbuans of Eastern Nepal constituting of martial castes like Rai, Limbu, Magar are demanding separate rule based on the contention that they came under the Nepal monarch, Prithvi Narayan Shah under a special arrangement, but now, since the monarchy is gone, they are no longer part of the country.

Even in the hills, therefore, the concept of Nepali nationalism is very vague. Some people attributed the lack of nationalism to the historical reason that Nepal comprised more than 50 different principalities/petty-kingdoms unified artificially by Prithvi Narayan Shah. In the small state of Nepal, there are a host of external players like China, US, UK and Pakistan. Its geographical proximity to China and the changes taking place there (Tibet) lends Nepal immense strategic importance. The lack of hostile neighbours and the Kathmandu centric orientation of the country have also contributed to the lack of nationalism. One political leader quipped that there is no one in Nepal who is ready to die for his country. One politician even made a euphemistic suggestion that if India were to somehow extend the Sixth Pay Commission to Nepal, the country would happily accede to India.

Fault Line

The people in the Terai region draw their political inspiration from the Indian political template. On the other hand, the people in the hills are little aware about the contours of Indian politics. Even domestically, compared to the people in Terai, they are less politically active because of their day-to-day hard struggle for subsistence and survival. Nevertheless, the hill people see the Terai and its people as an extension of India. They see the Maoists as just another political force rather than being influenced by any 'ism'. While the Terai people are apprehensive about any strong inroads by China and share the Indian perspective and concern, the hill people are hardly sensitive on the issue. Many people in the Terai region even supported the economic blockade by

> In Madhesh as well as in the hills, the overwhelming refrain was that if a referendum were to be held, 90 percent of Nepal would vote in favour of a Hindu state.

A village school in Terai with its principal in background. The Indian government has contributed three crore Rupees for expansion of the school, but has been held up due to extortion demands.

the Rajiv Gandhi government. They maintained that the blockade did much to compel the monarchy to restore democracy.

Apparently, the Maoists influence has been supplanted by the Madheshi movement, even though the Maoists leaders are trying their best to split the Madheshi ranks by instigating the cause of Tharus and Muslims. In 2007, more than 20 Maoists were slaughtered at Gaur in a public meeting. Last year fierce clashes took place between the Madheshis and the hill people (*Paharis*) in the Terai region. Video tapes of *Madheshi-Pahari* clash were shown in various places in Terai to arouse passions. The customs office at Bittha More on the Indo-Nepal border near Janakpur, was attacked and in its wake there were no border officials to be seen for the next 20 days. Most *paharis* were compelled to sell their properties at throughaway prices and migrate to northern regions. The Maoist government did nothing to stop this as part of a deliberate strategy to cause polarization and confusion in Nepal. Some petty *Pahari* businessmen, however, are trickling back since then.

> The Maoists do not seem to be perturbed over their waning popularity, since they have armed muscle. The peace pact and the democratic process, they consider, as just another halt or a stepping stone in their journey to a Maoist state.

The common people in Terai do not harbour much hatred for the hill people and they consider them extremely innocent, but are bitter about the *pahari* heavy dispensation over the years. Both, influential hill people and Terai people that I interacted with, were cagey and cautious while discussing the issue, but a sense of disquiet and apprehension was discernable.

A distinct fault line presently operates alone the East-West Highway dividing the hill people from the people in Terai. The chasm was growing by the day, but off late the realization is creeping in that the fault line is adversely impacting both on the hill people and the Terai population. As long as the hill people were there in the Terai, the markets were thriving. The exodus of hill people from the Terai has caused severe labour problems; as a result all economic activity has come to a halt. The only beacon of hope seems to be the President of Nepal Dr Ram Baran Yadav, who is increasingly being seen as a Gandhian and a statesman; the President, a qualified heart specialist, has been repeatedly stressing on the unity of the people of Nepal, which is being extremely well received by the people due to their growing exasperation with internecine violence and mutually ruinous hatred.

Hurtling towards a Failed State

When I crossed the Nepal border, there were no customs officials. Despite deployment of large number of police personnel in various areas in the Janakpur region, there was no indication of active policing. People were traveling on the roof top of buses with gay abandon, something which never happened under the monarchy. Schools are closed for most of the period. Cheating in exams, which was an unknown feature, has now become rampant. I visited a school in Pipra village near the border, where the Indian government has given three crore rupees for refurbishment and expansion, the foundation stone for which was laid by Ambassador Shyam Sharan. Construction work stopped midway due to extortion demands of the Maoists and other groups. People maintained that the education system in Nepal was better than India in many respects. However, now, to compensate for the loss of school hours, children could be seen in hordes with their school bags going for tuition classes. Students in Madhesh are considered to be very promising and hardworking, but do not see much future in Nepal.

There are now more than three dozen outfits espousing the cause of 'One Madhesh One Pradesh.' Most of these outfits are nothing but criminal organizations indulging in arson, loot, murders and extortion. I met a banker living bang opposite the residence of the SP, who confided to me that he was compelled to pay one lakh rupees to one of these organisations. These organisations are now flush with finances and new weapons. Most of these organisations have been infiltrated by ex-Maoists. Kidnapping has become a industry with money being shared with the police. The general feeling was that the situation was not as bad even during the peak of Maoist agitation, and the Maoist leadership was working to a plan of destroying the entire system.

Road blockades and *bandhs* in Nepal are so frequent that people have become inured to it. Road blocks and *bandhs* are never partial but complete, and it extends for days together, causing much hardship to the people in the hills due to acute shortage of essential supplies, triggering abnormal price rise of commodities. I could not proceed from

Janakpur to Kathmandu by road due to *bandh* imposed by the Tharu community, which had entered its 23rd day. There was not even a modicum of effort by the government, and its law and order agencies to enforce a solution. The Janakpur-Kathmandu road link constitutes the main artery for the Kathmandu valley. Again my travel from Kathmandu to Pokhra by road was interrupted by a road blockade created by a student group during student elections. More than hundered vehicles with tourists lay strung on the road. Large posse of policemen was seen to be moving up and down, but did not attempt to clear the blockade. After four hours, I and others were compelled to pickup baggage and walk 5 to 6 km before I could find another means of conveyance on the other side of the blockade. People were of the opinion that the culture of *bandhs* and road blocks in utter disregard to the needs and hardships of the countrymen was introduced in the political culture of the country by the Maoists, and therefore now when in the government, they do not have any moral authority to condemn and contain the very same method, which they engaged in with telling effect.

Both in the hills and Terai, power cuts range from 16 to 18 hours a day. This includes Kathmandu and Pokhra as well. The void created by the monarchy and its institutional framework has not been supplanted by other effective mechanisms. In fact, the existing institutions are in complete confusion and disarray. There is a growing feeling that it is a part of deliberate Maoist strategy to destroy or marginalize all existing institutions including the army.

Influence of the Maoists

Most people including those inhabiting the areas of Maoist stronghold maintained that the electoral success of Maoists was due to a combination of extraordinary factors. In the remote hill regions, there was no presence of any other political force other than the Maoists, therefore the poll results in favor of the Maoists was a foregone conclusion. In other areas, fear of the Maoists and intimidation by them were the factors. And in the areas where the Maoists were a weak force, they adopted a humble political posture requesting the voters to give them a chance, as they had tried all other political players in the past. The general public failed to see the danger posed by the radical *ism* of the Maoists. The Maoists even threatened to continue their armed struggle if not voted to power. Fed up with a decade of violence and hardship, many people decided to give the Maoists a chance. The Congress leaders disclosed that Mr Koirala, in the very late stages was given intelligence inputs regarding the emergence of Maoists as the leading political force, yet he did nothing to scuttle the elections. Therefore, in a way he did favor to the Maoists.

> Sans Gyanendra therefore, the people carry some very revered memories of the monarchy, something which the Maoist have to contend with, but are determined to efface. They therefore see the Nepal Army as a vestige of the monarchy, which must be radically altered in the colour of 'Red' and on the lines of the PLA of China.

To win over the people, the Maoist used a simple tactic. Mr Kamal Thapa, former home minister and now a member of the Constituent Assembly representing the Rashtriya Prajatantra Party, said that he was intrigued by the switchover of loyalties by the cycle-rickshaw pullers to the Maoists in his constituency 'Hetauda'. It was then revealed to him that the Maoist had asked the cycle-rickshaw pullers, as to what their daily earnings were, and how much did they pay everyday to rickshaw owners as hiring charges–which was Rs. 30 and Rs. 100 respectively. The Maoists issued a diktat that henceforth they would pay only Rs.70 to the rickshaw owner and contribute Rs.10 to the Maoist fund. Happy at the increase of their earnings from

The author with Mr. RC Jha, UML leader and Local Development Minister

ON THE SPOT REPORT

Rs.30 to Rs.50, they changed their loyalties overnight. Then they issued a diktat that no restaurant worker will be paid less than a stipulated amount. Such tactic worked, but now the politics of distribution of the Maoists is facing new hurdles on account of shortages, rising inflation, fast deteriorating infrastructure, and sharp decline in the tourism industry, which is critical to the Nepalese economy. Most Indian industries are either closed or have relocated on account of labor problems. Many industries in Birganj-Pathlayia corridor have been closed or on the brink of closure. Same is the case with industries at Itahri. All industries were there due to cheap labour and 15 percent duty difference, which will become nil after 2010 when WTO provisions come into force.

As per Mr Kamal Thapa, like the Congress, the Maoists were not averse to partnering with the monarchy. In fact, the Maoist leadership had sounded the King that the institution of monarchy could well fit in their scheme of things, as in the case of Cambodia. They urged the King to join forces with them to wipeout other political parties from the scene of Nepal, a proposal Mr Kamal Thapa said, the King refused to buy. When this did not work, the Maoists struck common cause with the political parties, which was part of their design of incremental progress towards establishing a Maoist state. There were others, who believed that the King was also not averse to use the Maoists as a counterpoise to the political parties. In that they cite the security forces operation in Holari, wherein the entire Maoist top leadership was surrounded and would have been easily eliminated but for the intervention of the King.

Maoists have also indicated to certain quarters I interacted with that in the event of being voted out in the Constituent Assembly, they would quickly seize power by force.

Acutely conscious of their limited influence the Maoists then joined hands with the other political parties. The King declared his resolve to destroy the Maoists and appeal to the political parties and the people for the need to prolong 'emergency' with the promise to restore democracy once the Maoist terrorism was vanquished. However, by then King Gyanendra and his son had become hugely unpopular, and ceased to enjoy any respect or patience with the monarchy. The Maoist then collaborated with other political parties to overthrow King Gyanendra, not because of their opposition to monarchy and love for democracy, but for sheer survival and for elimination of another rival power center to pave the way for the realization of a Maoist state. It may be mentioned here that some Maoist supporters still hold Gyanendra's predecessor King Birendra in very high regard, and so do many in the Nepali Congress and other political parties. I was told that in the late 80s, Mr G P Koirala had in fact expressed his desire to King Birendra to join forces with monarchy, but the latter insisted he should launch a movement, for democracy, as the other royal family members were targeting him (King Birendra) of being soft and overly disposed in favor of democracy at the cost of monarchy. Sans Gyanendra therefore, the people carry some very revered memories of the monarchy, something which the Maoist have to contend with, but are determined to efface. They therefore see the Nepal Army as a vestige of the monarchy, which must be radically altered in the colour of 'Red' and on the lines of the PLA of China.

It is with this objective that the Maoist leadership is insisting on absorption of their armed cadres into the Nepal Army and has objected to routine recruitments by the Army. They recently tried to deny extension to the eight Brigadier Generals against the established convention. Unfortunately, the Maoists do not have the numbers to bulldoze their agendas in the Constituent Assembly, but are nevertheless moving incrementally with a clear purpose. Interestingly and much to the discomfiture to the Maoist leadership, the Madhesh Liberation Tigers (MLT), during its negotiations with the government, demanded that its 10,000 armed cadres should be treated like the Maoist armed cadres, who are enjoying the facilities provided by the state and should be absorbed in the Nepal Army.

Ever since, the Maoists have taken over the mantle of governance they have been losing political ground and popularity due to increasing instability in the country. Even amongst the supporters, I did not find any reverence for the Maoist leadership. In some parts of the Terai region, the mere mention of the names of Maoist leaders invites peoples' wrath. The Maoist leaders do realize that they cannot override the rising Madheshi sentiments, therefore they have adopted different tactics. They are trying to drive a wedge in the Madheshi ranks by instigating ethnic groups like Tharus and Muslims to demand 'special identities and privileges.' The recent Tharu and Muslim agitation is believed to have been engineered by them. It is also alleged that they are floating Madheshi organizations under different names and secretly imposing their leadership in Madheshi avatars. There are insinuations that two former Maoist leaders, Upendra Yadav (Foreign Minister) and Maitrika Yadav, now heading Madheshi organizations, remain fundamentally Maoists. That these two leaders have so far strongly supported all controversial decisions lends credibility to the suspicion. For the Maoists, the foreign minister portfolio is most critical and it is intriguing that it should have been given to a political rival.

The decision of the government led by Maoists to increase the salary of the MPs (601 in the Constituent Assembly) from 14,000 to 50,000 has not gone down well with the people. Most people find the tax regime in Nepal oppressive. With regard to vehicles, the yearly tax slab is Rs 1,800 for 100 CC motorcycles, Rs 3,600 for 150 CC motorcycles, Rs 15,000 for 1500 CC cars, and Rs 50,000 for cars above 1,500 CC. Under the Maoist government, the state-run schools are hardly functional due to various reasons, and people are seeking recourse to private institutions. There are some 9,000 private schools in 56 districts of Nepal. Each of these schools has a minimum of 20 employees. A five percent tax has been levied on students studying in private schools. As it is private schools are paying 25 percent income tax, 1.5 percent tax for rural education development programme, 10 percent building tax, even if the school is being run from own premises. The Maoist leader Babu Ram Bhattarai had recently threatened to close all private schools. Exasperated the Private School Association threatened to close the schools from the very next day.

While I was in Nepal, the Students' Union Elections were being held throughout the country. A lot of significance was being attached to it so as to gauge the following of the Maoists amongst the youth. With 48 seats, the Student Wing of the Maoists ANNISU (R) were placed third after ANNFSU (student wing of UML) and NSU (student wing of Nepali Congress) with 86 and 61 seats respectively. The Maoists had placed a lot of premium on the elections and provided substantial funds to their student wing.

The Maoists do not seem to be perturbed over their waning popularity, since they have armed muscle. The peace pact and the democratic process, they consider, as just another halt or a stepping stone in their journey to a Maoist state. They are very well utilizing the present opportunity to bolster their armed might and infiltrating key institutions of governance. Before they entered the peace process, they carried out frantic recruitment of new cadres in their armed wing, which they insist on calling the PLA. During the peace process, they took the position that their PLA has 30,000 cadres. The UN Monitoring Committee reckoned it at 18,000. These cadres organized in special camps under the UN supervision continue to be trained. It is widely believed that some of hard core cadres and the most potent weapons remained outside to be used when required. In addition, the Maoists have raised the 'Youth Communist League' (YCL) with the membership of one lakh as claimed. They are being liberally armed and financed by the Maoist leadership, now running the government. It may be mentioned that the YCL cadres took out a protest march against the Supreme Court's stay on the defence minister's decision of not granting extension to eight Brigadier Generals. It may be mentioned that the defence minister Badal was the head of the armed wing of Maoists before joining the government.

> Many leading politicians were candid enough to tell me that to be counted in Nepal's politics; India-bashing is a compulsion, even as they fully realize that India has been more than indulgent, benign and generous towards Nepal all through.

As per some key sources, the Maoists are preparing for an eventuality of an armed show down with the assistance of China, in case they are politically overwhelmed by opposing forces. Maoists have also indicated to certain quarters I interacted with that in the event of being voted out in the Constituent Assembly, they would quickly seize power by force.

India Factor

The people in the Terai nurture a deep grievance that their pro-India orientation has been overlooked and subverted not only by Nepal, but India as well. They pointed out that without a liberal and open border regime, their very survival will be at stake. They asserted that for everything right from sustenance to good future for their children they have nowhere to look, but India. Even the hill people, who have the means are hedging their chances by acquiring properties in India. There are numerous advertisements in Nepalese newspapers regarding sale of flats in Delhi. As per report, more than 150 Gurkhas of the British Army have bought properties in Gurgaon. The complementarities between Nepal's Terai and India were accentuated during the recent road block by

Recruitment rally being conducted by the Indian Army at Pokhra.

model be replicated with regard to dental hospitals. In that India should assist in establishing dental hospitals at Jaleshwar, far-western Nepal, mid-western Nepal and eastern Nepal. Some of these hospitals will benefit India as well. It may be mentioned here that Nepal is ahead of India in anti-blindness programmes, Vitamin-A programmes, Polio eradication, mother and child health programmes, and oral health programmes (in Asia, only Thailand is ahead of Nepal).

the Tharu community, when people travelling from Birganj to Janakpur, two important towns of Terai, had to do so through the Indian territory. They also brought out the impact of happenings and internal administrative measures by the contiguous states on Nepal's Terai. For example, they cited that many criminals and anti-social elements have crossed into the Nepal's Terai region after tightening of law and order machinery by the Nitish Kumar government in Bihar. They therefore warned that a Maoist takeover of Nepal will have deep ramifications in India.

The stranglehold of China on the Maoist leaders was quite evident when it prevailed over Prachanda to decline invitation to participate in the recently held India Today Conclave. Not only the Maoist leaders, but also the Madheshi leaders like Upendra Yadav and Maitrika Yadav are also considered extremely close to China, and indirectly and secretly supporting China in furtherance of its agendas in Nepal.

A few other examples can be given with regard to the complementarities. The BP Koirala Institute of Medical Science at Dharan, established with Indian assistance has more than 70 percent patients from Bihar. There are also eye hospitals in the Terai at Lahan (established with German assistance), Janakpur, Birganj, Bhairawah and Getta. Again, 70 percent of patients in these eye hospitals are from the Indian side. The Indian patients find it very convenient and economical as treatment fees is fixed and there is no fleecing or hidden costs involved. The fixed rate for a cataract operation is Rs 1,000/-. A senior functionary of the National Academy of Medical Sciences proposed that the same

The people of Nepal are very impressed with India's economic growth and expect India to be more magnanimous in view of its burgeoning economy. I told the some Nepalese leaders in the government that without doubt Nepal is a sovereign country, but Delhi-Kathmandu state-to-state relations paradigm is detrimental to the development and well-being of Nepal. The geographical truism is that Nepal has borders with Sikkim, West Bengal, Bihar, UP, and Uttrakhand, some of which are presently not the best performing states of India. Development of Nepal can only take place if the complementarities of these Indian states with Nepal are taken into consideration by both the countries. There is a pressing imperative that the Chief Ministers of bordering Indian states are included in the decision-making loop with regard to the relations between the two countries and development activities undertaken in Nepal with Indian assistance.

Most people in Nepal, (lesser extent Terai), are unaware about India's security sensivities like externally sponsored terrorism and activities of the country's belligerent to India like Pakistan and China. Mired in their own problems, they tend to overlook the fact that India has direct security interface with five other neighbors. In fact, there is a propensity amongst some policy-makers to indulge in India-bashing, whenever they interact with other SAARC members. This propensity is exploited by powers inimical to India. Many leading politicians were candid enough to tell me that to be counted in Nepal's politics, India-bashing is a compulsion, even as they fully realize that India has been more than indulgent, benign and generous towards Nepal all through. There are others, who accuse India of suffering from big-brother syndrome. They portray the Indian embassy in Nepal as a state within Nepal. There is a tendency to blame the Indian embassy and the RA&W for all the shortcomings of Nepal. This constituency in Nepal completely ignores the fact that given the unique nature of India-Nepal geopolitical interface, a modicum of reciprocities is expected from Nepal. They are sensitive about their concept of 'sovereignty' to ridiculous extents. They chased away the Indian technicians working on the hydro-electric project on the River Karnali on the plea of preserving Nepal's sovereignty. They have done the same at other places as well. They also chased away Indian engineers and workers, who had gone to Nepal for repair of the embankment of the Kosi River. Nepal after Brazil has the highest potential for hydro-electric power, yet most of Nepal is today suffering from daily power-cuts of 18 hours.

An Indian pilot, who has flown extensively in the domestic circuit of Nepal observed that most of the airfields in Nepal have been constructed with the Indian assistance, and the plaques mentioning the same has deliberately been allowed to deteriorate and are obscured by wild grass.

The Nepal government has been selling the argument to its people that electricity shortages are due to disruption of 500 MW of power supply from India. It does not realize that India is a precarious power-deficient state and can ill afford to persist with the arrangement indefinitely.

About one thousand crore rupees is disbursed by India as pension for Gurkha ex-servicemen yearly by the Indian Pension Establishment in Nepal. The officers and the staff of the establishment travel to remote areas, but their movement has never been disrupted even during the peak of the Maoist insurgency. It is intriguing that many Gurkha ex-servicemen also get afflicted by 'sovereignty' and 'anti-India' syndrome. Same is the case with regard to recruitment of the Gurkhas of Nepal in the Indian Army. I attended a recruitment rally at Pokhra. In the preceding two years, the Maoists had created hurdles in holding recruitment rallies, again citing 'sovereignty'. These elements were conveyed that it was not India's problem but Nepal's, as India has enough voluntary aspirants for the Indian Army. After the reality sunk in, and under public pressure the Maoist leadership had no choice, but to finally yield.

Much of the Indian assistance to Nepal is not only taken for granted, but misused as well. As per a functionary of the Indian Consulate at Birganj, India had recently gifted some ambulances to Nepal, and a few months down the line, he said that he was horrified to see them being run a taxies.

China Factor

Some of very important non-Maoist ministers in the present government, conveyed their alarm in the abnormal increase in the number of visits by Chinese delegations to Nepal. There have been 28 official delegations from China to Nepal ever since the Maoists have come to power. It was pointed out that in the last four months, there have been nine Chinese delegations and only four Indian. As per sources in Nepal's Army, the number of unofficial Chinese delegations is even more. The non-Maoist ministers revealed that the current Nepalese dispensation and China are moving very fast on realization of the extension of Tibet Railway to Kathmandu. In fact, recently, the Nepal government has officially requested China in this regard. These leaders were of the opinion that if the preliminary work was to begin on the project, it would be impossible to thwart it, as public opinion would go against India. They therefore, proposed that India should immediately take cogent action towards extension of railway from India to Kathmandu and beyond upto the Chinese border.

> I also asked concerned authorities in the present dispensation, what would happen in Nepal if there were to be a rebellion by the police? Who will quell it if the ultimate institution 'Army' is humiliated and in disarray? I said that if the army ceases to be an effective institution, Nepal will quickly degenerate into anarchy.

A large number of Nepalese students are being

A very symbolic China Tourism hoarding outside Kathmandu airport with the message, 'Welcome to Nepal-Gateway to China'

NEPAL : FIFTY YEARS AGO...

Excerpts from the diary of Late Mr H Lal, ICS, Head of the Indian Aid Mission in Nepal, 1957–60

"I was at a loose end this morning and went and saw TPA (Tanka Prasad Acharya). We had the old type of banter...India was responsible for all the ills of Nepal. Then he explained, 'we politicians must have a scapegoat. I blame the political parties too, Dr KIS (K I Singh) and UDF as you may have seen. Actually the King is largely to blame for the present grave situation. But how can we blame the King. It would shake his position further; so India makes a satisfactory juicy scapegoat. You should be prepared for it and ignore these.' To the query, 'why not an occasional fling at China, or Russia as well...to give it more balance.' He said, 'they are not doing anything in Nepal at present.' I said, 'why paint us so black. Why not appear judicious and give us credit for some things also.' He said, 'the time for that will come later, when things have settled down. Then we shall need no scapegoats.'

He feared that the present situation was potent with grave possibilities. The King had already isolated himself. The movement to be launched on the 8th Dec (1957) will degenerate into one against the King, and there will be widespread disorder...the Knats and Limbus, the Newars, the Bhotiyas, and the language controversy in the Tarai...all these issues will raise their head simultaneously. It will shake the monarchy. If India is a friend of Nepal, the time has now come to show it. There are two courses...this conflict must be avoided. First: the King should be told firmly that he must take in the democratic forces into government otherwise he would forfeit India's sympathy. At the same time the democratic forces must be told that whatever gesture comes from the King, it should be readily accepted. Second: in case the King is not amenable, and a really serious situation develops, India should march in, prevent disorder and bloodshed, hold election and the walk out again."

"Nepal is an unfortunate country. The King who could make and mould the destinies of this country, is not well educated or experienced, is ill advised, is amenable to pressures, is indecisive, has a personal prejudice against B P Koirala (and consequently Nepali Congress) and is playing politics with TPA (Tanka Prasad Acharya) and KIS (K I Singh), has not had the courage to remove corruption and reform the administration, to take bold decisions on taxation, in fact to provide the leadership which the country needs at this stage. The politicians too have let down the country. They are self-seekers, running after personal glory and satisfactions. These people have never addressed themselves to the crying problems of the country...The picture is complex. Only bold steps can save the country. These can come either from the King or from the PM. With the King amenable to all influences and pressures, no PM can have a free hand. Compromises will ruin him and take the effect out of his measures. The King...ill-advised or advised only by interested parties close to him...is not likely to provide this leadership. There seems no hope for this country, but chaos...another rising against the actors, including the King who will fly to India...a more robust party or group in power...and he may return as a more chastened King to the throne..."

"...who are these communists? At one time they belonged to the Nepal Congress but out of frustration they joined the Communist party. If this kind of stalemate continues more and more people are going to leave Nepal Congress and join the Communists, while as a gladiator, you (the King) may cut off the heads of Nepal Congress leaders, you cannot cut off the heads of Communists. They do not expose their head. That lies in some other country. There are only limbs here. They will grow more limbs!..."

"...we are committed to support the King. We shall never draw back from that position. On the other hand we cannot give up the democratic course. Our nation has deliberately taken this decision. Our Constitution is based on this. We have supported Nepal Congress in the past. We are bound by the nature of our institutions to wish for the triumph of democracy...It is becoming difficult to distinguish a friend from a foe. Pakistan utters all those lies, about Indian troops massed on the border and there is not a word of contradiction from the Foreign Office. This could have been easily verified from the Bada Hakims on the border, there is vicious propaganda that we are financing the movement..."

(Courtesy: VP Sawhney–ex-IAS officer and son-in-law of Late Mr H Lal)

lured by China to avail technical education facilities especially created for them. These are basically those students, who fail to enter engineering and medical institutions in Nepal or India. It may be mentioned that Nepal with a population of 2.5 crores has 14 medical colleges. The Chinese have a very blasé attitude towards the fulfillment of academic and professional aspirations of the Nepalese students. The objective is not education, but to subvert these students and further Chinese influence. Extensive visits to the prosperous parts of China forms part of the curriculum. These institutions are very poorly equipped. For most practical classes, video tapes are shown. The standard of students graduating from the medical institutes is so poor that the Nepal Medical Association has begun to conduct exam for certification and practice in Nepal. Members of the Nepal Medical Association, who visited China told me that the institutions in China catering exclusively to Chinese students are much superior, rather state-of-art. Since such exams by the Medical Association cannot be confined to Chinese graduates, others including Indian and Nepal graduates have also been brought in the ambit. Very recently, some 600 graduates appeared for licensing exam of which only 40 percent qualified and most failures were graduates from China.

The stranglehold of China on the Maoist leaders was quite evident when it prevailed over Prachanda to decline invitation to participate in the recently held India Today Conclave. Not only the Maoist leaders, but also the Madheshi leaders like Upendra Yadav and Maitrika Yadav are also considered extremely close to China, and indirectly and secretly supporting China in furtherance of its agendas in Nepal. Maitrika Yadav has just returned from his visit to China. The recent statement by the Chinese Ambassador in Nepal to the effect that China will not allow Nepal's sovereignty to be interfered with is significant and unequivocally demonstrates the Chinese resolve to wean Nepal from its special relationship with India. The evolving contours between Nepal and China under the Maoist dispensation is best signified by a huge hoarding of Chinese tourism just outside the Kathmandu airport. It reads 'Welcome to Nepal, the Gateway to China.'

Marginalization of the Army

The Maoists have been consistently humiliating the Nepal Army. In fact, they have been treating the army as an enemy force. They feel that the Nepal Army is the only institution, which can challenge their armed might. They have been raising hue and cry over recruitment by the army to fulfill vacancies, which occur routinely on account of retirement and other reasons. The present Army Chief General Rookmangad Katawal has been fighting a lonely battle against the government headed by the Maoists, and the defence minister is a one time foe being the head of armed wing of the Maoists. The Army Chief earlier enjoyed a very high protocol status under the monarchy and was entitled to state sendoffs and receptions. The Maoists have ensured that today he is no one. Nevertheless, General Katawal, who was the adopted child of King Mahendra, is a powerful personality and the only one in the army hierarchy, who can protect the Nepal Army from subversion and marginalization attempts of the Maoists. Unfortunately, he is to retire in June.

During my visit to Nepal, the Maoist insistence of absorption of its armed cadres into the Nepal Army was a hotly debated issue, and then during my stay, another extremely contentious issue regarding the extension of eight Brigadier Generals came up. These Brigadier Generals are Pradeep Bikram Rana, Pawan Bahadur Pandey, Kumar Budhathoki, Narendra Bahadur Rawal, Raju Pratap K C, Ramesh Bista, Nara Bahadur Kandel and Shiva Poudel. It has been an unbroken tradition in the Army to grant three years extension to a Brigadier General and as such is provided in the Army Act as well. Some of these officers are considered to be highly qualified and experienced, having done their courses in India and some other western countries. It may be mentioned that the expansion of the Nepal Army from 50,000 personnel to the present strength of about 90,000 personnel took place in the later stages of Maoist insurgency and therefore, 70 percent of the personnel are below seven years of service.

When Mr GP Koirala was the Prime Minister, who also had the defence portfolio in the interim government, was persuaded by General Katawal not to delegate powers of deciding on the issues pertaining to the army to the cabinet, as he was apprehensive that the Maoists leadership would further its agenda of destroying the institution of the Nepal Army. Unfortunately, it was this very provision that Badal, as the defence minister, used to deny extension to the Brigadier Generals. This move of Badal was meant to send strong signals within the army ranks that for future career prospects, the Nepal Army officers had to depend on the largesse of the Maoist leadership. The move was opposed by other political parties including the UML. The President appeared to be constitutionally helpless under the circumstances, and to make matters worse, none of the political parties, who had opposed the move, approached him to remonstrate. It would have certainly been lapped up by the media and strong signals would have been sent to the Maoist leadership. Fortunately, a few days later, the Supreme Court put a stay order on the retirement of the concerned Brigadier Generals.

When prominent members of the cabinet and opposition leaders asked for my opinion on the issue of absorption of Maoist cadres into the Nepal Army, I gave the example of the Indian National Army officers and men, who were not reabsorbed into the Indian Army despite stiff pressures from the political class on the Army Chief General Cariappa. I said that any army, which has any kind of ideological stream, ceases to be an impartial and effective force. I also quoted the examples of two distinguished Indian Generals, General Thimayya and General Bhagat, who as young officers had offered Mahatama Gandhi their services in the freedom movement after quitting the British Indian Army. Mahatama Gandhi was sagacious to advice them that they must remain in service and serve loyally as their services and experience would be critical to post-independence India. I reminded them that the Bangladesh Army could never become a non-partisan and apolitical force because of the two streams that emerged in the army after creation of the country, i.e. the freedom fighter lobby and the repatriated lobby. I also asked concerned authorities in the present dispensation, what would happen in Nepal if there were to be a rebellion by the police? Who will quell it if the ultimate institution 'Army' is humiliated and in disarray? I said that if the army ceases to be an effective institution, Nepal will quickly degenerate into anarchy. I cited the recent quelling of revolt in the BDR by the Bangladesh Army. One politician expressed that in Nepal the people feel that the army has never been employed for any purpose and therefore has little regard for them. I then gave the example of Sri Lanka, which had a ceremonial armed force of 18,000 personnel in the 70s, but circumstances compelled it to increase its size to more than one lakh personnel and over the years have evolved into a formidable fighting machine, so no one knows what role the Nepal Army may have to perform in future. I further added that like the Indian Army, the Nepal Army could become a symbol of national integration and effective instrument of nation-building.

Future Scenarios

Based on my interactions with the general people, politicians, administrators and members of the government, I foresee three very unpleasant scenarios in the immediate future of Nepal, which most institutional players in Nepal concur.

Scenario-A: A total Maoist takeover of Nepal with the tacit support of China.

Scenario-B: An violent clash between the Maoists versus the rest. The latter will include all other political forces and the army as well. As per my inputs, the Nepal Army is not inclined and united to interfere in the political happenings of the country, but if it continues to be humiliated and the situation in Nepal becomes untenable, they may well step-in to salvage the country from the brink of collapse.

Scenario-C: Split of Nepal into various entities.

Evolving Situation in Nepal : Implications for India

The impact and implications of the evolving political and security scenario in Nepal on India are:

- Advent of Maoist government has not ushered political stability in Nepal and for both India and Bhutan. Consequently the seven states of the NE region face renewed challenge to their stability and security. Coupled with this the Maoists can be expected to influence like minded groups in the 80 odd districts in the Red Corridor along our eastern sea board. PRC is already known for its intervention/interference in NE region
- Rise of this trend coincides with that of PRC influence in Nepal. Significantly the proposed treaty between Nepal and China will lead to unprecedented regional developments. In this the Tibet card will be effectively lost. PM Prachanda will perhaps make more concessions to PRC when he visits Beijing next. With the western bloc bending over backwards to please Beijing, Prachanda's position will be alarming. Loss of Tibet card in Nepal for India will have incalculable effects on Delhi.
- Beijing's growing assertiveness is exemplified in the manner of preventing Prachanda from participating in the India Today conclave citing the Dalai Lama's presence. A number of countries have had to bite dust on this subject.
- With Nepal in its bag, Beijing's next target will be Bhutan with whom it has a border problem. China has settled this issue with 12 out of 14 neighbours. Its next target of course will be assertion of claims on maritime boundaries that has witnessed increasing shrill in past couple of weeks.
- While Pakistan remains a source of major threat, the larger role of China cannot be viewed in isolation.
- The recent US DOD report on China is eloquent on Chinese threats.

Unity of Nepal is critical to India. A divided Nepal will usher in many other forces inimical to India. The gradual but determined imposition of their totalitarian 'ism' by the Maoists on the people of Nepal is percitibly turning Nepal into a volatile state, even as history, relegious moorings and sociology of the nation is at severe odds with ultra-left philosophy, notwithstanding the limited success of the Maoists in the Constituent Assembly elections held under extraordinary circumstances. As it is, elections are temperamental affairs and the largest political bloc with armed muscle cannot be the sole arbiter of a nation-state during its rebirth. The Maoists cannot be allowed to hijack the country in the garb of democracy, in which they fundametally do not believe in. It is a foregone conclusion that the Maoists at no cost will ever be prepared to sit in the opposition, therefore the present democratic process for them is only an avenue towards establishment of a Maoist state.

LTTE'S Self-Destruction

BY LT GEN SC SARDESHPANDE

INSURGENCY-GUERILLA WAR AS A combination in the struggle of the weak against the strong has established itself as a strong and successful method of waging an armed struggle. It is said that the combination may not win but forces the opponent to lose, thereby bringing success (victory) to the former. Experts have listed various conditions where it can thrive, expand, grow in strength and achieve success, like - binding cause, people's support, outside help, safe areas, difficult terrain etc; and classified various stages through which it passes, i.e. growing local resistance and discontent, expanding armed resistance, hit-and- run-merge with the public, guerilla operations, liberating chunks of territory, organizing conventional forces, resorting to conventional wars, with necessary flexibility to get back to the lower stage depending on the situation, while considering time to be on its side and a means of wearing down the opponent. Examples are Mao's China, Vietnam, Cuba, Algeria, some of the Central and Latin American countries. Afghanistan has a long history of resisting intruding powers and sending them to their doom, as none of the Central, West or South Asian powers or those of Great Britain, Russia or now the USA have succeeded in subjugating and ruling the fiercely independent Afghans, despite Hindu, Buddhist and Islamic influences over them. We have our own Naga, Mizo, Manipuri and now Maoist insurgencies still biting at us. The Bangladeshi insurgency also turned its full circle in 1971.

In all this where does the Sri Lankan Tamil genre stand? Besides a history of over three decades, it has had an unassailable "cause", people's support, safe haven (India), foreign assistance (India, Western and Southeast Asian world), a highly trained, disciplined, dedicated, motivated and innovative cadre based organization (one of the best in the world). Its militant cadres withstood the 80,000 troop onslaught of the IPKF for 30 months in the difficult terrain of lagoons, kulams, marshes and forests in its vast expanses. Yet in these last few months its militant wing, the LTTE, has been at the losing end with astonishing rapidity, though it lost the eastern wing some time ago. From its real estate of 2500 sq km, it is reduced to a 250 sq km swathe of marshy forest, with nearly three lakh hapless civilians trapped–virtually imprisoned–within. It seems to be a matter of time before the armed resistance of the LTTE is reduced to zero.

Has the Sri Lankan Tamil insurgency failed? Even as it had almost all the plus points and favorable conditions? The answer will very soon be 'yes.' The question then for the warfare specialists and military thinkers is why has it failed?

It is said that war is politics by other means. In return can it also be said that war should revert to politics at an opportune moment? The LTTE seems to have missed this aspect. Identifying the opportune moment depends on many factors–stages of success achieved in the continuum of the conflict; people's welfare and well-being, levels of favorable factors obtained which help the further pursuit of the ongoing struggle, i.e. people's feelings, outside support, safe areas, effectiveness of operational methods, availability of resources, international opinion and so on. Fascist, dictatorial, self-righteous regimes find it difficult to identify such a moment. This much emerges clearly.

It is said that war is politics by other means. In return can it also be said that war should revert to politics at an opportune moment? The LTTE seems to have missed this aspect.

Over the years the LTTE earned more international opprobrium over its numerous assassinations, explosions, obduracy, deceit, intolerance, continuation of violence and stark rigidity. It even earned the terrorist tag and has been internationally banned. It torpedoed successfully all peace efforts, all development and reconstruction projects and plans in the war ravaged North and East, and obviously paid little attention to the woes and weal of the people. A 4.5 billion dollar aid offered by Japan and other donor countries in 2003 was rejected by the LTTE as it

Lt Gen SC Sardeshpande was the Divisional Commander of 54 Infantry Division in Sri Lanka, and later Deputy GOC, Headquarters IPKF, Chennai linked the peace process to the offer. Indian's proposal for a safe zone for the lakhs of civilians caught or forcibly retained in the war zone was not respected by the LTTE. It lost major part of Indian sympathy by killing Rajiv Gandhi and eliminating other Sri Lankan Tamil leaders on Indian soil. It stood to lose even in Tamil Nadu itself, notwithstanding the outpourings of Vaiko. Its Sri Lankan Tamil representational charter appears to have been lost, giving way to the Tamil people themselves, perhaps a worst blow to the LTTE. That has cleared the way for the Sri Lankan military to methodically destroy the LTTE. The Sri Lankan military and government have not distinguished themselves as the practitioners of winning people's hearts and minds, a cardinal principle of counter-insurgency. And yet the LTTE has been losing people's support. That is a point of significance.

The Indian government concentrated on the well-being of the Sri Lankan Tamil people, and cast away the LTTE as terrorists. The feeling making rounds is that the fight is against the obstinate LTTE which cares little for the people, and not to jeopardize the Tamil people as such. The LTTE in the name of the Sri Lankan Tamil insurgency has brought about this situation upon itself through its thoughtlessness, rigidity, selfishness and political arrogance. Its injunction that the people too have to suffer in the cause of freedom has perhaps backfired in the face of its obstinacy, overemphasis amounting to force, and lack of political wherewithal to bring succor to the people.

The Sri Lankan military and government have not distinguished themselves as the practitioners of winning people's hearts and minds, a cardinal principle of counter-insurgency. And yet the LTTE has been losing people's support. That is a point of significance.

There is a parallel here when we juxtapose the instance of Pakistan–its military and the people it holds in thrall as their sole protector. It is becoming obvious that the crack and the chasm between the people and their militant instrument and activities are emerging as dominant factors in the scale of success. It is particularly noticeable in insurgency–guerilla war combination. Same is the case with the waning insurgency in the J&K–chasm between the insurgents and the people. It is clear therefore that while insurgency, guerilla operations, militant activities are only means, the main thing is the mindset of the people and their active support. The militant leadership of the Tamil insurgency seems to have missed this reality in the conduct of insurgency, and the role of political activity in carrying on the struggle from the point armed activity has brought it to.

In this light the blame on the IPKF for its so-called failure in the three years of its involvement in Sri Lanka seems to be less than justified as its operations brought about a situation of devolution of power to the Tamils there in a suitable political arrangement , and which is once again being talked about as the best solution in the present situation as well, even as the mindset of not only the Tamils but also of the Sri Lankan and Indian governments has changed in favor of the people, relegating their leadership arrogated by the LTTE. *The Times of India* issue of 1 Feb'09 says, "In the past year India made a careful distinction between the LTTE and ordinary Tamils. It said the LTTE must be crushed even as ordinary Tamils are helped to reclaim political, economic and social rights. It is this distinction that drives India's Sri Lanka policy". The emphasis everywhere is on reconstruction and rehabilitation. Rambukwella, a Sri Lankan minister says "India's influence will be greater after the demise of the LTTE" – a sea-change from the earlier LTTE's image as India's leverage in Tamil affairs to that of its demise! MJ Akbar writes in the same issue, "...Colombo has reason for continued suspicion of Delhi...But it has exchanged past bitterness for common sense, refused to let animosity interfere with trade, benefited from the ensuing economic partnership and created a sustainable and equitable relationship with Delhi".

Prabhakaran alienated his eastern brethren, lost their support, cleared the way for their elected representation in the Sri Lankan parliament, adding another heavy blow to the LTTE's Eelam idea and cause. His leadership is established and accepted more out of fear and ruthlessness than through persuasion and consideration for people's will. Nearly two generations have suffered thus, with little to show by way of worthwhile progress. In Nagaland it was within a decade of their uprising that the Nagas got their statehood. In Mizoram their chief insurgent leader took over as the state's chief minister, democratically elected, and within the constitutional framework.

The LTTE started seeing itself as a military power and started building its conventional forces–artillery, air force, navy. That led to its undertaking its conventional, positional war. These forces were at the particular stage no more than fancy stuff, as it turned out, when in opposition to the regular Sri Lankan military units, and offered set-piece territorial targets for attacks by superior forces. In the interregnum the fight with the LTTE over three decades saw the graduation of the largely ceremonial Sri Lankan military into a professional fighting force, with sufficient experience and military hardware. LTTE's premature conversion to conventional forces and positional war seems to have been its undoing. Worse, its traditional tactic of pushing upfront its civilian human shield, and ruthlessly resorting to it even in conventional war holding captive hordes and lakhs of helpless civilians in the shrinking war zone may have set afire human rights activists, and certainly must have displeased and endangered the human gun fodder.

LTTE is a banned terrorist organization, it cannot even change its name like Lashkar-e-Toiba, so famous and prominent the world over. In its Eelam obsession, in its irredeemable demand for enormous sacrifices by the people over years upon years, in its boorishly uncompromising self-righteous attitude which can only be called irrational and obstinate, and in its treating the very people as secondary and expendable, the LTTE has let a breach appear between itself and the people. Its senseless and demoniac exercise of terror, violence, assassination, destruction and elimination, with no thought, leave aside efforts, on reconstruction and relief for the people are widening the chasm. Its self-delusion of graduating to conventional forces and positional warfare has been leading it to self-destruction as is becoming clearer as days pass. Its failure or refusal to judiciously mix political efforts, armed violence and flexibility of approach to arrive at an agreeable solution for the common weal of the people has left no friends, no help and little sympathy. India's standing aside has already resulted in the Sri Lankan government seeking arms and ammunition from Pakistan as reported a TV channel. China eyes the Indian Ocean with renewed hope and desire. It has remained on sympathetic and helpful terms with the Sri Lankan government over these four decades and more. LTTE's treatment of Sri Lankan Muslims is cause enough for the latter's neutrality, and for extending welcome to Arab largesse. These possibilities will impact on Indian interests since "Sri Lanka is critically important to India's big power ambitions" as one journalists puts it.

> The blame on the IPKF for its so-called failure in the three years of its involvement in Sri Lanka seems to be less than justified as its operations brought about a situation of devolution of power to the Tamils there in a suitable political arrangement , and which is once again being talked about.

Despite being its northern neighbour's (India's) protégé and leverage, despite their role as the Sri Lankan Tamil's protector, as their champion of demand for a place in the sun, and as the shield against Sinhala infliction, the LTTE has been found wanting in waging a successful insurgency war because of its wanton practice of excessive violence and terrorism, failure to ensure the people's well-being and development, refusal to wisely and judiciously practise use of force and political dialogue in achieving their political goal; and because of their inflexible, obstinate rigidity, holding them captive to their fascist, dictatorial, brutally self-righteous tendencies. Fantancy of graduation to conventional forces and conventional war has capped its failure because of it being premature.

Indian Army and Management of Stress

BY MAJOR GENERAL MRINAL SUMAN

MILITARY'S PARAPLEGIC Rehabilitation Centre (PRC) at Pune provides rehabilitation support to paraplegic and tetraplegic soldiers. Most of the inmates are victims of bullet or other injuries sustained during action in war and counter-insurgency operations. During 1990s, a military delegation from a European country visited PRC. One foreign delegate wanted to know the suicide rate amongst the inmates. He found it difficult to believe that it was nil. In his country, he admitted, nearly 30 percent paraplegic soldiers exhibit suicidal tendencies and have to be kept under constant supervision. He wanted to know what made Indian soldiers so tough mentally to be able to withstand such trauma without losing the will to live. "The Indian soldier is inherently very strong mentally and can withstand extreme privations without breaking down. Additionally, faith in religion and unflinching family support act as shields," Director, PRC explained.

The above incident has been recalled to compare it with the spate of suicides and fratricides occurring in the recent past. As per reports appearing in the press, the Indian Army lost 333 soldiers due to suicides and 75 soldiers to fratricide during the period 2004 to 2006. It has been a cause of major concern. Such incidents were unheard of earlier. Where have these things gone wrong? Why have the soldiers become so weak mentally? Agreed that the increased level of insurgency imposes additional strain on the troops, but then Indian troops have been used to prolonged deployments in uncongenial areas. The Army that could fight war in sub-zero temperatures in lofty Himalayas without proper winter clothing in 1962 without a whimper of protest could possibly not become so frail as to be unable to withstand the current hardships. Have there been any disquieting changes? Has the stress level reached such alarming proportions that the soldiers are unable to cope with them and resort to desperate acts?

As per reports appearing in the press, the Indian Army lost 333 soldiers due to suicides and 75 soldiers to fratricide during the period 2004 to 2006. It has been a cause of major concern. Such incidents were unheard of earlier.

Maj Gen Mrinal Suman is India's foremost expert in defence matters.
mrinalsuman@gmail.com

A number of studies have been carried out to identify reasons for unacceptable levels of stress felt by Indian soldiers. Unfortunately, the emphasis has always been on material, obvious and well-known reasons - prolonged deployment in highly dangerous environments protracted separation from families, financial inequities and lack of liberty (as enjoyed by other citizens). These are all very relevant factors and do contribute in generating considerable stress. However, as mentioned earlier, these factors have always been in existence and soldiers have been braving them with fortitude. Therefore, there ought to be other reasons that generate stress which crosses the threshold of endurance of some soldiers and makes them break-down. What causes stress to become distress? This paper attempts to highlight those aspects which have generally remained unidentified.

Soldiers and Stress

Although stress is a biological term, it is commonly used in a metaphorical sense. It has also come to be accepted as a euphemism for describing difficulties faced by an individual. Every one faces challenges in life. These could be due to professional, societal and domestic environment. These challenges vary in intensity and are handled appropriately by human bodies, both at physical and emotional levels. Failure to adapt to challenges results in perceiving them as threats, which in turn generates pressures. When pressures become severe, human organism gets strained to respond. Extreme pressures become stress. Some experts consider stress to be as a subjective sensation as it differs with individuals with varied symptoms. When stress surpasses ability to handle, it becomes a threat to both physical and emotional well-being. While stress refers to the reaction of the organism, stressor implies perceived threat.

However, stress within manageable limits is not only desirable but essential. It acts as an engine that drives humans to excel. Unless a human experiences sufficient stress, enough adrenaline does not get produced to propel him to strive for achieving objectives beyond his normal capabilities. Stress is thus, an integral part of human functioning and is a catalyst for fulfillment of aspirations.

Stresses faced by soldiers are entirely different from those faced by civilians, both in nature and intensity. These stresses threaten emotional and psychological equilibrium of soldiers and generate the "fight-or-flight" response. Some of the major peculiarities are as follows:-

- Whereas stresses faced by civilians generally relate to material and societal issues, soldiers face both physical (threat to life) and emotional stresses. Civilians have their families with them to share their concerns unlike a soldier who has to bear it all alone – lack of family support in times of emotional disturbances is thus, a major contributory factor.
- Military's highly disciplined, hierarchal and restrictive environment deters giving vent to or sharing pent up frustrations. Howsoever disturbed a soldier may be he has to put up a façade of bravado. Bottled up discontentment with no escape valve results in a 'pressure cooker effect'. Additionally, military service is a long term commitment. Unlike civilians, soldiers cannot switch jobs if not satisfied.
- Serving in isolated, lonely and oxygen-starved high altitude areas of the Himalayas affects physiology and psychology of soldiers. For example, many soldiers fear that continued exposure to ultra-violet rays and lack of oxygen would affect their reproductive organs. Fear of impotency becomes highly stressful.
- Inability to be with parents and family in times of domestic emergencies weighs heavily on the minds of many soldiers. They do understand problems relating to exigencies of military service and distances from home, but tend to suffer from guilt complex. They feel that they have failed their parents or family. Earlier joint family system took care of many such exigencies.
- The search for recognition is one of the pursuits which all human beings indulge in and continuously strive for. The same is equally applicable to soldiers. They draw strength to face privations from the love and respect that their countrymen extend to them. Conversely, they are very sensitive to unfair and ill-informed criticism. They wonder if the nation recognises their services and values them. It causes immense despair to them. Consequently, their capacity to withstand adversities suffers.

When Stress becomes a Threat

As has been discussed earlier, stress within limits is desirable. However, once the threshold gets crossed, warning signals must be taken note of and preventive mechanism activated. As prevention is always better than cure, it is best to identify stressors and initiate advance action to minimise their intensity. Additionally, troops and commanders should be trained and prepared to manage them. Some of the major stressors faced by Indian soldiers have been discussed below.

Overstretched Functioning

Given India's geographical compulsions with long boundaries with inimical neighbours and internal unrest, Army's commitments are going to remain heavy in the foreseeable future. Therefore, troops will continue to have prolonged tenures in remote and dangerous environments. National security can never be compromised as that is the raison d'être of the Army. What can, however, be done is to minimise, and even eliminate, avoidable and extraneous work load. There is immense scope for the same.

The Indian Army is a command oriented organization. Promotions are totally dependent on command performance. All commanders in their respective short tenures have to earn their spurs and hence cannot allow any leisure time to the troops.

One of the primary reasons for excessive work load is unduly short command tenures, as increase in command vacancies has not kept pace with increase in higher ranks. A unit commander stays in command for two years normally. In such a short period he has to make his mark and earn good reports to get nomination for career courses and promotion to the next rank. He drives his unit hard without any let up. Similarly, a brigade commander gets only 18 to 24 months to impress his military bosses to get nominated to the prestigious National Defence College course. He keeps his brigade on its toes, lest any undue relaxation spoils his career prospects. The same is the case with divisional commanders as their tenure rarely exceeds 18 months.

The Indian Army is a command oriented organization. Promotions are totally dependent on command performance. All commanders in their respective short tenures have to earn their spurs and hence cannot allow any leisure time to the troops. Such a state of affairs results in continued engagement of troops on field exercises, demonstrations, sand model exercises, training camps and field firing camps. Leaves get curtailed to ensure maximum presence at all activities. Troops get exhausted with no respite whatsoever.

Army Wives Welfare Association (AWWA) is considered by most to be an avoidable encumbrance. Though well intentioned, it has degenerated into a parallel command structure with immense nuisance value. Every single unit commander wants to be freed from AWWA activities. There have been cases where unit commanders have preferred Siachen Glacier to peace tenures as they dreaded AWWA irritants. An infantry unit, when offered extended stay in a peace station, declined to accept it for similar reasons. AWWA activities are considered extraneous, burdensome, taxing and stressful. Most soldiers feel that the only purpose served by AWWA is to satisfy the ego of senior ladies and give them a façade/cover to meddle in normal military functioning.

The magnitude and frequency of celebrating unit days and other occasions has increased considerably during the last few decades. Organization of social functions for visiting dignitaries on five-star scale has become a routine. As these social dos are taken very seriously by the seniors, units get hard pressed to ensure flawless organization. In one of the divisions in a peace station, all units were asked to organize picnics by rotation and the unit commanders were graded accordingly for their organizational skills. Soldiers understand the absurdity of such employment and resent it. Such social activities mean additional work load for the troops with resultant reduction in leisure time.

Army Wives Welfare Association (AWWA) is considered by most to be an avoidable encumbrance. Though well intentioned, it has degenerated into a parallel command structure with immense nuisance value. Every single unit commander wants to be freed from AWWA activities.

Lack of Adequate Communication between Leaders and the Led

Group cohesiveness is the best protection against stress related break-downs and group cohesion is totally dependent on the degree of rapport built between commanders at various levels and their subordinates. Rapport, on the other hand, is a function of inter-personal communication in a group. Soldiers willingly repose unflinching faith in a commander who establishes an equation based on empathetic relationships. In other words, a commander assumes the role of a friend, guide and mentor. A soldier feels assured of his immediate commander's support in all matters, both official and domestic.

Earlier, immense stress was laid on commanders knowing their men and their problems. Visiting officers used to check this aspect diligently. Platoon 'make-and-mend parades' and games with troops contributed in promoting rapport. Additionally, *'arzi report'* and *'sainik sammelan'* provided ample opportunities to the soldiers to put up their personal and collective points to commanders in the chain of command. Serious cognizance was taken of all issues raised and feedback provided to the concerned personnel. Commanders used the platform of *'sainik sammelans'* to keep troops informed of various policy issues and other developments.

Unfortunately, over the last few years, there has been a complete breakdown of communication between commanders and their subordinates. Platoon parades and games with troops have gone out of practice. *'Arzi reports'* and *'sainik sammelans'* are given perfunctory importance. Soldiers are discouraged to put up any issue lest records show dissatisfaction of troops.

Acute shortage of officers is the primary cause for this state of affairs. Units which are authorized 24 officers are being made to function with 7–9 officers. A company which should have 4–5 officers is being manned by a single officer. It is well nigh impossible for him either to know all soldiers in the company or to look after their welfare adequately. "Who has time to know men?" is the common refrain. Shortage of officers coupled with overloaded working environment make a deadly combination in which the officers have no time for their troops. Such a situation lends itself to acts of desperation by some over-stressed and distressed soldiers.

Social Inequalities and Discrimination

Social interaction is encouraged in the services to promote cohesion amongst officers. They also provide an opportunity for senior commanders to gauge the morale of their junior officers by engaging them in casual and informal conversation. Earlier, this aspect was taken very seriously by all commanders. Commanders and their wives considered it to be their bounden duty to mingle with all to feel the pulse. Any undercurrent of dissatisfaction was noticed by them and corrective action initiated to nip the problem in the bud. Field Marshal Manekshaw had issued informal orders that he did not want his senior staff officers to surround him in social gatherings as he wanted to interact with junior officers and their spouses. Same was the practice followed by Lieutenant General Bhagat and others.

Sadly, social functions have got reduced to networking opportunities. Senior officers and their ladies, surrounded by their cronies, remain confined to a separate VIP corner. Every function today has separate tables and enclosures for senior officers to ensure that they get exclusive hospitality. On one hand, such social discrimination and stratification keeps commanders totally ignorant of brewing dissatisfaction, while on the other hand, subordinate officers consider such treatment as an affront to their self respect. Thus, social interaction which should promote cohesion ends up creating dissentions. A minor grievance may take the form of major dissent if not noticed and addressed in time.

Rashtriya Rifles and Counter Insurgency Operations

Rashtriya Rifle (RR) units have been raised for fighting internal insurgency. The format may have been working well operationally but has many negative attributes as regards man-management. Officers and soldiers are drawn from different units. They come together for a single tenure and revert to their respective parent units thereafter. Therefore, while serving in RR units the troops miss their regimental buddies and officers. Many soldiers feel insecure and resent absence of mutual camaraderie.

As all RR units are located in high risk insurgency-infested areas, soldiers are subjected to intense physical pressure. Without the support of familiar regimental environment, emotional anxieties rise to precarious levels, thereby depleting soldiers' strength to withstand prolonged exposure to stresses.

Another issue dogging RR units pertains to burgeoning court cases. Making false allegations against the armed forces is a standard ploy of anti-national elements the world over. It is the easiest way to win public sympathy while discrediting and demoralizing soldiers. Militants in Kashmir have understood the power of such misinformation campaigns. Whenever under pressure, phony accusations are made against soldiers for alleged molestation of women or for looting civilian property. Every single case of misdemeanor by soldiers has been thoroughly and diligently probed by the armed forces and almost all of them have found to be baseless.

As politicians can never miss an opportunity to exploit such issues, they jump in the fray and start demanding legal action against falsely accused soldiers. Media and self-styled human rights activists start a hate campaign to malign the forces. Cases are registered by the local police. Beleaguered soldiers have a miserable time responding to court summons and proving their innocence. Unfortunately, little help is extended to them by the services. They are left to fend for themselves. They feel let down. Many soldiers wonder whether aggressive anti-terrorist actions are worth the risk of getting embroiled in false court cases. There have been numerous cases where such predicament has generated unbearable stress.

Inadequacy of Grievance Redressal Mechanism

Although the importance of an effective grievance redressal mechanism is well understood, inadequate attention is being paid to this critical aspect of man-management. This is proved by the fact that over one lakh armed force related cases are pending in different courts in India with more than 10,000 cases in various High Courts. As per the rules, all service personnel are allowed to seek audience with their commanders to apprise them of their complaint and seek redressal. In case not fully satisfied, they can submit written appeals to the Chief (non-statutory complaints) and the Government (statutory complaints). Time-bound action has been mandated on such complaints. Against the laid down time span of six months for final disposal, a complainant considers himself fortunate if he receives dispensation during his service. Most complaints shuttle up and down the bureaucratic hierarchy on technicalities.

Another issue dogging RR units pertains to burgeoning court cases. Making false allegations against the armed forces is a standard ploy of anti-national elements the world over. It is the easiest way to win public sympathy while discrediting and demoralizing soldiers.

The Military Secretary's Branch, tasked to handle all complaints, has acquired notoriety for inaction and total lack of empathy and urgency. Complainants have to pull strings or visit Delhi repeatedly to coax action on their representations. The whole system is so insensitive that unless an individual can exert pressure, nothing moves. In some cases, complainants retire before their cases are finally disposed off, making the whole exercise meaningless. Handling of complaints by the Ministry of Defence is even more slipshod. Functionaries have to be approached to have the files moved. There are also allegations of some favors being sought as quid pro quo.

Entry of Women Officers

Concern for equality of sexes and political expediency forced the Government to allow intake of women as officers in select arms and services in 1992. Although no formal attempt has ever been made to study the effect of women's entry on the officer cadre, discussions with most commanding officers reveal that the presence of women has created additional and totally unwarranted stress amongst officers. Over 40 commanding officers were spoken to and all were of the view that there has been a discernible increase in inter-personal tensions.

Presence of women amongst males tends to make the environment formal and stiff. Men miss their light hearted banter which is considered essential to release work tensions and promote group cohesion. They consider women to be intruding on their privacy. Moreover, many officers resent additional work load that they have to take on as many tasks cannot be delegated to women.

Mutual comfort level between men and women colleagues is low as societal and cultural ethos continue to be mired in sex discrimination. Most of the women opting for a career in the services belong to families where their upbringing has been in a highly sheltered environment. A career in the military is at the other extreme. Even casual friendship between a woman officer and her male colleague is construed as a developing relationship. At times the emotional quotient becomes so high that it generates jealousies and envy. There have been a number of cases where either a woman officer or a male colleague have taken friendship as long term emotional commitment and suffered mental breakdown when things went awry.

Symptoms of Different Stages of Stress amongst Soldiers

BY MAJOR GENERAL MRINAL SUMAN

Stress is essential for human existence as it impels him to excel, much beyond his normal capabilities. In other words, stress is a driver for the fulfillment of aspirations. However, it must remain within manageable limits. When it crosses the threshold of tolerance, it threatens emotional and psychological equilibrium. Stresses faced by soldiers are entirely different from those faced by civilians, both in nature and intensity. Whereas stresses faced by civilians generally relate to material and societal issues, soldiers face both physical (threat to life) and psychosomatic stresses. If not managed in time, they generate "fight-or-flight" response with severe consequences.

	Useful Stress	Threshold	Stages of Harmful Stress Experienced by Soldiers			
			Alarm	Resistance	Exhaustion	Breakdown
Nature	Stress is the primary motivator for soldiers to strive for mission fulfillment	Differs with individuals depending on individual degree of sensitivity and coping mechanism	Body starts sensing demands and challenges which exceed normal levels	Body's defence mechanism tries to adapt to the stresses and gets stretched	Body's defence mechanism reaches close to breaking point	Body's defence mechanism collapses and normal functioning ceases
Symptoms	• High degree of arousal and excitement • Urge to excel and stand out		• Anxiety • Tension • Restlessness • Inability to concentrate • Dissatisfaction	• Irritability • Impatience • Short temper • Mood swings • Indecisiveness • Loss of appetite • Constant worrying	• Cognitive impairment • Memory problems • Pessimism • Insomnia • Weight loss • Alcoholism • Drug use	• Aggression • Depression • Trauma • Agitation • Sense of isolation • Feeling of being overwhelmed

Managing Stress and the Way Forward

Undoubtedly, the problem is serious. It will not be incorrect to describe it as a failure of command. Therefore, reforms must start at the command level. A three-pronged approach should be followed as discussed below.

- *Command Level Initiatives.*
  - All efforts should be made to increase command tenures at all levels to provide continuity, as short tenures result in hectic pace of activities for troops. Such a measure will have to be implemented in a graduated manner.
  - Maximum period in a year for which troops can be exercised must be unequivocally laid down. Adequate period for recuperation and recreation must be ensured.
  - Intake of officers should be increased by making Short Service Commission attractive by assuring second careers to all.
  - Commanders must identify themselves with their troops by close and regular interaction. They should also be trained to read symptoms of stress building up in a soldier and initiate corrective action in time.
- *Organizational Level Reforms.*
  - Status of soldiers must be improved. They should be made to feel wanted and respected. Civil authorities should be impressed upon to extend all possible help to the families of the soldiers who are posted in field areas.
  - Platoon parades and games with the troops must be made compulsory and given as much importance as operational training.
  - The system of redressal of grievances must be made more responsive and considerate. Troops must be convinced that their genuine concerns would be attended to in a just, fair and time-bound manner.
  - Policy on induction of women officers should be regularly reviewed and modified as per the feed back received.
  - Maintenance of cantonments and other routine tasks should be outsourced to civilian agencies to reduce administrative load on units.
- *Psychological Level Measures.*
  - Every unit should have a few officers trained in elementary counseling functions. Timely and on-the-spot counseling can prevent many potentially risky cases.
  - Religious teachers should be capable of giving discourses which soothe strained nerves and put troops at ease during tough times. They should also be given training in handling sensitive soldiers and help them in ridding negative thoughts.
  - Yoga is another effective method of helping soldiers to cope up with stresses. It should be done regularly and under expert supervision.
  - Buddy system should be promoted. Every soldier should have a buddy who acts as his companion, confidante and alter-ego. Buddy provides a shoulder to unload fears and apprehensions. Secondly and more importantly, an alert buddy can gauge abnormal behavioral changes at an early stage and bring the matter to their commander's notice.

Intensity of stress is always based on the perceptions and responses of humans trying to adapt to the challenges of everyday life. These challenges in military life are different than those faced by civilians, both in terms of threat of physical harm and emotional security. In the case of the Indian military, these stresses acquire heightened severity due to prolonged deployment in challenging environments and absence of family support.

Finally, introduction of much-needed organizational and institutional changes to keep the environment free of excessive stress is the ideal way of dealing with the problem. As the threshold of tolerance varies in individuals, it is equally essential to keep a close watch on soldiers who display signs of getting stressed. In case local commanders feel that expert medical or psychiatric help is required, there should be no hesitation in seeking that. Management of stress is a function of command for which innovative measures are needed.

An Analysis of China's White Papers on Defense

BY CLAUDE ARPI

HAVE YOU EVER HEARD OF THE term 'Informationization'?

The word is used 48 times in the new White Paper (WP) on Defense[1] published by The Information Office of State Council of the People's Republic of China. It is the sixth WP since Beijing started the biennial exercise in 1998. It is considered (by Beijing at least) to be an attempt at transparency.

But what is this 'Informationization' about?

While most classical dictionaries have never heard of the word, *Wiktionary* says that it is a synonym for 'Informatization'.

In the White Paper, 'Informationization' is mostly used for Information and Communication Technology (ICT). The extensive repetition of the word shows an important direction in which the Chinese Armed forces are engaged.

A research paper, *Who Owns Informationization?* published by Kathleen Hartford of University of Massachusetts/Boston gives a better explanation: "The term, increasingly employed [in China] to describe an overall process, has in recent years become a linchpin of central and many local development strategies, and a talismanic device that is supposed to modernize the party-state system, upgrade ailing parts of the economy, turn the Chinese into true denizens of the 21st century, and plug China into the wider world. And all without undermining the dominant position of the Communist Party and the Chinese state – indeed, while increasing its effectiveness and its reach."[2]

Claude Arpi writes regularly on Tibet, China, India and Indo-French relations in *The Pioneer*, the *New Indian Express*, *rediff.com* and other Indian and French publications. He is the author of *Tibet: The Lost Frontier* and his forthcoming book is *The Negotiations That Never Were*.
claudearpi@gmail.com

In the WP, 'Informationization' is mostly used for Information and Communication Technology (ICT).

The extensive repetition of the word shows an important direction in which the Chinese Armed forces are engaged.

This trend is not restricted to the defense sector, Hartford rightly writes: "China's highest leaders have, increasingly over the past two decades, encouraged, urged, and embraced not only the development of ICT industries but the application and use of ICTs in all spheres of government, industry, education, culture, and even… agriculture."

Interestingly, Hartford describes the general characteristics of ICTs; they usually do not belong to the domain of the State:

- These are technologies characterized by the rapid pace of innovation, a process that by its very nature defies planning.
- These are technologies that both transcend and undermine geographic borders, the foundation of modern state structures.
- These are technologies that alter the state/individual balance of powers resting upon control of, or access to information and communication, placing more autonomy in the hands of individuals.

Though the above particularities are also true in China, the State and more particularly the defense establishment seem determined to make the most of the new technologies in information and communication.

This is certainly one of the most striking features of the WP.

'Informationized conditions' is also described as an operating environment characterized by communications jamming, electronic surveillance, precision weaponry and of course, cyber war.[3]

When Beijing speaks of 'local wars under conditions of Informationization', its defense establishment means to "take into overall consideration the evolution of modern warfare and the major security threats facing China, and prepares for defensive operations under the most difficult and complex circumstances."

For China which has been more inclined to protracted People's Wars, it is a new concept of war. The WP explains that it is: "Designed to bring the operational strengths of different services and arms into full play, combine offensive operations with defensive operations, give priority to the flexible application of strategies and tactics, seek advantages and avoid disadvantages, and make the best use of our strong points to attack the enemy's weak points."

The capacity to sustain a war at a distance against a more powerful adversary should be added. In 2006, the Quadrennial Defense Review Report had noted, "[China] has the greatest potential to compete militarily with the United States and field disruptive military technologies that could over time offset traditional U.S. military advantages."[4]

It is apparent in the WP that it is one of the objectives of the modernization of China's defense forces.

Release of the WP

Though entitled *China's National Defense in 2008*, the paper was released in January 2009; and not on any odd date. The Chinese, always fond of symbols, chose the day of the swearing-in ceremony of President Barak Obama. Pundits will also point out that it was the Martin Luther King Day, a day dedicated to non-violence: the choice of the State Council is certainly not fortuitous.

Adam Wolfe, an analyst based in New York, comments on the WP in 'ISN Security Watch:'[5] "As with previous reports, 'China's National Defense in 2008' is short on specifics about equipment and technology. Also, the US intelligence community remains convinced that China has understated its military budget by about 50 percent and is deliberately hiding its intentions. What is notable about the new paper is that it directly addresses the budget."

Though, it may not be a 'breaking news' type of publication, many interesting trends emerge while going through the preface and the 14 chapters of the WP[6] apart from the 'Informationization' being the most important trend.

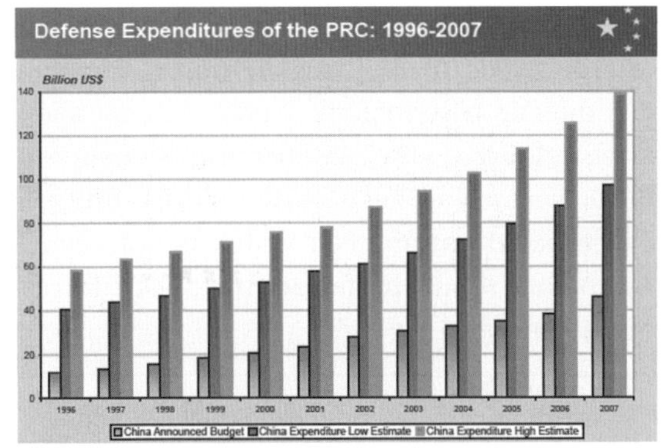

Figure 6. Defense Expenditures of the PRC: 1996-2007. *The graphic depicts China's official defense budget since 1996, and associated DoD estimates of actual defense expenditures. Announced budgets are from State Council announcements during the annual National People's Congress meeting. DoD estimates include projected expenses for strategic forces, foreign acquisitions, military research and development, and paramilitary forces. All figures are in 2007 U.S. dollars*

Public Relation exercise

Undoubtedly, the WP is first and foremost an exercise in public relations for the People's Republic of China which wants to project a new image: that of a responsible nation, fully involved in global issues facing the planet and ready to help find solutions to these problems.

In the Preface itself, the WP explains: "Historic changes have taken place in the relations between contemporary China and the rest of the world. The Chinese economy has become an important part of the world economy, China has become an important member of the international system, and the future and destiny of China have been increasingly closely connected with the international community. China cannot develop in isolation from the rest of the world, nor can the world enjoy prosperity and stability without China."

One of the most salient pieces of information in the WP is the evolution of Beijing's view on Taiwan which has traditionally been used as the pretext for the navy and artillery build-up.

The Cultural Revolution's days, when Mao Zedong did not care about the rest of the world, are gone. This is certainly a progress, though the declared policy and the facts do not often tally in practice.

In consonance with President Hu Jintao's theory of the Peaceful Rise of China, the WP affirms: "Starting from this new historical turning point, China is unswervingly taking the road of peaceful development, unswervingly carrying out its policies of reform and opening-up its socialist modernization, unswervingly pursuing an independent foreign policy of peace and a national defense policy solely aimed at protecting its territory and people, and endeavoring to build, together with other countries, a harmonious world of enduring peace and common prosperity."

Once again, the profession of faith is worth recording, even if the reality is often different, mainly due the one-party regime which does not allow diversity to express itself. Further, in order to survive, the present regime has a tendency to use an over-exacerbated nationalism which is not always compatible with its professed concern for the rest of the world.

Revolution in Military Affairs

The concept of Revolution in Military Affairs (RMA) is recurring, as is the idea of 'active defensive'. Practically it means a military strategy in which China does not initiate wars, but engages in war to defend its national sovereignty and territorial integrity: "Strategically, it adheres to the principle of featuring defensive operations, self-defense and striking and getting the better of the enemy only after the enemy has started an attack," says the WP which also introduces the notion of 'RMA with Chinese characteristics'.

Beijing, minimizing the importance of the sources of conflicts (not only Taiwan) continues to insist that its armed forces are playing an active and constructive role in multilateral affairs and that this new attitude is "notably elevating its international position and influence".

The WP gives the history of the concept: "Entering the 1990s, the PLA began to vigorously promote RMA with Chinese characteristics. It established the military strategic guideline of active defense for the new era, based on winning local wars in conditions of modern technology, particularly high technology. It began to adopt a strategy of strengthening the military by means of science and technology, and a three-step development strategy in modernizing national defense and the armed forces, and promoted the coordinated development of national defense and economy."

For the leaders in Beijing and especially the Central Military Commission (CMC) which rules over defense matters, this is the best way to move forward for the PLA: "Regarding RMA with Chinese characteristics as the only way to modernize the military, it put forward the strategic goal of building an informationized military and winning informationized wars."

All this gives us an idea of the general direction in which the PLA wants to go in the years to come, but nothing very specific is mentioned.

The Taiwan issue

One of the most salient pieces of information in the WP is the evolution of Beijing's view on Taiwan which has traditionally been used as the pretext for the navy and artillery build-up.

The newly released document explains that "the society remains stable and unified, and the capability for upholding national security has been further enhanced." And further adds: "The attempts of the separatist forces for 'Taiwan independence' to seek '*de jure* Taiwan independence' have been thwarted, and the situation across the Taiwan Straits has taken a significantly positive turn. The two sides have resumed and made progress in consultations on the common political basis of the '1992 Consensus' and consequently cross-Straits relations have improved."

This is good news and can only help in reducing the tensions in the region. However, later in the WP, the Chinese defense ministry admits that: "Impact of uncertainties and destabilizing factors in China's outside security environment on national security and development is growing. In particular, the United States continues to sell arms to Taiwan in violation of the principles established in the three Sino-US joint communiqués, causing serious harm to Sino-US relations as well as peace and stability across the Taiwan Straits."

In the years to come there is no doubt that Chinese defence forces will continue to concentrate on the rebel island which remains the main external (through Beijing would object to the use of the term 'external') threat for Beijing.

Cheng-Yi Lin in an article, *China's 2008 Defense White Paper: The View from Taiwan in the China Brief* however asserts: "The White Paper fails to address concerns over Chinese missile deployments targeting Taiwan and US forces stationed on bases surrounding Taiwan."

The same author notes that there was hardly any reaction in Taipei after the publication of the document. "Taiwan's defense ministry shunned away from making a public statement on the 2008 White Paper, [but] experts in Taiwan argue that there is little new information revealed in the White Paper".

Beijing, minimizing the importance of the sources of conflicts (not only Taiwan) continues to insist that its armed forces are playing an active and constructive role in multilateral affairs and that this new attitude is "notably elevating its international position and influence". The main objective of the WP is, let us not forget, to project to the outside this post-Olympics image of China as a responsible nation which cares.

Budget growth

One could ask, if the situation has improved so much and the threat perception decreased, why increase the defense budget by 20 percent?

The WP in a way answer this question: the defense budget had to be increased for three reasons:

- Increasing the salaries and benefits of servicemen.
- Compensating for price hikes such as the rise in price of food, building materials, fuel, etc.
- Pushing forward the RMA [Revolution in Military Affairs]. China has augmented the input into military informationization and moderately increased the funds for equipment and supporting facilities, so as to raise the defense capabilities in conditions of informationization.

The transformation of the PLA into a modern force is one important component of the budget increase.

Beijing justifies thus its approach: "Both the total amount and per-service-person share of China's defense expenditure remain lower than those of some major powers. In 2007 China's defense expenditure equaled 7.51 percent of that of the United States, 62.43 percent of that of the United Kingdom. China's defense expenses per-service-person amounted to 4.49 percent of that of the United States, 11.3 percent of that of Japan, 5.31 percent of that of the United Kingdom, 15.76 percent of that of France and 14.33 percent of that of Germany."

It is the RMA field which absorbs most of the budgetary increment (hidden or disclosed). It is

	Active Force	Reserve Force	Militia	Total	
				Amount	Percentage
Personnel	118.971	1.044	0	120.015	33.76
Training & Maintenance	112.268	1.515	7.258	121.042	34.05
Equipment	112.200	1.134	1.100	114.434	32.19
Total	343.439	3.693	8.359	355.491	100.00

Chart 1: China's Defense Expenditure in 2007 (unit: RMB billion)[8]

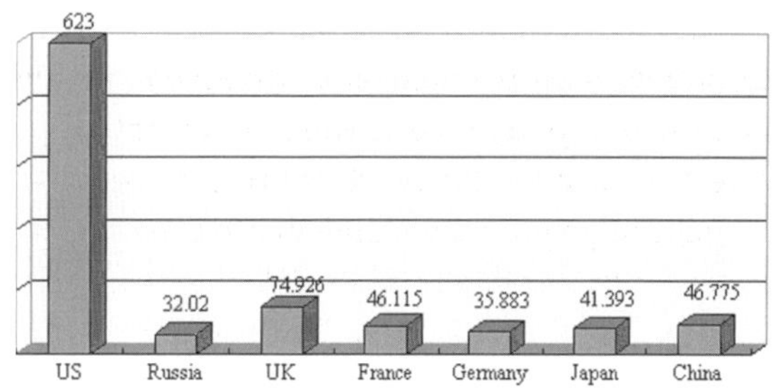

Chart 2: Comparison of Defense Expenditures of Some Countries in 2007 (unit: US$ billion)

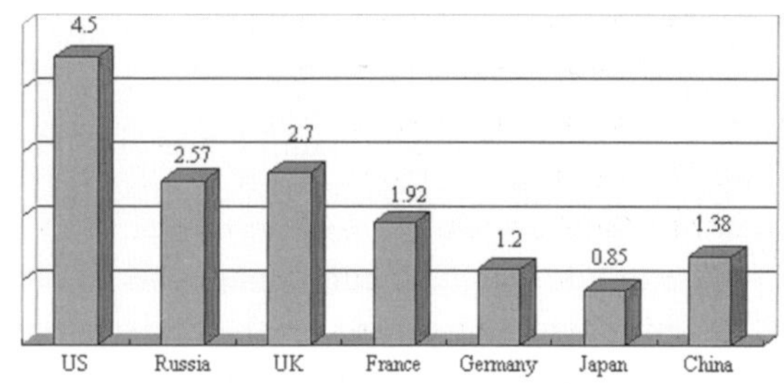

Chart 3: Comparison of Percentages of Defense Expenditures in the GDP of Some Countries in 2007 (%)

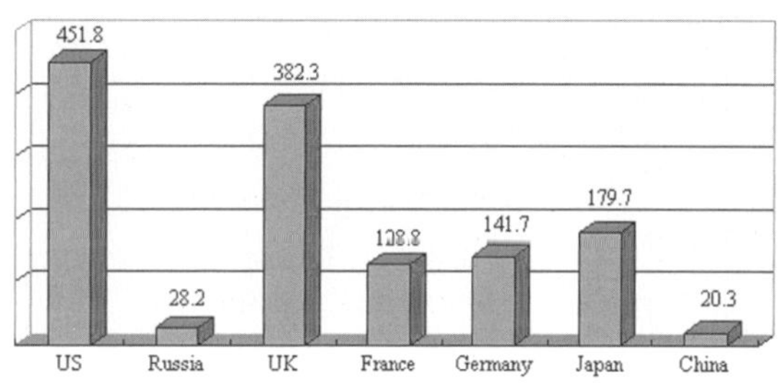

Chart 4: Comparison of Per-Service-Person Share of Defense Expenditure of Some Countries in 2007 (unit: US$ 1,000)

clear from the Chinese declaration of intention that a large chunk of the defense budget's increase goes towards preparation of 'informationized wars'.

Two months after the release of the WP, Premier Wen Jiabao delivered his annual speech at the National People's Congress. According to Xinhua, he reaffirmed that: "China will transform its military training based on mechanized warfare to that based on informationized warfare. In the coming year, we need to make our army more revolutionary, modern and standardized."

In his report, the Premier explained: "The building of computerized armed forces has entered a new era of all-round development." It was also announced that Beijing planned to increase its defense budget by 14.9 percent to US $ 70 billion in 2009.

The Chinese Premier reiterated the other

arguments for larger budget needs (rise increase in salary and compensation for inflation).

Outreach Diplomacy

As already mentioned, China's positive image in the world is a significant motivation for Beijing. The WP states: "It takes military operations other than war (MOOTW) as an important form of applying national military forces, and scientifically makes and executes plans for the development of MOOTW capabilities. China participates in international security cooperation, conducts various forms of military exchanges and promotes the establishment of military confidence-building mechanisms in accordance with this guideline."

It is in this context that India appears in the WP: "China has begun to hold defense and security consultations with India."

Though the United States "welcomes the rise of a stable, peaceful, and prosperous China", the Pentagon admits that: "Much uncertainty surrounds China's future course, in particular in the area of its expanding military power and how that power might be used."

The WP elaborates: "Since 2007 China has held over 20 joint military exercises or joint training exercises with a score of countries. ...In December 2007 and December 2008, armies of China and India staged joint counter-terrorism training exercises respectively in Kunming, China and Belgaum, India."

We shall refrain from commenting about these exercises, though it seems strange that India needs to train China in 'counter-terrorism.'

The participation of the Chinese navy in the anti-piracy operations off the coast of Somalia is certainly an important development for China. It is "probably more of a sign of things to come than a one-off publicity stunt," says Adam Wolfe in his *ISN Security Watch*'s article.

Further, China has about 1,950 military peacekeepers serving in nine UN missions last year. It is an unprecedented effort.

The US view

Washington does not see Beijing's growing defense budget through the same eyes. Though the United States "welcomes the rise of a stable, peaceful, and prosperous China", the Pentagon admits that: "Much uncertainty surrounds China's future course, in particular in the area of its expanding military power and how that power might be used."

According to the latest *Annual Report to Congress – Military Power of the People's Republic of China, 2008,*[9] "The PLA is pursuing comprehensive transformation from a mass army designed for protracted wars of attrition on its territory to one capable of fighting and winning short-duration, high intensity conflicts along its periphery against high-tech adversaries – an approach that China refers to as preparing for local wars under conditions of informatization."

The US Report believes that the PLA is developing capabilities for use in other contingencies, such as conflict over resources or disputed territories.[10]

This is of course not mentioned in the WP.

Though the publication of regular updated WPs is a small progress towards a greater transparency, China's military development remains very opaque. As the Report to the Congress asserts: "The international community has limited knowledge of the motivations, decision-making, and key capabilities supporting China's military modernization. China's leaders have yet to explain in detail the purposes and objectives of the PLA's modernizing military capabilities. For example, China continues to promulgate incomplete defense expenditure figures, and engage in actions that appear inconsistent with its declaratory policies. The lack of transparency in China's military and security affairs poses risks to stability by increasing the potential for misunderstanding and miscalculation. This situation will naturally and understandably lead to hedging against the unknown."

The report added: "The pace and scope of China's military transformation have increased in recent years, fueled by acquisition of advanced foreign weapons, continued high rates of investment in its domestic defense and science and technology industries, and far reaching organizational and doctrinal reforms of the armed forces."

This is particularly true for China's nuclear force modernization and particularly worrying not only in Washington, but in several other capitals (probably excluding Delhi, as it is not in the Indian psyche to worry).

Beyond the Words

For the first time, the WP goes into details on how and when Beijing may use its nuclear forces: "If China comes under a nuclear threat, the nuclear missile force of the Second Artillery Force will go into a state of alert, and get ready for a nuclear counterattack to deter the enemy from using nuclear weapons against China. If China comes under a nuclear attack, the nuclear missile force of the Second Artillery Force will use nuclear missiles to launch a resolute counterattack against the enemy either independently or together with the nuclear forces of other services. The conventional missile force of the Second Artillery Force is charged mainly with the task of conducting medium and long-range precision strikes against key strategic and operational targets of the enemy."

and a day later, the refusal for the *USS Kitty Hawk* to anchor in Hong Kong harbor. Even if the PRC subsequently reversed its decision, it was too late and the harm was done.

The WP does not give any details on the new Chinese destroyers, frigates, submarines and warplanes that have greatly improved the PLA Navy capability as a regional power.

The building of an aircraft carrier is also not mentioned in the WP.

The US Report on the *Military Power of the People's Republic of China* confirms what is known in defense circles: "China has an active aircraft carrier research and design program. If the leadership were to so choose, the PRC shipbuilding industry could start construction of an indigenous platform by the end of this decade."

But once again no specifics are mentioned, not even about the fielding of the new DF-31 and DF-31A intercontinental-range missiles which have greatly enhanced Beijing's strategic strike capabilities.

Transparency has some limits in China.

Morever not a word has been said to explain the anti-satellite (ASAT) test in January 2007, though Beijing is aware that it marked a major turning in Sino-U.S. military relations.

Another issue which led to the deterioration of the US-China relations was the last minute denial of entry into Hong Kong of the *USS Patriot* and *USS Guardian*, two small mine sweepers, seeking temporary bad-weather refuge in the Chinese port

Ditto for submarines: "Two new SHANG-class (Type 093) nuclear-powered attack submarines (SSN) and one JIN-class (Type 094) SSBN may soon enter service alongside four older HAN-class SSNs and China's single XIA-class SSBN", and the submarine launched missiles: "China is also working on a new submarine-launched ballistic missile, the JL-2, for deployment aboard the new JIN-class (Type 094) nuclear-powered ballistic missile submarines (SSBN). The JL-2 is expected to reach initial operational capability (IOC) between 2009-2010."

In China, transparency is still a limited commodity.

Interestingly, an incident involving the *USNS*

Impeccable and five Chinese vessels occurred early March 2009.

A senior Pentagon official affirmed that a US oceanographic ship was 70 miles south of Hainan Island conducting routine operations in international waters when some Chinese ships approached: "We view these as unprofessional maneuvers by the Chinese vessels and violations under international law to operate with due regard for the rights and safety of other lawful users of the Ocean."

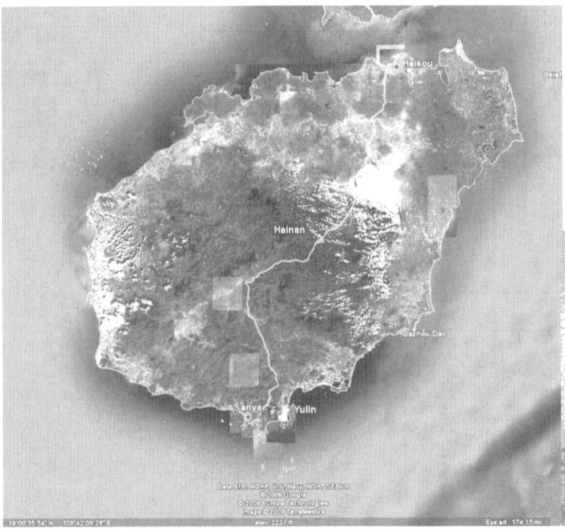

The Chinese ships, including a Chinese Navy intelligence collection ship, a Bureau of Maritime Fisheries patrol vessel, a State Oceanographic Administration patrol vessel and two small Chinese-flagged trawlers, surrounded the *Impeccable* and two ships closed into within 50 feet.

Soon after the incident, Hans Kristensen posted an article, *US-Chinese Anti-Submarine Cat and Mouse Game in South China Sea* in the Federation of American Scientists Strategic Security Blog.[11] He wrote that the incident "appears to be part of a wider and dangerous cat and mouse game between the U.S. and Chinese submarines and their hunters."

The U.S. Navy collects data on submarines and seafloor "to improve its ability to detect the submarines in peacetime and more efficiently hunt them in case of war".

Kristensen explains that the *USNS Impeccable* has the important military mission of using its array of both passive and active low frequency sonar arrays to detect and track submarines.

The US 'civilian' ship was probably monitoring the Shang-class SSN, the new class of Chinese submarines which will soon replace the old Han-class. The Shang-class submarines were recently spotted at the nearby Yulin base.

The incident shows that despite the new image of a 'Peaceful Rise of China' promoted by President Hu, Chairman of the CMC, the Chinese forces can still be very aggressive and do not care much about international laws when their national interests are at stake.

Situation Inside Tibet

When it comes to the security threat facing China, the WP does not hesitate to admit: "Being in a stage of economic and social transition, China is encountering many new circumstances

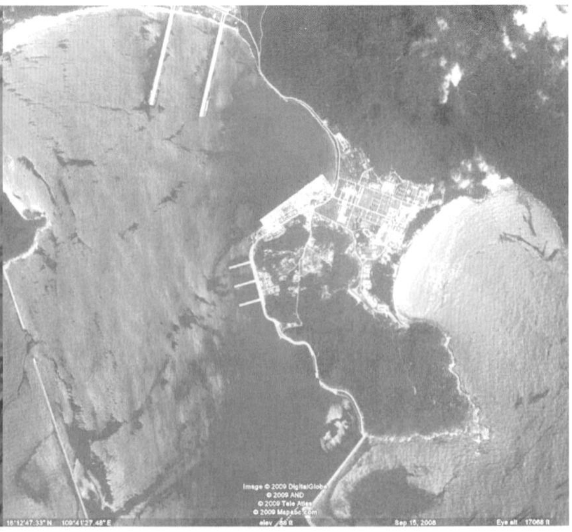

and new issues in maintaining social stability. Separatist forces working for 'Taiwan independence,' 'East Turkistan independence' and 'Tibet independence' pose threats to China's unity and security."

Though these three above threats cannot be put into the same category, it is necessary to say a few words about Tibet.

The March-April 2008 unrest on the Tibetan plateau demonstrates one of the weaknesses of Beijing's defense set-up. Due to deep resentment against the Chinese migrants and the People's Armed Police Forces (PAPF)[12], the local population in Tibet took to the streets. The Chinese authorities immediately accused the Tibetans of "hitting, smashing, stealing and burning". The 'Dalai's clique' was blamed for the incidents. The repression was ferocious; more than 200 Tibetans were killed.

Wang Lixiong, a well-known Chinese author, married to the Tibetan famous blogger, Woeser wrote an article, *Roadmap of Tibetan Independence,* in which he expressed the opinion that the violent reaction of the Chinese leadership can only create more problems for Beijing.

He made a judicious remark: "Street protests with violence similar to the '3.14' [March 14, 2008] incident repeatedly occur in Mainland China. The tactics used to handle these incidents have already been very obtusely unskillful. But if the same tactics – news blockade, passively cooling down, not stimulating further conflicts, cracking down the hardcore while providing comfort to others, and finding scapegoats in lower level bureaucracy to calm down the anger – were used to deal with the March incident, the chain reactions throughout the Tibetan area that we had seen would not have been forthcoming."

Why is it not done in Tibet?

If one thinks about it, the recurrent resentment of the Tibetan population against the Chinese is strategically extremely dangerous for Beijing. The only answer is the Great Han Chauvinism which has been plaguing China since Mao's days and has often been denounced by Chinese intellectuals.

For Mao and his colleagues, the 1962 attack against India was probably only a spank to an ill-prepared Indian Army and once the blow was given, the PLA immediately returned to its barracks in Tibet.

Many things have changed since then in the Middle Kingdom, but the Tibetan factor has remained. Regretfully, the discontent in Tibet in 1959–1962 and its implications for the Chinese defense preparedness has never been studied.

The Tibetan resentment manifested in a 70,000-character petition sent by the Panchen Lama to Mao in April 1962. In September, during a CCP Conference, Mao denounced the 'poisonous arrow' sent by the Tibetan Lama and called him 'an enemy of our class.'

In October–November 1962, a longer war with its supply base in Tibet would have been very difficult to sustain in the atmosphere of 'rebellion' prevalent on the Roof of the World at that time.

For Mao and his colleagues, the 1962 attack against India was probably only a spank to an ill-prepared Indian Army. Many things have changed since then in the Middle Kingdom, but the Tibetan factor has remained.

Whether the unrest in Tibet should be considered as a threat to China's unity and security is debatable (today the Dalai Lama only asks for a genuine autonomy within the People's Republic of China), but the leadership in Beijing should be aware that the situation is tricky and if a conflict arises in the region, the Chinese forces will have to face unprecedented difficulties.

Unfortunately, Beijing still reacts like an ostrich. On March 11, Kang Jinzhong, the Political Commissar of Armed Police Corps in Tibet told the media: "The people in Tibet and armed police stationed there enjoy harmonious relationships." He added: "The armed police earnestly implement the country's ethnic and religious policies. They love the people in Tibet and contribute to the stability and development in the region, while the local residents have shown sincere support for the armed police."

Though an entire chapter of the WP is consecrated to the People's Armed Police Force (PAPF), nothing is mentioned about Tibet except the above short sentence.

Conclusion

China's 2008 National Defense White Paper is a small leap forward on the path to transparency. It projects China as a responsible stakeholder. This is probably the main objectives of those who drafted the text.

The overall feeling while going through the WP is that the leadership in Beijing is serious about the 'modernization' of the Armed forces, though many serious issues have been kept under the wrap of secrecy dear to the Chinese leaders. The defense budget is the most obvious case, though for the first time a chapter is consecrated to the subject.

Notes

1 The WP is available on http://www.gov.cn/english/official/2009-01/20 content_1210227.htm
2 See http://web.mit.edu/chinapolicy/www/conference1/hartford.pdf
3 See our article in a previous issue of the IDR.
4 Quoted in: www.defenselink.mil/pubs/pdfs/070523-China-Military-Power-final.pdf.
5 See article in http://www.isn.ethz.ch/isn/layout/set/print/content/view/full 73?id=95974&lng=en.
6 The chapters are the following: I. The Security Situation; II. National Defense Policy; III. Reform and Development of the PLA; IV. The Army; V. The Navy; VI. The Air Force; VII. The Second Artillery Force; VIII. The People's Armed Police Force; IX. National Defense Reserve Buildup; X. The Armed Forces and the People; XI. Science, Technology and Industry for National Defense; XII. Defense Expenditure; XIII. International Security Cooperation; XIV. Arms Control and Disarmament.
7 China Brief of Jamestown Foundation, Volume 9, 3, February 5, 2009, see: http://www.jamestown.org/programs/chinabrief/
8 Source: http://www.china.org.cn/government/whitepaper/2009-01/21/content_17162799.htm
9 See www.defenselink.mil/pubs/pdfs/070523-China-Military-Power-final.pdf.
10 India has the largest areas of 'disputed territories' with China.
11 http://www.fas.org/blog/ssp/2009/03/incident.php
12 According to the WP: "As a component of China's armed forces and subordinate to the State Council, the People's Armed Police Force (PAPF) is under the dual leadership of the State Council and the CMC. The PAPF consists of the internal security force and various police forces. The border public security, firefighting and security guard forces are also components of the PAPF. The PAPF is charged with the fundamental task of safeguarding national security, maintaining social stability and ensuring that the people live and work in peace and contentment. Routine guard duties refer to duties the PAPF performs to maintain internal security, which are mostly carried out by the internal security force. The basic tasks are: to guard against all forms of attempted attacks and sabotage; protect designated individuals and facilities; ensure the security of important international and national conferences and large-scale cultural and sports events; protect important airports, radio stations, and key and confidential units, and vital places in such sectors as state economy and national defense; protect important bridges and tunnels; ensure the security of prisons and detention houses; and maintain public order in state-designated large and medium-sized cities or specific zones." The PAP has a strength of 6,60,000 personnel.

China's Maritime Thrust in Africa

BY S RAJASIMMAN

CALL IT CHINA'S NEW MILITARY diplomacy or birth traits of its emerging naval strategy, a Chinese naval fleet arrived in the Gulf of Aden off Somalia on 6 January, 2009 to carry out the first escort mission against pirates. In an efficient display of its growing naval operational capabilities, the fleet completed its twenty first mission (the largest held so far in the series) of escorting merchant ships in this region on 18 February, 2009. Ten Chinese merchant ships were convoyed while three foreign ones, including *Hermione* from Germany, *Viking Crux* from Singapore and *Princess Nataly* from Cyprus, who requested protection, were escorted by the Chinese fleet. The fleet had left sail from a port in Sanya city of China's southern-most island province of Hainan on 26 December, 2008. The fleet comprises two destroyers (*Haikou* and *DDG-169 Wuhan*) and a supply ship (*Weishanhu*) from the South China Sea Fleet. The fleet carried about 800 crew members, including 70 soldiers from the Navy's special force, and was equipped with ship-bourne missiles and light weapons.

It is worthwhile to explore this issue given the implications this would have for India and the Chinese motivation behind this decision to conduct naval operations far away from the mainland for the first time in 500 years. There seems a general consensus among many Chinese military and non-military experts that it was in China's favor to project a force far away from its shores. Firstly, China has gained enough experience in long distance naval force deployment due its frequent military exchanges with other countries. The logistics problem of supply and refueling was seen no more as a constraint. The fleet, while on its way to the Somalian coast, displayed its supply and refueling capability as it entered the India Ocean at the Malacca Straits. The supply ship *Weishanhu* refueled the two destroyers with several hundred tons of oil, an operation that an official for the fleet support described as "highly efficient".

The fact that two Chinese ships, a fishing vessel and a Hong Kong flag ship with a 25-member crew, were seized by Somalia pirates in October 2008 do not qualify as potential reasons for this long distance naval deployment. These hijacks occurred off the Kenyan coastline, and the total number of hijacks of Chinese vessels so far constitutes only 0.7 percent of the total passages. Therefore the decision may involve other factors apart from one involving immediate Chinese interest. Prior to deployment, China explicitly believed that any action in the Gulf of Aden must be carried on within the "United Nations Framework". In his address to the UN on 16 December, 2008 the Vice Foreign Minister said: "China is seriously considering sending naval ships to the Gulf of Aden and waters off the Somali coast for escorting operations in the near future." The minister also added that it appreciated the efforts made by other navies to curb the problem of piracy. This needs to be contrasted with the Chinese government's stand on growing intervention based military strategies.

> Another important motivation behind the decision to deploy the Chinese naval force off Somalia could be the fact that this involves African continent if not directly. Chinese leaders have been frequenting Africa since 2000. As a leading importer of crude oil, China depends on 25 percent of this import from Africa. This is projected to up to 40 percent by 2020.

The China Defence White Paper, 2000 stated that the UN role in securing international peace was on decline because of unilateral actions taken by some countries outside the United Nations Security Council framework (eg. Yugoslavia). In the same address to the UN (mentioned above) the Vice Foreign Minister said that the UN should also attempt to resolve the root causes of piracy in Somalia. The Chinese believe that piracy is the direct consequence of the domestic politico-military-economic condition within Somalia. The transitional federal government in place in Somalia worked up the power ladder with US support and displaced the Islamic Courts Union (ICU) which still holds huge mass support, especially in Southern Somalia. This is indicative of the US efforts on its war against terrorism.

S Rajasimman is a Research Assistant at the Institute of Defence Studies and Analysis, New Delhi

Further, in the absence of multilateral operations under the UN, Somalia may at future point become a case for unilateral intervention by the US or Britain or both. Therefore piracy seems to be only the tip of the iceberg. However, Chinese behavior is inconsistent with its political rhetoric at least at a practical level. On 24 June, 2007 the Chinese oil company, C.N.O.O.P singned a deal with Somali President Abdullah Yusuf to explore the northern puntland region for oil. This deal was signed in a hurry prior to the Somali government framing National Oil Rules (NOR). Chinese firms backed by its government seem to be willing to take economic and political risks which western firms would shy away from. A unilateral military action by western powers would effect Chinese equations in the region. Like the anti-satellite missile tests in early January 2007, China seems to project its capabilities as part of its extending diplomacy without breaking any rules.

China, which became a permanent member of UN Security Council only in 1971, did not engage in peace-keeping operations until 1989. In 1989, China began its first exploratory foray into UN peacekeeping missions, sending non-military observers to join the UN Namibia Transitional Period Aid Group overseeing a general election. In 1990, China dispatched military observers to the Middle East in support of the UN Truce Supervision Organization (UNTSO). One reason for this transition was the incident of Tiananmen Square, when the People's Liberation Army was caught on the wrong foot with its own people. This incident stimulated the need for the PLA to conduct more people oriented activities such as disaster relief, domestic security, and other measures, but also, very importantly, participation in UN peacekeeping operations. This transition now makes China the largest contributor by a permanent member of the UN Security Council (in close competition with France). The second reason is the PRC's concern for sovereignty and its liquidation by interventions. China was unsupportive of the blue helmet due to its national experience. During the entire Cold War, United Nations sanctioned the use of force only once. The target nation of this decision was China herself (Korean War). With the Cold War world order shaking and reshaping in this era of intense economic interdependence, China's concern seems to be reorienting. The third reason could be the Chinese concerns for Taiwan, Tibet and Xinjiang, which if left uncontrolled could become cases for intervention. [It may be worthwhile to explore this aspect a little more in terms of other factors that have led to China's engagement in peacekeeping missions.]

On 24 June, 2007 the Chinese oil company C.N.O.O.P singned a deal with Somali President Abdullah Yusuf to explore the northern puntland region for oil. This deal was signed in hurry prior to the Somali government framing National Oil Rules (NOR). Chinese firms backed by its government seem to be willing to take economic and political risks which western firms would shy away from.

Another important motivation behind the decision to deploy the Chinese naval force off Somalia could be the fact that this involves the African continent if not directly. Chinese leaders have been frequenting Africa since 2000. As a leading importer of crude oil, China depends on 25 percent of this import from Africa. This is projected to up to 40 percent by 2020. It has extensive debt packages given to Africa on a no fringe attached basis and its bilateral trade is expected to touch $ 100 billion by 2010. Suffice to say that its stakes and advantages in Africa are high. The overall expected output on oil by a Chinese firm in Africa is 78 million tons (presently the output is 40.3 million tons). China also depends on Saudi Arabia for its crude oil imports and has huge markets in Europe. Chinese merchant ships will have to necessarily frequent the Gulf.

With limited power or force projection capability, Chinese action is consistent with its overall policy strategy of creating an international order that is different to the Cold War order. Securing international peace and development is currently an objective of it foreign policy. This international environment will only help China in achieving its strategic and development goals. It will enhance its image as a responsible power in the 21st century and give it the experience to conduct operations of this nature.

A few decades back while articulating over new ways to use the National Defence Force, Deng Xiaoping's strategic thought mentioned that "...when our country is developed and more prosperous, we shall have a bigger role to play in the world". After almost three decades this seems to be coming true.

PUBLIC SECTOR
survival through circumventing competition

BY MAJOR GENERAL MRINAL SUMAN

THE CURRENT EQUIPMENT PROFILE of the Indian Armed Forces has been a matter of serious disquiet to all those who are concerned with national security issues. Many wonder if India possesses the necessary punch to safeguard its national interests. Articles appearing in the press indicate a requirement of 100 billion dollars and a time span of 10 years before a semblance of balance can be achieved. Why have matters been permitted to drift to such alarming levels? Who is responsible for the current state of affairs? By jeopardizing national security, India has been rendered a 'soft state', as amply proved by the sheer audacity of the Mumbai terrorist attack of November 2008.

Funds have never been a problem. The Government has been making adequate allocations to the defence. The Ministry of Defence (MoD) has been surrendering funds. Despite the fact that the services carry a long list of items urgently required to fill critical gaps, no major proposal appears to be getting fructified. A close examination reveals that major impediments to the modernisation of the armed forces are Defence Research and Development Organisation (DRDO) and the defence public sector. They make a lethal combination that effectively stalls all equipment procurement proposals.

Earlier, no procurements from abroad could be carried out unless DRDO, which was a member of all sanctioning boards, accepted that the product could not be produced/developed in the country in the required time frame. DRDO was always wary of conceding this for two reasons. One, it reflected adversely on its research and development competence, and two, every new project meant an opportunity to expand its own domain with the associated budget. There has hardly been any equipment which DRDO has developed in the promised time-frame and conforming to the formulated parameters. In almost every case, it was only after years of failed trials that DRDO reluctantly allowed the services to resort to imports. It has been a history of false claims, tall promises, unexplained delays and sub-optimal products, thereby forcing the services to live with huge voids.

> Very often the services are given only one option – 'take whatever the public sector offers or do without it'. In a way, the public sector has contributed directly to the current state of affairs where the armed forces are saddled with mediocre and outdated equipment.

DEFENCE PUBLIC SECTOR AND ITS HEGEMONY

The Indian defence public sector consists of nine public sector undertakings and 39 ordnance factories. Despite getting preferential treatment through the patronage provided by the Department of Defence Production (DDP) in MoD, they have singularly failed to keep pace with

Maj Gen Mrinal Suman is India's foremost expert in defence procurement procedures and offsets. He has been directing much acclaimed defence acquisition management courses in India and abroad
mrinalsuman@gmail.com

technological developments. They thrive on assured orders from the services and periodic infusion of transferred technology. No indigenous competence has been developed. Most unfortunately, the Indian military is a captive customer of the public sector and is forced to buy what it produces. Very often the services are given only one option – 'take whatever the public sector offers or do without it'. In a way, the public sector has contributed directly to the current state of affairs where the armed forces are saddled with mediocre and outdated equipment.

> Another exasperated officer went to the extent of saying that DDP's intransigence smacks of unpatriotic and anti-national behaviour. "How can officials deny modern systems to the services for purely partisan interests? I wish the national leadership takes notes of such negative elements and takes action against them."

In all cases where technology is purchased for subsequent production within the country, a public sector entity is nominated as the recipient even if a private sector company can manage production by receiving only incremental technology. At times the technology is totally alien to the nominated public sector entity entailing long delays in its absorption and subsequent production.

The public sector is adept at taking preemptive action. Being a part of MoD, it gets to know the military's likely projections of equipment acquisitions in advance. Armed with this information, it promptly signs and MOU with foreign vendors to forestall competition from the private sector, thereby presenting a fait accompli to the decision makers. Once orders are in hand, it displays no urgency in delivering quality goods in the promised time frame.

To illustrate the clout that the public sector enjoys to guard its exclusive turf, the case of Tactical Communication System (TCS) has been discussed in detail herein. It is indicative of the extent to which the public sector can go to retain its monopoly. Although, promotion of 'free competition' is one of the stated objectives of the much touted defence procurement procedure, every subterfuge is being used to award the contract to a public sector favourite underhandedly by eliminating competition.

Tactical Communication System

There is an urgent need to put in place a system which can handle communication requirements (voice, data and video) of a field force in the Tactical Battle Area. The current system called Army Radio Engineering Network (AREN) is totally outdated. TCS is a force multiplier and the current void can result in grave consequences.

A case for replacement of AREN by TCS was initiated way back in 1996. Initially, TCS was proposed to be an upgrade of AREN and a case was processed accordingly. After five years of bureaucratic travails, in 2001, MoD directed that the project be taken up as a fresh procurement proposal. Accordingly, the Army Headquarters (AHQ) initiated the case and obtained Acceptance of Necessity. Under the provision of the defence procurement procedure, the case was categorized as a hybrid of 'Buy and Make' and 'Make'. It was stipulated that the first two systems would be imported and the balance manufactured in India with imported technology. The latter 'Make' part of categorization related to indigenous development of secrecy and Network Management System by DRDO.

The case took another turn in November 2007 when it was proposed to recategorize the proposal as 'Make (Hi-Tech)' under the newly issued 'Make' policy as a part of Defence Procurement Procedure –

violated in a blatant and brazen manner.

When the private sector came to know of the above subterfuge, it cried foul and appealed to the top MoD leadership. It demanded that it be given a fair chance to compete on a level playing field and whosoever emerges best should be selected. Defence Acquisition Council (DAC) appeared inclined towards open competition. Realising that the DPSU may have to face competition, DDP came up with another innovative stratagem. It demanded that a committee be constituted to carry out a feasibility study of the Indian industry's competence to develop TCS. It was a totally unwarranted demand as a number of market scans had already been carried out and it had been well established that the Indian industry possessed adequate capability. In any case, competence assessment of participating vendors is required to be carried out by IPMT after the formulation of Project Definition Document. The sole aim of DDP was to delay the whole process till the existing DAC was replaced by a more pliable DAC after May elections.

Notwithstanding total irregularity of DDP's demand, a multi-disciplinary committee was

MoD continues to play favourites, brooking no challenge to the monopoly of an inefficient, insecure and inapt public sector. All efforts are made to thwart attempts of the private sector to get an equal opportunity.

2006 (DPP-2006). Here a word about the new 'Make' policy would be in order. As per the policy, development of all strategic, complex and security sensitive systems are required to be undertaken by DRDO while projects entailing high-tech complex systems would be identified as 'Make (Hi Tech)'.

'Make (Hi Tech)' projects would be based on proven or matured technologies where fundamental research is not required. The policy unambiguously states that both public sector undertakings and private sector companies are eligible to participate in 'Make (Hi Tech)' cases on a level playing field.

In a move smacking of gross partisanship and in total violation of Government's own policy, TCS was surreptitiously categorised differently. In a pre-emptory move, a Defence Public Sector Undertaking (DPSU) was nominated as the sole design and production agency and the private sector was totally eliminated. The old practice of favouring public sector was continuing, belying Government's often repeated claims of opening the defence sector to private companies.

'Make (Hi Tech)' policy clearly lays down that a duly constituted Integrated Project Management Team (IPMT) under the Acquisition Wing would shortlist a minimum of two Development Agencies (DA) after inviting Expression of Interest of participating vendors. Thus, in the said case of TCS, both the spirit and the provisions of the policy were

constituted on 22 January 2009 to carry out feasibility study. A representative of DDP was also made a member. As the services were keen to expedite the process, the committee held its first meeting on 04 February, wherein modalities of carrying out feasibility study were finalised. It was decided to request both the public and the private sectors to make presentations of their competence to enable the committee to conclude its finding. Consequently, detailed presentations were made on 11 February and the committee unanimously concluded that both the public and the private sectors possessed necessary competence. It was decided to meet on 17 February to sign the report.

When the committee met on 17 February, representative of DDP sprang a surprise by demanding that the committee should visit companies to see their competence on ground before finalising its recommendations. Apparently, he had been directed by the officials of DDP to stall conclusion of the committee's report. The committee decided to satisfy DDP to obviate subsequent questioning. Hurried visits were organised to different private sector facilities at Pune, Mumbai and Bangalore. Ground visits further reinforced the committee's findings as regards the competence of the private sector.

> Private sector should also be considered for the receipt of imported technology. In many fields it is far ahead of the public sector. Therefore, it is in national interest that the most suitable company be selected to receive technology.

The committee met on 04 March and draft of the final report was approved. As no issues were raised, all members were asked to meet the next morning to sign the report. But DDP was not done as yet. Its representative declined to sign the report. Continuing with its delaying tactics, DDP now demanded that a few more private sector companies should also be visited and cost benefit analysis of adopting 'Make' route should be carried out. Such a flagrantly outlandish conduct of DDP surprised and shocked even those who are familiar with its past track record. Interestingly, DDP has not empowered its representative to sign the report without reference to DDP functionaries, thereby stalling progress.

The Current Status

Through its clever delaying tactics, DDP has been able to derail the whole process indefinitely. The stand taken by the nominated DPSU is totally unreasonable to say the least. It claims that it is the best in the country and has invested huge resources in creating the test bed, yet is mortally scared of competition. It wants TCS project through the back door and not in an open, transparent and equitable environment. Very rarely one comes across behemoths which suffer from such a sense of insecurity. Apparently, the DPSU lacks confidence in its own capability to win the contract on sheer merit and is trying all tricks to eliminate competition – even seeking the help of its trade union to pressurize the Government.

Requirement for TCS was initiated in 1996 and today, after 13 years India is still to take the first step. DDP has made its stance clear that if TCS is not awarded to the nominated DPSU and it is asked to compete, DDP will not let the project proceed, whatever be the degree of desperation of the services to acquire the said equipment. Surprisingly, the higher leadership of MoD appears helpless and reconciled to the tantrums thrown by the predisposed elements of DDP.

As regards the past track record, the designated DPSU has acquired notoriety for time and cost overruns. When asked to provide time and cost details of completed projects during its presentation, the DPSU's reply was a juvenile exercise in dodging the real issues. (See box.)

"The Indian military will continue to be dumb and deaf in the battle field. Given our current communication system which is archaic, we will not be able to exchange voice, data and video. I wonder if the mandarins of DDP understand the damage they are doing to India's defence potential," commented an officer.

Another exasperated officer went to the extent of saying that DDP's intransigence smacks of unpatriotic and anti-national behaviour. "How can officials deny modern systems to the services for purely partisan interests? I wish the national leadership takes notes of such negative elements and takes action against them." "How can officials get away with actions which are inimical to national interests?" he wondered.

The services want the best equipment in the given time frame. Therefore, they prefer competition and want the most competent entity to get the contract. As regards the private sector, it seeks an equal opportunity to compete and does not grudge a public sector company winning the contract if it emerges the best. It is a very fair and reasonable demand.

The Way Forward

The Defence Minister has been expressing his unhappiness at the slow pace of modernization. TCS presents itself as a study case for MoD to draw lessons and introduce corrective measures. Policy statements and frequent assertions mean nothing unless followed by honest ground implementation. As seen in the case of TCS, a mockery has been made of the much touted 'Make' policy. An impermissible new categorization, 'Make by DPSU,' has been fraudulently introduced to favour the public sector. The Government's claims of providing level playing ground to both public and private sectors have been belied. TCS case has certainly raised questions regarding the Government's sincerity and dented its credibility.

MoD continues to play favourites, brooking no challenge to the monopoly of an inefficient, insecure and inapt public sector. All efforts are made to thwart attempts of the private sector to get an equal opportunity. As has been the history, the public sector continues to thrive on patronage, monopoly and captive customer base. Adverse effects on the fighting potential of the services appear to matter little to the protectors of the public sector. As a dismayed expert observed, "It appears that the survivability of an inefficient public sector is being given precedence over national security."

"Either the Government should stop claiming equal treatment of public and private sectors, or reign in its errant officials who make a mockery of its policy," stated a private sector functionary. "We have been taken for a ride. Trusting Government's repeated assertions of fair play, we have invested heavily in technology and infrastructure. However, nothing has changed on the ground. Every major project continues to go to the public sector and we are left looking for left over crumbs," he added.

If the Government is serious about according equal status to the private sector, it should initiate the following steps immediately:

- As DDP's sole charter is to sustain monopoly of the public sector by keeping the private sector out by all means fair or foul, it should be abolished and replaced by Department of Defence Industry (DDI). DDI should be tasked to look after the interests of the Indian defence industry as a whole. Officials of DDI should possess breadth of vision to view all issues in larger national interests, rather than in narrow parochial and blinkered manner as at present. A dedicated Joint Secretary should be detailed to facilitate entry of the private sector.
- Private sector should also be considered for the receipt of imported technology. In many fields it is far ahead of the public sector.

The Art of Dodging Issues

BY MAJ GEN MRINAL SUMAN

During the presentation made to the Feasibility Study Committee on 11 Feb 2009, a Defence Public Sector Undertaking (DPSU) announced that it had executed orders worth 4,100 crore rupees during the previous financial year. Further, it claimed that it was the sole enterprise which could undertake Tactical Communications System as it had already executed many projects for the services successfully. Two questions were posed to the DPSU. Questions and written replies provided by the said DPSU are tabulated below.

Delivery dates and costs have no sanctity as regards the public sector. Being part of the Ministry of Defence, it dictates terms to the powerless services. Notwithstanding the high sounding claims made by the public sector in their publicity material, almost all projects undertaken by them have seen massive time and cost overruns. Unfortunately, things continue to drift in the same manner even now and the services continue to suffer. As seen above, the DPSU's reluctance to reply to simple questions displays a distinct sense of insecurity.

Interestingly, the said DPSU's mission statement on its website reads, "To be a customer focussed, globally competitive company in defence electronics and in other chosen areas of professional electronics, through quality, technology and innovation." While claiming aspirations to be globally competitive, it lacks confidence to face competition even from Indian companies and resorts to unfair practices to grab business for survival.

Question	Reply by BEL	Remarks
Out of rupees 4,100 crores of revenues for the year ending March 2008, how many orders were won by the DPSU in open competition against other bidders and how many orders were managed through single vendor nomination?	Experience of the company in competitive markets dates back to the 80's, where the policy initiatives in the Telecom and Broadcasting sectors brought in competition. Operating in these sectors, the company has successfully managed competition and won many contracts. Majority of the transmitters of All India Radio and Doordarshan are of the company's make. More than 15 lakh telecom lines of BSNL are supplied from the company. While the company has been facing competition in civilian sectors in the 80's and the 90's, the recent policy reforms in MoD have brought in competition in various defence electronics sectors also in the last 5 years. The company has been participating in Global RFPs and has been successful in developing business, even in the multi-vendor competitive environment in defence.	The question posed to the DPSU was very specific and pertained to the previous financial year alone. Instead of enumerating orders won in competitive environment with their gross value, the company has tried to evade the issue by unnecessary hogwash. As can be seen, no information has been furnished. Apparently, facts would have exposed hollowness of its claims.
Please provide in a tabular format details regarding date of PO, date of original delivery stated in the PO, date of actual delivery, current project status and PO value and the final value claimed in respect of the projects undertaken as shown in the presentation slide.	The company has always delivered systems on time or ahead of time except when there have been design changes due to change in specifications or due to non-availability of components due to reasons like sanctions, etc. Even in such cases, the company has always found solutions and delivered the systems under most difficult situations also.	Instead of giving details in a tabular form as asked for, the DPSU resorted to irrelevant generalities. It is clear from their convoluted response that their claims of having completed projects ahead of schedule and without cost overruns appear false and unsubstantiated.

Therefore, it is in national interest that the most suitable company be selected to receive technology. This will save considerable time and resources as only incremental technology may be needed to be purchased.

- Private sector associations (viz. CII & FICCI)

should also be represented in categorization committees and DAC, albeit within the constraints of security considerations. Potential of private sector should be exploited by treating them as partners in progress rather than as a threat to the public sector. Their prowess should be considered as a national asset.

- A mechanism should be put in place to redress grievances. In case an entity feels wronged by a partisan and subjective decision, it should be able to seek immediate relief. Disciplinary action should also be initiated against delinquent officials.
- There should be an institutionalized interface between MoD, services and the private sector for regular interaction at the policy making level. Such a platform will go a long way to promote mutual confidence and remove unnecessary irritants.

The private sector was delighted to hear Defence Minister Pranab Mukherjee declare publically in New Delhi in June 2005, "The Government is committed to the development of a vibrant and proactive defence industry in India. It should be ensured that the available capability, infrastructure and resources, including intellectual capital, are harnessed to the fullest extent as our national assets and optimally utilised in achieving this objective." He further advocated a strong and healthy partnership between the public and private sector for enhancing the defence capability and in sustaining a powerful domestic industrial base for the future.

Undoubtedly, the public sector possesses excellent infrastructure, manufacturing facilities and a highly experienced task force. Unfortunately, due to its monopolistic pre-eminence it has failed to keep pace with the latest technology, managerial practices, marketing skills and financial management. It is fully aware of its weaknesses and knows that it cannot survive in an open competition with the private sector. This sense of insecurity makes it wary of the private sector and it tries all stratagems to block its entry. The Government has to realise that both public and private sectors are national assets and harnessing of their potential is essential if India wants to achieve self-reliance in defence production. It should not play favourites and treat both as equal partners in progress.

PAOLO CARMASSI
PRESIDENT, HONEYWELL AEROSPACE, EMEA AND INDIA

"Honeywell will provide safety and mechanical systems..."

INTERVIEW BY BHARAT VERMA

Can you kindly briefly describe the profile of Honeywell, its range of products and technologies across the spectrum of military as well as non-military applications.

Honeywell Aerospace is a leading global provider of integrated avionics, propulsion engines, aircraft and engine systems and full-service solutions for our customers.

Honeywell's products make flight safer, more reliable and more cost-effective. In the air and on the ground, Honeywell's aerospace products can be found on virtually every type of aircraft in use, in nearly every region of the world.

Honeywell has delivered integrated defense solutions that improve mission readiness for 60 years. Honeywell's great technologies power military readiness. From turbine engines for the Abrams M1 Main Battle Tank and the CH-47 Chinook helicopter to systems that power unmanned vehicles and avionics for jet fighters. Our technology is important because it saves lives and money.

Honeywell is activiely involved in Air Traffic Management programs around the world including

Paolo Carmassi (right) and Steven J. White, Deputy Chief of Mission for the US Embassy at Aero India 2009.

the FAA (US) NextGen program, Eurocontrol's Single European Sky ATM Research Programme and China's Air Traffic Management Bureau.

What are the areas of interest and opportunities for Honeywell in the thriving Indian aerospace industry? To what extent has Honeywell been successful in penetrating the market in the defence sector in India?

As the skies become increasingly crowded with commercial and business aircraft, today's flying public, and the airlines that carry them, demand a focused priority on safety.

Honeywell Aerospace has a tradition of pioneering comprehensive safety systems and we continue to be a leading supplier of safety products by offering state-of-the-art products and systems for large and regional air transport, business and general aviation aircraft, military aircraft, surface vehicles, defense systems, and space applications.

Honeywell's F125IN engine, a 9850lbf (43.8kN) thrust engine that will deliver high performance, improved pilot safety, lower maintenance and outstanding reliability, is currently being considered for the Indian Air Force Jaguar re-engining program.

This thrust class engine is built around Honeywell's proven expertise in the design and production of aircraft systems, which is evident in the F125IN engine, an outstanding propulsion system for military aircraft. The engine will transform the Indian Air Force Jaguar aircraft by improving mission performance, enhancing pilot safety, reducing pilot workload, and reducing maintenance events and costs.

The F125IN power plant is significantly lighter and much more powerful than the aircraft's current engine. It has an advanced dual full-authority digital engine control (FADEC) system, modular construction, integrated engine health monitoring system and best in class thrust-to-weight ratio – all designed to give the military the best engine with the lowest operating and maintenance costs.

The F125IN will provide the Indian Air Force Jaguar fleet with a modern, reliable and safe propulsion system that will transform the capabilities, performance and safety of the aircraft in combat. In significantly improving single engine thrust performance, this increase pilot safety and aircraft survivability.

Recently, Honeywell announced it will provide its Traffic Collision Alerting System and other key safety and mechanical systems for the Indian Air Force C-130J program. Honeywell expects to deliver the key aircraft systems that enhance flight safety – including our Military Aircraft Collision Avoidance System. The Indian Air Force C 130J will also operate with other Honeywell avionics, mechanical and lighting systems and components.

Honeywell has several partnerships in India, including the licensed manufacture of the TPE331 engine by Hindustan Aeronautics Limited (HAL). A diversified technology and manufacturing leader, Honeywell has significant operations in cities throughout India, with more than 8,000 people working in multiple locations.

Honeywell's F125 IN engine is currently being considered for the Indian Air Force Jaguar re-engining program. The engine will transform the Indian Air Force Jaguar aircraft by improving mission performance.

In the context of the rapidly increasing density of global air traffic what are the newest technologies that Honeywell has to offer in the regime of global air traffic management and aerial navigation that not only ensure optimum utilization of airspace but would also meet with the stringent environmental standards the world expects and provide for higher levels of air safety?

Required Navigation Performance or RNP uses a

Honeywell's next-generation SmartPath Precision Landing System technology supports precision approach and landing using Global Positioning System (GPS) satellite data and transmits digital guidance signals to aircraft systems. Honeywell's SmartPath system saves acquisition and maintenance cost while providing aircraft operators and airports with safer, more efficient operations.

combination of on-board navigation technology, precise sensors and the GPS satellite network keep aircraft within a tightly specified airspace corridor. Aircraft can precisely fly a wide variety of desired flight paths including curved paths to avoid terrain and obstacles, thereby overcoming limitations of conventional instrument procedures. Operators will benefit from better access to terrain-challenged airports, fewer delays and diversions, and a reduction in noise and emissions, in part due to more direct routes to the airport – advantages some airlines are already achieving with the technology.

For decades, modern aviation has relied on ground-based navigation aids, but recent industry developments are driving the adoption of RNP techniques as a method of increasing capacity and improving traffic flow. RNP enables aircraft to fly more precise approaches, providing benefits for lower minimal operations, more favorable routing in congested or terrain challenged airspace, noise abatement compliance, improved safety and lower operating cost.

Honeywell offers all of the avionics necessary to equip an aircraft for RNP – from Flight Management Systems (FMS) to Enhanced Ground Proximity Warning Systems (EGPWS) to Inertial Reference Systems (IRS). And Honeywell continues to raise the standard year after year by providing a broad selection of innovative systems that enable RNP and help operators navigate the skies more simply, safely and efficiently. Honeywell continues to strive to offer new RNP technologies guided by a pilot-focused vision to provide solutions that offer the right capabilities to airlines' operating procedures.

IntuVue™, Honeywell's Weather Hazard Detection System, is the only system on the market to provide 3-D capability to help pilots avoid weather-related turbulence and delays. Honeywell's IntuVue offers flight crews the ability to detect and avoid previously unforeseen turbulence, wind shears and dangerous storm activity so they can make more informed route decisions – thereby increasing passenger comfort and safety while decreasing weather-related costs due to injuries and aircraft damages.

In addition, Honeywell has developed technology that provides information on all other traffic directly to pilots. Currently, pilots hear from controllers where the traffic is around them. Honeywell's Airborne Traffic Situational Awareness (ATSAW) system provides that directly to pilots. It allows pilots to more quickly move to smoother air for more efficient fuel use and a smoother ride for passengers, and it also lets them know what traffic is around them.

Honeywell technology address another rapidly growing class of accidents – runway incursion and other on-ground incidents. Honeywell has been a thought-leader in safety systems designed to prevent accidents at and around airports since the early 2000s.

Honeywell's Runway Awareness and Advisory System (RAAS) was certified in 2003 and remains the only runway incursion system available for use in air transport, regional, business and general aviation aircraft.

The RAAS is a software upgrade to the Enhanced Ground Proximity Warning System, making it economical for aircraft operators to add RAAS capabilities.

RAAS uses the EGPWS on-board computer and terrain database, combined with data from the aircraft's Global Positioning System and other navigation systems, to provide flight crews with enhanced situational awareness on and around airport runways.

The system provides an aural warning when an aircraft approaches a runway while taxiing, to help pilots avoid entering an active runway unintentionally. System features also ensure that pilots are taking off or landing on the correct runway; in both cases aural announcements confirm runway identification information.

There are clear signs that Autonomous Unmanned Aerial Systems are set to play an increasingly important role both in respect of military and civilian applications. What solutions can Honeywell offer to ensure safe integration of this new generation of aerial vehicles into high density civil air traffic and resolve issues related to certification?

Honeywell's avionics solutions broadly used for flight safety in manned aircraft can also be part of a UAS avionics solution. Our Traffic alert and Collision Avoidance System (TCAS) is an aircraft collision avoidance system designed to reduce the incidence of mid-air collisions between aircraft. It monitors the airspace around an aircraft for other aircraft equipped with a corresponding active transponder, independent of air traffic control, and warns operators of the presence of other transponder-equipped aircraft which may present a threat of mid-air collision. Enhanced Ground Proximity Warning System (EGPWS) serves as an independent monitor of an aircraft's position relative to the surrounding terrain utilizing the aircraft inputs such as position, attitude, air speed and glideslope along with internal terrain, obstacles, and airport databases to predict a potential conflict between the aircraft flight path and terrain or an obstacle. Other products, such as our radar altimeters, provide all-weather, high performance and low detectability in small form factor, single card implementations. Current applications include Hunter, Eagle Eye, and Fire Scout. Honeywell's Integrated Guidance, Navigation and Control (INS/GPS) for Unmanned Systems provides users with precise and independent inertial position information for navigation, targeting and altitude reference. Adaptive configurable embedded INS/GPS are featured on platforms such as General Atomics Predator B, Reaper, and Warrior UAS.

What solutions does Honeywell have to offer beyond those existing at Indira Gandhi International Airport at Delhi to ensure uninterrupted departures and arrivals in conditions of very low or even zero visibility which afflicts the airport frequently in the winter?

Honeywell's SmartPath™ Precision Landing system uses GPS data to provide a cost-effective Ground Based Augmentation System (GBAS) solution to increase airport capacity, decrease air traffic noise, and reduce weather-related delays.

By providing aircraft with very precise navigation data, SmartPath represents the latest technology for precision approach and landings, enabling aircraft to fly either complex or straight-in approaches. Easy to install, at major cost savings compared to traditional Instrument Landing System, SmartPath is now available. FAA certification is expected in third quarter, 2009.

Currently, aircraft use Instrument Landing System (ILS) technology, an older technology with technical limitations that impact flight path flexibility and airport throughout. ILS is also susceptible to signal interference by weather and obstacles, including large aircraft like the A380. This can result in significant disruptions to airport traffic and cause delays. Replacing ILS with GBAS has been identified in the FAA's NextGen and Eurocontrol's SESAR programs as critical enablers for improving air traffic capacity.

The improved safety from the accuracy and stability of the approach provided by Honeywell's SmartPath GBAS versus the older ILS technology is one of the major benefits to pilots. A single GBAS can support landing operations on multiple runways simultaneously, eliminating the need for multiple ILS systems at airports with more than one runway. This new system will reduce acquisition and maintenance cost while providing aircraft operators and airports with safer and more efficient operations.

The global economic downturn has in turn affected the Indian economy as well. What in your assessment are the future prospects in the near and long term for the aerospace industry and the airline business in India?

It is definitely a challenging time as flight hours are down across the globe. However, there is still a strong backlog for the region.

The diversity of Honeywell's business, spanning across military, space, air transport and business aviation, helps to ensure that our financial performance is not as severely impacted by economic upheaval as other less diversified aerospace companies may experience. Aerospace is a long-cycle business, and when coupled with the company's business backlog, provides a good basis for weathering this economic downturn.

Aero India 2009
defence industries news

BY BHAVNA PANDEY

BOEING C 17 GLOBEMASTER

In response to the Request for Information (RFI) on strategic airlift aircraft from the Indian Ministry of Defence received in 2008, Boeing IDS responded with an offer of the C 17, Globemaster III. This most advanced military airlift aircraft in the world can undertake diverse mission demands around the globe.

The C 17 Globemaster III is the newest airlift aircraft to enter the Air Force's inventory of the US Air Force. It is a high-wing, four-engine, T-tailed aircraft with a rear loading ramp. With its 160,000-pound payload, the C 17 can take off from a 7,600-foot airfield, fly 2,400 nautical miles and land on a small, austere airfield in 3,000 feet or less. The C 17 can be refueled in-flight. On the ground, a fully loaded aircraft, using engine reversers, can back up a two percent slope.

The first C 17 Squadron was operational in January 1995. Since then the fleet has amassed more than 75,000 flying hours and has been involved in numerous contingency operations, including flying troops and equipment to Operation Joint Endeavor to support peacekeeping in Bosnia and the Allied Operation in Kosovo. Eight C 17s, in 1998, completed the longest airdrop mission in history, flying more than 8,000 nautical miles from the United States to Central Asia, dropping troops and equipment after more than 19 hours in the air. The C 17 is capable of rapid strategic delivery of troops and all types of cargo to main operating bases or directly to forward bases in the deployment area. The aircraft is also able to perform theater airlift missions when required.

The C 17's system specifications impose a demanding set of reliability and maintainability requirements. These include an aircraft mission completion success probability of 93 percent, only 18.6 aircraft maintenance man-hours per flying hour and full/partial mission capable rates of 74.7/82.5 percent respectively for a mature fleet with 100,000 flying hours.

The C 17 is approximately 174-feet long with a 170-foot wingspan and is powered by four fully reversible Pratt & Whitney F117-PW-100 engines. Each engine is rated at 40,900 pounds of thrust. The thrust reversers direct the flow of air upward and forward to avoid ingestion of dust and debris.

With more than 170 C 17s now in service with the United States, the United Kingdom, Australia and Canada, the C 17 has become a defining force in the global war against terrorism, performing strategic and tactical missions in both Afghanistan and Iraq. A number of C 17s with upgraded capabilities are performing Special Operations missions. The aircraft has also been ordered by Qatar and a consortium of NATO members.

The C-17, which was on flying and static display at the Aero India air show in Bangalore, participated in aerial demonstrations on a daily basis impressing one and all with its size and maneuverability. Members of the international media and defence experts were taken aboard during demonstration flights to witness some of its capabilities first hand. The aircraft has been on India's radar for some time. Boeing expects to engage in further discussions with India and believes that a Request for Proposal (RFP) would come soon.

India's rapidly growing aerospace and defense industry offers significant opportunities for growth and productivity and participation at Aero India underscores Boeing's enduring commitment to India and its efforts at fostering stronger ties with Indian customers and partners.

Bhavna Pandey
kooks85@gmail.com

BOEING P-8 I POSEIDON FOR INDIA

Just a month ahead of Aero India 2009, competing against a number of others in the field, Boeing bagged a $2.1 billion order from India for eight of its P-8 I Long Range Maritime Patrol Aircraft. Derived from Boeing's commercial 737 airframe, it is similar to the P-8 A Poseidon that Boeing is developing for the US Navy. This fleet is intended to replace Russian-built TU-142 fleet as the Indian Navy's long-range patrol aircraft and will be capable of anti-submarine warfare apart from a number of other capabilities.

The Boeing P-8 I Poseidon will provide the Indian Navy the capability to fulfill its enhanced responsibility in the Indian Ocean as a consequence of India's rise to the status of a regional power. The aircraft is capable of operating effectively over land or water while performing search and rescue, maritime interdiction and long-range intelligence, surveillance, target acquisition and reconnaissance. It is estimated that India may need as many as 30 such aircraft by the year 2020. The decision in favour of the Boeing P-8 I still under development was made when negotiations for the two retrofitted P-3C Orion maritime-optimized patrol and surveillance aircraft of the US Navy did not succeed for a variety of reasons.

Boeing's P-8 I Maritime Patrol Aircraft contract is with the Indian Ministry of Defence. The sale includes associated support equipment, spares, training and logistical support through June 2019. Direct arms-trade "offsets" were expected to include engineering services, manufacturing and integrated logistics-support projects to the tune of $641.3 million. The first P-8 I would be delivered within four years of the date of the contract. The remaining seven would be delivered by 2015.

The aircraft are built in a secure assembly building in Renton, USA, separate from the commercial 737s. In December 2008, Boeing completed assembly of the second P-8 test aircraft, which will be prepared for extensive ground tests in a fixture inside the assembly building. Loads calibration testing of the first P-8 A Poseidon test aircraft was completed two weeks ahead of schedule. This is one of the pre-requisites for the U.S. Navy flight clearance process. First flight of the P-8 is expected later this year. In 2004, the U.S. Navy chose Boeing to build 108 of the P-8s, with initial operational capability slated for 2013.

It is understood that the $2.1 billion sale to India of eight Boeing Co P-8 I maritime patrol aircraft has been cleared by the US government. This is regarded as the largest US arms transfer to India to date. The Indian Navy is the first international customer for this aircraft.

EADS Defense & Security : Eurofighter

Germany's EADS has proposed a long-term strategic partnership with Indian aerospace and defence companies. Speaking to the media during Aero India 2009 Bernhard Gerwert, CEO of Military Air systems – an integrated business unit of EADS Defence & Security – said, "We have a strong interest to create a long-lasting strategic partnership with the Indian aerospace industry. India is our partner of choice and therefore we invite India to join the Eurofighter Typhoon programme."

Gerwert went on to say "We are ready to provide our operational, support, engineering and development capabilities to the Indian aerospace and defence sector, which is growing fast, and we want to grow together." The CEO of Eurofighter GmbH, Aloysius Rauen, said the Eurofighter Typhoon is currently the most modern combat aircraft in the world. The company has orders of more than 700 aircraft for six nations."

The Eurofighter Typhoon which made its debut appearance in the Indian sub-continent at Aero India 2009 at Bangalore ahead of a projected deployment in Afghanistan, is a highly agile, multi-role/ swing-role air superiority fighter. This fourth generation fighter fielded by EADS is one among the six contenders in the running for the 126 Medium Multi-Role Combat Aircraft (MMRCA) contract for the Indian Air Force. Both single and two-seat variants took part in the flight displays conducted daily at the air show.

A Eurofighter Typhoon bid proposal and a comprehensive offset offer were submitted to the Indian authorities in 2008. Since then, 25 Memoranda of Understanding (MoU) have been signed to enhance the cooperation with India's aerospace and defence industry. The Eurofighter Typhoon partner companies are confident of fulfilling the 50 per cent offset obligation of the request for proposal (RFP), and will offer India access to an international sourcing network of "unparalleled" scope.

The production of the Eurofighter Typhoon will create thousands of new jobs in India according to EADS. The leading-edge combat aircraft has a tremendous built-in growth potential and therefore the Eurofighter partner companies can offer India new opportunities for cooperation in design, development and manufacturing.

The ongoing campaign is fully supported by the four European nations involved in the Eurofighter programme – Germany, the United Kingdom, Spain and Italy; their air forces and Europe's leading aerospace companies Alenia/Finmeccanica, BAE Systems and EADS.

EADS which has the lead of the Eurofighter Typhoon campaign in India, is currently preparing its participation in the flight trials of the Medium Multi Role Combat Aircraft (MMRCA) competition. The flight trials are expected in 2009 after a short listing of the bidders and intensive preparations have been launched to meet this important milestone.

EADS will help India's Aeronautical Development Agency and Hindustan Aeronautics Limited which manufactures the country's indigenous Tejas Light Combat Aircraft to expand the flight envelope of the fighter and help speed up the test flights leading up to the initial and final operational clearances. EADS will also help India to refine some of the existing simulation models.

EADS is already in a strong position to exploit advantages in India. The company's strategy of setting partnerships in India will likely win it a lot of subcontracting and prime contracts.

Lockheed Martin

Lockheed Martin Aeronautics had a large presence at the Aero India 2009 where it showcased the F-16 IN Super Viper and the C-130J Super Hercules. The F-16 IN Super Viper is one of the six contenders for the Medium Multi Role Combat Aircraft (MMRCA) contract for the Indian Air Force. The aircraft is tailored exclusively to meet all of India's MMRCA requirements and it is ready for integration into India's infrastructure and operations. Evolutionary integration of technologies makes the F-16 IN the most advanced Fourth Generation fighter in the world today. It is a unique new fighter sharing a heritage with the world's only fifth generation fighters – the F-35 Lightning II Joint Strike Fighter and the F-22 Raptor.

The ability of Lockheed Martin Aeronautics to incorporate the latest technologies into the F-16 IN is the key to expanding mission roles and improving combat capability, thereby creating the most effective multi-role fighter today. The F-16 IN can be readily equipped with emerging capabilities throughout its life cycle.

India's partnership with Lockheed Martin can provide access to the highest technology, opportunities for technology co-development, low-risk licensed production, transfer of technology, and opportunities for extensive long-term business. The Super Viper will facilitate a key strategic partnership with the US and the USAF including joint training, logistical and operational concepts. The company has a proven history of successful partnerships. The F-16 is the fighter of choice for 24 nations with 52 follow-on buys, including successful international licenced production of 928 aircraft. Lockheed Martin's worldwide industrial partnership success is unsurpassed.

Deliveries of the C-130J Super Hercules to India will begin in 2011. This will be the "stretched" variant of the C-130J, similar to those being delivered to the USAF. This is the most advanced air lifter ever built. It combines the latest in aerospace technology with a proven, rugged airframe design, resulting in an aircraft that gives an operator more capability with greater operational efficiency. Equipped with an Infrared Detection Set (IDS), the aircraft will be able to perform precision low-level flying, airdrops, and landing in blackout conditions. Self protection systems and other features are included to ensure aircraft survivability in hostile air defence environments. In addition the aircraft is equipped with in-flight refuelling capability for extended range operations. Lockheed Martin will integrate this equipment and other capabilities into the Indian configuration as agreed between the two governments. With the acquisition of this aircraft, India joins the growing number of nations with C-130J fleets including the US, Australia, Canada, Demark, Italy, Norway and the UK.

The C-130J carries eight 463L pallets, 97 medical litters, 24 CDS bundles, 128 combat troops and 92 paratroops. While the exterior looks very much like previous versions, the C-130J mission and propulsion systems have been completely redesigned. Primary features of the C-130J include a new digital avionics architecture and propulsion system, twin head-up pilot displays that are certified as primary flight instruments and dual mission computers that automate many functions allowing the aircraft to be operated by only two pilots and a loadmaster. The net effect of these improvements is enhanced performance of the aircraft, and greater reliability of the systems.

Northrop Grumman

"India represents an important market in Asia for Northrop Grumman's industry-leading technologies and capabilities and we recognize India's changing needs particularly in homeland defence," said John Brooks, president Northrop Grumman International Inc and Vice-President Business Development for Northrop Grumman Aerospace Systems sector. At the Aero India 2009, Northrop Grumman showcased the E-2 Hawkeye, 737 AEW&C and a model of the AN/APG-80 (AESA) radar for the F-16 IN Super Viper. Other exhibits included its multi-role electronically scanned array (MESA) radar, an E-2 Hawkeye airborne early warning and battle management system crew workstation and flyable cockpit simulator aimed at demonstrating maritime reconnaissance. The Fire Scout vertical take-off and landing unmanned aerial vehicle was also featured.

Other programs available for viewing were models of Directional Infrared Countermeasures (DIRCM), the LITENING advanced airborne targeting and navigation pod and the Longbow Apache radar and Longbow Hellfire missile system. The company also promoted its LPD San Antonio-class Amphibious Warfare and Transport ship and the International Patrol Frigate, a versatile warship based on the multi-mission National Security Cutter currently operated by the U.S. Coast Guard.

Northrop Grumman's German subsidiary, Northrop Grumman LITEF, was also present displaying its navigation systems for land vehicles, sensors for weapon stabilization, inertial guidance systems for missiles and AHRS/navigation systems for fixed-wing and rotary-wing aircraft.

Bharat Electronics Limited (BEL) and Dynamatic Technologies Limited were selected by Northrop Grumman to manufacture components of the F-16 APG-68(V)9 fire control radar, used on recent advanced versions the F-16. Northrop Grumman and Lockheed Martin are offering a more advanced radar system, the AN/APG-80 active electronically scanned array (AESA), for the F-16 IN Super Viper multi-role fighter aircraft proposed for the MMRCA program. The agreement is part of a broader initiative to engage Indian industry as strategic business partners. The engineering teams will collaborate on all aspects of the manufacturing process, beginning with a formal Production Readiness Review (PRR), and concluding with First Article Inspection (FAI) and First Article Test (FAT) milestones. Initial radar component deliveries are expected in the second quarter of 2009.

Lockheed Martin had a choice of three radars. Raytheon's Advanced Combat Radar (RACR) and Northrop Grumman's Scalable Active Beam Radar (SABR) fit in an F-16, but Lockheed ultimately chose Northrop Grumman's APG-80, in service in the United Arab Emirates' F-16E/F. Two reasons are behind this, says Northrop Grumman: the proposed F-16 IN for India is similar to the E/F and can accept the APG-80, which needs more power and cooling than RACR or SABR, and is lower risk. Northrop Grumman says no APG-80 antennas have had to be repaired, in normal use, since tests started over four years ago. "The antenna will outlast the airframe," the company says. A few modules might fail over its lifetime, but they won't affect performance enough to make it worth unsealing the radars and replacing them.

Northrop Grumman strives to be a trusted partner with India to provide advanced defence capabilities enabling India to meet whatever challenges arise. The 737 Airborne Early Warning and Control (AEW&C) system is the right choice for airborne surveillance and control autonomous 24-hour, all-weather precision strike capability for the F-16, including synthetic aperture radar. Other systems include the AN/APN-241 radar which was developed specifically for the C-130 mission and operational requirements.

MBDA

MBDA is a subsidiary of BAE Systems, EADS and Finmeccanica. In response to a global Request for Proposal (RFP) issued by DRDO in 2008 for co-development of a Short Range Surface-to-Air Missile (SRSAM) with range of over 15 kilometres, the European company is holding talks with the Indian Ministry of Defence, DRDO procurement office and MBDA's local industrial partner, Bharat Dynamics Ltd (BDL). MBDA is hopeful that talks with the Indian authorities will yield a contract for the development of the new Surface-to-Air Missile with the DRDO, CEO Antoine Bouvier said on February12 at the Aero India air show. "We are discussing the development of missiles with Indian agencies in this regard and are hoping for a positive outcome," MBDA spokesperson Mati Hindrekus told the media at Aero India 2009. At the government-level transfer of technology to India will be the prime focus and is likely to sail through without difficulty.

MBDA is the only group capable of designing and producing missiles and missile systems that correspond to the full range of current and future operational needs of the three wings of the armed forces. In all, the group offers a range of 45 missile systems and countermeasure products already in operational service and more than 15 others currently under development.

If the deal goes ahead, MBDA would co-develop the new missile and launcher, using technology and capabilities of the European company and DRDO. BDL would be the prime contractor to produce and integrate the weapon system. The choice of radar would be an Indian one. The missile would have a range of beyond 15 kilometers. The SRSAM will be developed as part of a strategic agreement between the two countries to meet an Indian armed forces requirement.

With development funds for new arms programs virtually non-existent in Europe, an Indian contract would mark an important source of fresh financing for MBDA and a step toward an internationalization, which reduces dependence on cash-strapped home markets. Some of the development on the Indian missile could help feed MDBA's technology base in Europe.

MBDA is also involved in the modernization of the Indian Mirage 2000 fleet. The project involves upgrade of the fighter's capabilities to fire the infrared and electromagnetic versions of the Mica air-to-air missile. There were no plans for a ground strike capability, he said. As part of the upgrade of the Jaguar, the deep strike aircraft would be capable of firing the ASRAAM short range air-to-air missile.

In December 2008 MBDA signed an agreement with the Indian Ministry of Defence and Bharat Dynamics Limited (BDL) which transfers the licenced production rights of the Milan anti-tank missile to India for a period of at least four years. The deal allows BDL to meet Indian demand, but there are discussions in progress on exports of the Indian produced Milan, Bouvier said. MBDA has worked with BDL for 30 years. After the 26/11 terror strike at Mumbai, the Indian Army placed an order for 4,100 Milan-2T Anti-Tank Missiles from MBDA.

MBDA is also supporting the three European fighters - Eurofighter Typhoon, SAAB Gripen and Dassault Rafale, all three in the race for India's Medium Multi-Role Combat Aircraft contract.

Hindustan Aeronautics Limited (HAL)

HAL was present at Aero India 2009 in a big way showcasing a number of indigenous products completed, under development or in the pipeline. One product that has been eminently successful is the Advanced Light Helicopter, Dhruv, a twin-engine machine in the 5.5-tonne class. The Dhruv can carry 13 passengers and has a price tag of $7 million (Rs 35 crore). Currently HAL has orders to deliver 270 Dhruvs worth Rs 16, 000 crore to the Indian armed forces. The overall order book position with HAL for the entire range of products is in excess of Rs 50,000 crore.

During the air show, HAL executed its first export order for ALH Dhruvs valued at $51 million (Rs 250 crore) from Ecuador for five machines. Union Defence Minister A K Anthony handed over the keys of the helicopters on display at Aero India 2009 to the Ecuadorian Air Chief in an impressive ceremony marking an important milestone in the history of India's aerospace major. HAL has orders for three helicopters, a deal worth $20 million (Rs 100 crore) from Turkey. This country has a potential market for 17 helicopters worth $ 150 million (Rs 7500 crore). HAL is in dialogue with Mauritius as well for securing similar orders.

Currently HAL's most prestigious rotary wing project is India's Light Combat Helicopter (LCH), the prototype of which is presently being built and is expected to fly by the end of the year. The LCH has been crafted on the basic design of the ALH and as such many of its components, including the engine, crucial moving parts like the rotor and the instrumentation of the LCH, have already been tested on the Dhruv. Cockpit and fuselage design for LCH was complete and the mock up trials were over last year. All dynamic systems of the LCH and weight class are identical to the Dhruv and only the fuselage and the landing gear have been designed afresh for the combat version of the helicopter. The LCH however is technologically far more complex than the Dhruv. On display at the air show was a black leopard-painted prototype of the armed Dhruv Advanced Light Helicopter. Called the Weapons Systems Integrated Dhruv (WSI Dhruv), this is the machine on which the LCH's armaments and sensors are being validated.

In the recent past, the Union Cabinet has approved HAL's Light Utility Helicopter (LUH) project, a helicopter in the three-tonne class.

The Indian Ministry of Defence has placed orders for 187 LUHs to be delivered by 2015-16. HAL and Israeli Aerospace Industries (IAI) have agreed to jointly develop helicopter UAVs.

In the fixed wing regime, the Tejas Light Combat Aircraft (LCA) has overcome many of the impediments. HAL will soon deliver 40 LCA Mark I including eight limited series production, 20 fighters and 12 trainers. HAL would then take up development of Light Combat Aircraft (LCA) Mark II which will be a new aircraft with a more powerful engine and redesigned fuselage and wings. IAF is expected to eventually order up to 220 LCAs and the Indian Navy another 20. The remaining aircraft will be in the Mark II configuration.

HAL is also negotiating with Russia for the manufacture of the Fifth Generation Fighter Aircraft expected to enter service in 2015 and a tactical military transport aircraft to replace the fleet of AN32 aircraft of the IAF.

Defence Procurement Update

BY SUMIT WALIA

BrahMos Mark II is ready for induction

The last three months have been really important for Brahmos Aerospace and the Indian Army. Brahmos tasted failure and success during these three months. On January 20th, 2009 Brahmos Aerospace conducted a test in Pokhran test ranges that was witnessed by Dr A Sivathanu Pillai, chief executive officer and MD of the company, General Deepak Kapoor, Chief of Army Staff and the top brass of the Indian Army. The missile took off successfully but due to a software glitch, it missed its target and the mission was aborted. The test of 20th January was declared a failure.

But this failure did not stop Pillai, who came back with a bang in less than 2 months. He requested the Army to witness another test on March 4th. This time the Deputy Chief of Army staff Lt Gen MS Dadwal witnessed the test. As per Pillai, the second test met all the required parameters and it hit its target, a factory sized building; but the Army was evaluating the test results and unfortunately did not come up with any results for three weeks. Finally another test was conducted on 29th March which was seen by a team led by the Director General of Military Operations, Lt Gen AS Sekhon. This time, the target was even tougher.

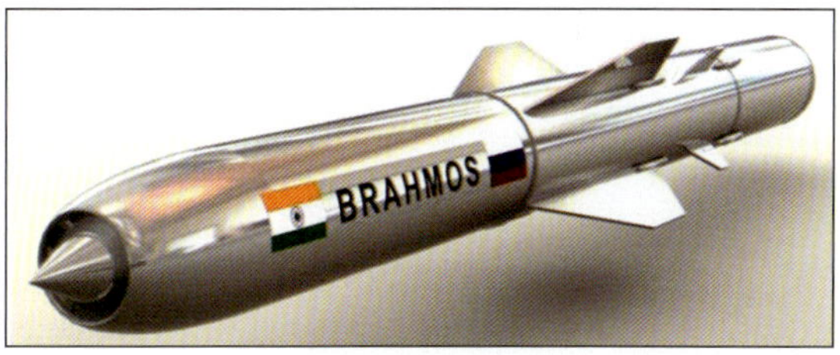

The BrahMos missile

During the first two tests, the missile was to hit a factory size building but in the third test on March 29th, the missile was to identify a building among a cluster of buildings in an urban environment. And the missile did it with precision. This test proved that the missile was all set to join the Army. It will give the Indian Army an unparallel capability with which the Army will be able to pick the target of its choice in any weather, day/night and in any location. Enemy's missile defence will not be able to engage the missile that travels as low as 10 meters in it's terminal phase and has stealth technologies and guidance system with embedded software. BrahMos travels at a speed of 2.8 Mach and up to a range of 290 km and can cruise at a maximum altitude of 15 km. The only cruise missile in active service is the US Tomahawk missile, which has proven its mettle in the Gulf war and the Afghanistan war, but the Tomahawk is a subsonic missile. Two other known supersonic land-attack cruise missiles under development are Fasthawk by Boeing and the French ANS.

A mounted BrahMos

The Indian Army has already raised one regiment (numbered 861) of the BrahMos Mark I missile that has an inferior quality of seeker or homing device. Now Vice Chief of Army Staff has confirmed that the BrahMos Mark II is ready for induction. Army will, reportedly, raise two regiments (numbered 862 and 863) of the BrahMos Mark II, which has an improved seeker and homing devices that can discriminate and zero in on a small target in an urban clutter. These regiments will have four to six batteries of three to four Mobile Autonomous Launchers.

Sumit Walia
sumitw11@gmail.com

DEFENCE & TECHNOLOGY MONITOR

But this is not the end of the road for Dr Pillai who is now working to take the missile to new heights. He is working on developing a Hypersonic BrahMos missile that can travel at Mach 5 to 7 which will make it almost impossible to engage the missile with anti-missile defence systems. Dr Pillai confirmed that lab tests had already started and test missiles would be ready by 2010. Test missiles would be flown over rockets motors and would use aviation kerosene and atmospheric air, mixed at a proportionate volume, as the fuel. Looking at the track record of BrahMos Aerospace, the target of 2010 for the hypersonic missile looks realistic.

Indian Missile Defnce System

Three tests of Ballistic missile defence (BMD) system and all of them successful. This is the most successful and surprising development plans of the DRDO. After the third consecutive successful test that was conducted on 06 March 2009 at 1624 hrs, DRDO's chief controller and air defence programme director VK Saraswat said, "All building blocks of the BMD are ready at the moment. Only part that remains to be developed is the interceptor missile and by the time they are in place, we will have our full mechanism in place. The programme will be completed by 2011."

Advanced Air Defence

The first test was conducted on 27th November 06 when Prithvi Air Defence (PAD) system successfully intercepted a projected enemy missile in Exo-atmospheric region at an altitude of 48 km and in another test Advanced Air Defence (AAD) intercepted an enemy missile on 06 Dec 2007 in Endo-atmospheric region at 15 kms.

This time, Dhanush missile (projected enemy missile) was launched from a ship 100 km off the Orissa coast and went to an altitude of 120 km and was successfully intercepted by advanced two stage missile at an altitude of 75 km. Dr Saraswat informed that the current missile was 30% more powerful and more advanced than the missile used in first test in December 06. The current missile had more energy, improved guidance and control system and above all had a Gimbaled Directional Warhead. The weight of the new warhead was 30 kg but was able to produce an impact of a 150 kg omni-directional warhead. New guidance system of the missile helps the missile to tackle maneuvers of the enemy missile just like Russian Topov M missiles that can perform Zig Zag (S shape) maneuvers in order to avoid interception.

DRDO would require 5 successful tests to complete Phase I which they hope to complete by 2011. Once Phase I is complete, BMD system will be able to take on missiles with a range of 2000 km like the Chinese M-9 class missiles. DRDO said that an integrated test will be conducted at the end of the year in which PAD will intercept enemy missiles in Exo-atmospheric regions and AAD will take care of missiles/debris in Endo-atmospheric regions.

Phase II of the BMD system will be developed to tackle missiles with a range of 6000 km. In phase II, hypersonic missiles will be developed that can travel at speeds of Mach 6 – 7 and with far more advanced guidance and control system, because the missile will have less time to guide itself to the incoming enemy missile.

Once deployed, the system will be fully automated and will not require any human intervention. Missiles will always be on "Hot Stand-by Mode" that will take-off within 120 seconds of the detection of the incoming missile by the tracking radars. During the war, a volley of interceptor missiles will be fired to ensure kill. Interceptor missiles will be constantly updated about the coordinates of the enemy missiles from the ground based radars through a data link that would be difficult to jam.

Impact of Mumbai Attacks on defence Procurement

'A stitch in time saves nine' is something we did not learn in the last 62 years. We have been putting our national security at stake and have been waiting for the enemy to attack and teach us a lesson. Weapon

Locating Radar procured right after the Kargil war is one such example. The Government did not listen to the Army for years and consequently, the Pakistani artillery took a number of army as well as civilian lives.

Elta EL/M-2083 Aerostat Radar

Same thing happened in Mumbai when we saw that NSG did not have their own planes or helicopters to come to Mumbai. They had to wait till an IAF plane came from Chandigarh to carry them from Delhi to Mumbai and wasted 5-6 precious hours. A 60 hour long battle forced the Government to take quick decisions of getting planes/helicopters and different equipments for a NSG like body - worn video and audio bugs, mini-remotely operated vehicles, real time x-ray viewing system, night vision equipments for assault rifles, laser listening devices and light support weapons. The MoD has already given the go-ahead for general purpose machine guns (with night sight and ammunition), under barrel grenade launchers, 2,724 night vision equipments, 6,908 reflex sight, 612 radio-controlled detonators, 372 remote detonating devices (including receivers, transmitters) and 93 guided parafoil air delivery systems.

Weight of the night vision devices that the NSG needs should be less than 2 kg and should be water resistant. They should have a non-reflective surface, shock-proof optics to sustain prolonged recoil, a zoom facility and should be able to detect a man standing at 300 metres on a starlit night without the moon. The laser listening device mentioned in the shopping list is a laser-based audio monitoring system that can allow surveillance operation from a distance of at least 400 metres.

The Navy has also geared up and has decided to raise a 1000 strong Sagar Prahari Bal, a specialized force to protect its assets. The Navy is also acquiring two EL/M-2083 aerostat radars built by Elta Systems, Israel. These balloon mounted radars will have a range of approximately 500 km and will be able to detect low flying aircrafts. These radars have been in the Navy's wish list for a long time.

On paper, MoD has also given approval to a Rs 6000 crore package to increase force level of the Coast Guard and has sanctioned an increase of 20% in the number of vessels. The proposal that was dying under stockpile of files in the MoD for years, involves induction of 40 new patrol vessels, 30 helicopters, 12 surveillance aircraft and 20 interceptor boats. Coastal radars are also expected to be procured to setup a chain of static coastal radars. But all these plans have just got their approval on papers; these will be implemented when a new Government takes charge after the elections.

10 Marine Police Stations were setup about 2 years ago but none of them was fully functional during November, 2008. Except the one in Somnath, none of these stations have their own building, forget boats and other equipments. Now new boats are being purchased for these stations. West Bengal has learnt its lesson from the Mumbai attacks and will set up 9 Marine Police Stations. Two of these stations, Hemnagar and Kishorimohanpur, have already started working. The State will purchase 18 patrol boats from Greece, which would be modified at the Garden Reach Shipbuilding Limited to meet Indian requirements. State Government will provide 400 men to man these police stations with latest weapons and gadgets. To deal with a Mumbai like terror attack a team of elite Navy commandos Marcos and state police commandos will be deployed at Kolkata port.

Even if all these gadgets are in place, the main question would still be unanswered: will all these agencies work in co-ordination? All these agencies will have to work like a well-oiled machine in order to avoid any other Mumbai like terror attack. Otherwise, we will see the same blame game again, where one agency will be holding another agency responsible for the failure.

Indian Air Force is going to get sharper teeth

IAF is facing severe problems of an ageing fleet. There has been very little induction in the last 20 years. Mig-29s were inducted in the late 80s and Su-30MKI in late 90s. The initial deal of Su- 30 MKI was of buying 40 aircraft off the shelf and manufacturing 140 aircraft in India by HAL. In September 1998, India bought another 10 Su-30s that were originally built for Indonesia. Cash strapped Indonesia could not take the delivery and that opportunity took the number of Indian Su-30 MKIs to 50. In 2007, Russia received another order of 40 Su-30 MKIs from India. Although HAL has been asked to complete the delivery of 140 Su-30 MKIs by 2013-2014, it will not help maintain a strength of 39.5 squadrons as the IAF is bound to phase out Mig-21s, Mig-23s and Mig-27s. Last month, the IAF phased out Mig 23 BN, operated by 221 Squadron, after service of 27 years and will phase out some 300 Mig-21s by 2010-2011. Induction of 126 aircraft, for which a tender was floated last year, will take at least 6 years. The IAF even tried to get second hand 12 Mirage 2000 aircraft from Qatar, but Qatar wanted a very high price. Those aircraft were almost new and would have joined the IAF in no time. But during the last 10 years, the IAF ordered force multipliers like mid-air refueling tankers IL-78s, Phalcon AEWandC, 80 Mi-17 1V helicopters and Hawk trainers. These would provide the much required thrust to the IAF's punch. Let's have a look at the systems that the IAF is about to receive and is intended to acquire in near future.

BrahMos on Su-30 MKI

- The IAF will receive its first of the three Phalcon Airborne Early Warning and Control (AEWandC) radar systems from Israel after a delay of 18 months. These three 'eye in the sky' systems were ordered in 2004 at a cost of $1.1 billion. Russian IL-76 aircraft was selected as platform for these systems, probably because the IAF is already operating these aircrafts and would not have to develop a separate line of maintenance. Second system is scheduled to be delivered in late 2009 and the third one would arrive by mid 2010.

  The most likely reason for the delay of the project seems to be integration of the Israeli, Indian and French electronics and sensors including long-range, high-powered transmit/receive (T/R) modules on Russian IL-76 aircraft. Once in active service, AEWandC will be integrated into a network of land based radars, Aerostat radars, UAVs and dedicated spy satellite that the IAF is going to get in near future. Phalcon's Active Electronically Scanned Array Radar will allow 360 degree coverage of sky up to a distance of 400 km and will track high maneuvering targets and low-flying objects in all weather day and night conditions. the IAF is looking to order three more such systems.

- Considering the threat posed by LTTE's recent attacks on Sri Lankan Air Bases, IAF has also decided to install Israeli EL/M-2083 Aerostat Radars to keep a close watch on low flying aircrafts. IAF has already moved its mobile radar units all along the Southern coast to avoid any such misadventure by the LTTE. For better coordination, control of Maritime Air Operations (MOA) would also be moved to Southern Air Command from South-Western Air Command.

- IAF has also issued Request for Proposal for 56 Advanced Jet Trainers (AJTs) to six aerospace companies. Earlier it was expected that BAE systems will get a follow on order of Hawk trainers. But IAF dropped the idea because of the delays in supplies of spare parts from BAE to HAL, who is responsible of assembling the Hawk trainers in India. However the RFP was sent 6 companies - BAE Systems for new Hawks, Italy's Alenia for its M346, South Korea's T-50, the Czech Republic's L-159 and Russia's Yak-130 and MiG AT trainer.

- Giving another surprise, some senior MoD officials have also confirmed that it is close to finalize a 1 billion euro contract for six Airbus A-330 Multi-Role Tanker-Transports (MRTT). The IAF is already using 6 IL-76 tankers and Russia was expecting a follow on order of more tankers, but the IAF has selected A-300 MRTT because of its large fuel loads and dual transport capability. The A330 has a large internal fuel capacity of 111,000 kg in the wings; fuel capacity can be further increased with under floor tanks, which would not compromise the main deck cargo capacity or seating in the strategic transport role. Standard fuel capacity allows the carriage of an additional 43,000 kg of cargo. It has won almost all international orders in the recent past.
- Currently, the IAF is upgrading its existing fleet of Mig-29s and its fleet of An-32. Under this upgrade programe, Anotonov will:
  - prolong an aircraft service life up to 20 years with further prolongation of up to 25-30 years. At that, it is proposed to carry out less laborios reconditioning repair instead of overhaul;
  - increase an engine life to 1st overhaul from 1,000-2,000 up to 4,000 hours, and specified life from 3,000-6,000 up to 20,000 hours;
  - increase payload;
  - extend a flight range by 1,000 km due to installation of additional fuel tanks, total of 3,000 liter capacity;
  - advance electronic equipment;
  - reduce noise level in cockpit;
  - perform maritime patrol and search-and-rescue missions.
- In 2006, India reportedly finalized the deal with RSK-Mig of Russia for $888 million to upgrade its fleet of Mig-29s. Under this upgrade, Mig-29s will be fitted with new avionics, electronic warfare suites and Phazatron Zhuk-M radar with a wide scan and tracking area of + / – 85 deg. in azimuth and + / – 60 deg. in elevation, terrain following mode, and ground target acquisition including high-resolution modes. Phazatron Zhuk-M radar range is 1.5 times than the Zhuk radar. RD-33 engines will also be worked upon to deal with some known issues. Planes will be provided ground attack and mid-air refueling capabilities. Currently 6 aircrafts are in Russia undergoing upgrades and the rest of the aircraft will be upgraded in Ojhar AFB, Nasik. This upgrade system will increase the life of Mig-29s from 25 year to 40 years.
- In the late 1990s, an agreement was signed between HAL and Turbomeca for installation of TM333 turboshaft engine on the Indian Dhruv helicopter.After the successful installation, HAL decided to develop a new engine with Turbomeca with 25% more power to enable Dhruv to operate in extremely cold and high terrains, like Siachin and extremely hot, like Rajasthan. The new engine was to be of the same size as the TM333 but it provided more power to perform missions at high altitudes. Dhruv flew with these Ardiden 1H (Shakti) engines on August 13, 2007 and was certified by the European Aviation Safety Agency in December 2007.

Shakti engines were further developed to Ardiden 1H1 with power output of 1032 kW. Five prototypes of these engines were delivered in December, 2008. Test flight of the Dhruv with twin Ardiden 1H1 engines took place on 12th January, 2009. The engine will be certified by EASA by March, 2009. Currently engines are being tested at Siachin. Once successfully installed on Dhruv, they would add punch to Dhruv's reliability and performance and help the Army to replace the ageing fleets of the Chetak and Cheetah helicopters.

- MoD has also scrapped a tender of 22 attack helicopters for which three international companies submitted their proposals. These companies were Russia's Kamov, the European Aeronautic Defence and Space (EADS) company and Italian-British group Agusta Westland. Two US based companies Boeing and Bell had already quit the race. The deal was supposed to be worth $550 million. The RFP was cancelled as the three companies could not meet the qualitative requirements. A fresh RFP will be floated shortly by the MoD.

KMW KRAUSS-MAFFEI WEGMANN

Remote-controlled weapon stations delivered.

Krauss-Maffei Wegmann (KMW) has carried out the first partial delivery of seven light FLW 100 weapon stations to the Federal Office for Defence Technology and Procurement (BWB). The contract signed in July last year allows for the production and delivery of 230 light (FLW 100) and 190 heavy weapon stations (FLW 200) in all.

Only four months after signature of the contract, the first weapon stations, which can be mounted on any type of vehicle, have now been handed over to the Bundeswehr.

Weapon Station FLW 100

This was only possible because all participating firms, under the leadership of KMW, began advance production immediately after the selection decision at the end of 2007, at their own financial risk, in order to meet the planned delivery deadlines. With the prompt delivery of the first seven weapon stations, KMW has been able to make a valuable contribution to the security of Bundeswehr soldiers in their missions abroad.

In order to respond to the resulting increased need for protection, the Bundeswehr decided to equip its vehicles with light and heavy weapon stations of the types FLW 100 and 200 in the framework of its 'GFF' ("protected command and role-specific vehicle") procurement programme. KMW was thus able to convince the Bundeswehr as to both modular weapon stations in a comparative test, and prevailed against competing international products.

Remote-controlled weapon stations

Both the FLW 100 and the FLW 200 can be operated by remote control by the vehicle crew from within the armoured interior, using a monitor with integrated day-and night-vision devices. A further technical feature of the system is the so-called gyroscopic stabilization, which enables an extremely precise and controlled deployment of the weapons even during high-speed movement through rugged terrain. In addition, the stations permit a rapid change in armament. The respective equipment range – from machine guns up to automatic grenade launchers – is automatically recognized, and the station adapts its ballistics accordingly.

A further advantage is that the system can be mounted on the vehicle without making roof openings, due to its modular design. This means that no moving parts are located in the interior of the vehicle and the level of protection of the vehicles is not reduced by the integration. The integrated security system of the weapon stations also takes the vehicle silhouette, the vehicle-specific arrangement of hatches, doors and body areas, into account. The weapon station will thus not fire on the vehicle itself by mistake.

RHEINMETALL DEFENCE

Wins big Bundeswehr ammo order

The German Bundeswehr has awarded a major contract for artillery ammunition to the Düsseldorf-based Rheinmetall Group. Worth around •63 million and set to run until 2014, the order encompasses 30,000 rounds of high explosive 155mm ammunition, type DM 121. The Federal Agency for Defence Technology and Equipment (BWB) in Koblenz announced the order on 20 March 2009, following approval by the Budget & Appropriations Committee of the German Parliament.

Procurement of this new ammunition technology bridges a significant gap for the Bundeswehr, one of Rheinmetall's most important reference customers. Thanks to special handling features, the DM 121 offers major advantages with regard to operating safety and reliability. Made possible by Rheinmetall's newly developed Rh26 Insensitive explosive, this feature places the new round on the global cutting edge of artillery shell technology. It also makes an important contribution to force protection.

Owing to its 30 km-range (with maximum charge load) and ability to penetrate bunkers, this ammunition is suitable for engaging hardened enemy positions at a safe standoff without endangering friendly forces.

With a view to current and future operational scenarios, Rheinmetall sees significant market potential for the new ammunition in a number of nations whose artillery forces deploy 155mm 39-/52 cal. artillery systems, especially users of PzH 2000 and M109 self-propelled howitzers and Rheinmetall's RWG-52 wheeled howitzer.

BWB's decision to source ammunition from Rheinmetall followed a customer product management process with an international market review and test campaign to evaluate competing products. Rheinmetall's DM 121 HE round proved to be the best choice both technically and economically.

The contract underscores once again Rheinmetall's leadership in the field of large calibre artillery systems, ammunition and propelling charges.

DCNS Sets up Indian Subsidiary

Patrick Boissier, Chairman & CEO of DCNS Group, a European leader in naval systems, inaugurated DCNS India, a wholly-owned subsidiary specializing in naval services in Mumbai on March 25.

DCNS Group is in charge of a contract for the transfer of technology of Scorpene submarines to Mazagon Dock Ltd (MDL) shipyard. Six Scorpene submarines will be delivered by 2018 under P75 Indian Navy's project.

DCNS India will contribute to this technology transfer by providing consultancy and technical assistance services and by helping to source and qualify Indian suppliers for submarine components and equipment.

Additionally, DCNS India will conduct detailed engineering studies and provide consultancy, sourcing and procurement services for other DCNS projects with Indian shipyards. It also plans to provide similar services to DCNS units abroad.

Mr. Xavier Marchal will be the Managing Director of DCNS India. He was associated with the Indian Navy's P75 project since its commencement 3 years back. The new entity is headquartered in Mumbai and expects to employ over 100 people by the end of 2010.

Mr. Patrick Boissier, Chairman & CEO of DCNS Group said, *"I am pleased to formally announce the launch of the Indian subsidiary of the DCNS group. India is one of the key strategic focus markets for DCNS group and we are looking at it from a very long term perspective. We hope to make significant contribution through our global experience and expertise to the Indian companies and will be able to add a lot of value through our technical know-how and programme management capabilities."*

The launch of DCNS India reflects the group's commitment to step up its international development and strengthen its presence in India in particular, primarily by facilitating the technology transfer process and establishing long-term ties with the local engineering and manufacturing industry, both public and private sectors.

The DCNS India opening ceremony was attended by prominent members of the Indian Navy and naval industry.

BAE SYSTEMS

Participation at Aero India 2009

BAE Systems had its biggest ever presence at Aero India 09, an event BAE Systems has attended every year since its inception. The company took a large stand alone pavilion, not a booth inside the halls.

BAE Systems' theme for the event was Autonomy - specifically autonomous air vehicles.

Mantis, a new autonomous UAV being developed by BAE Systems made its international debut at the show. A full size Mantis and Herti (pics attached) graced the area outside the BAE Systems pavilion.

Inside the pavilion, BAE Systems displayed products from across our aerospace capabilities, including Typhoon, Hawk but also some product not displayed in India before, such as the special seating for helicopters that protect aircrew from spinal injuries in crashes and hard landing - the leading cause of injury to helo pilots.

The Mantis UAS Advanced Concept Technology Demonstrator programme brings together technologies, capabilities and systems that will demonstrate the potential of a large unmanned autonomous aircraft

Phase one of the programme will see BAE Systems working alongside the UK MOD and industrial parties including Rolls-Royce, QinetiQ, GE Aviation, SELEX Galileo and Meggitt.

Mark Kane, Managing Director of Autonomous Systems and Future Capability at BAE Systems, said: "Mantis is another important step forward in the development of UAS capabilities. The aim is to prove that the integrated technologies on Mantis, that build on several years of autonomous UAS experience within BAE Systems and the wider UK industry, can provide the tangible military capability and levels of performance required for the future."

The Mantis benefits from low-cost advanced construction techniques developed on earlier BAE Systems UAS programmes and provides for a wide range of "plug and play" systems and equipment, as well as enabling flexible external stores carriage. A triplex flight control system will give high system reliability and integrity, with full exploitation of onboard autonomy reducing operator workload and increasing system performance. The novel design will also explore how low logistical footprint and ease of support could reduce through-life operating costs.

EUROSAM Systems

Headquartered near Paris, EUROSAM was established in June 1989 by three major European aerospace companies (Aerospatiale, Alenia and Thomson-CSF) known today as MBDA Missile Systems and THALES. It is a joint venture set up by Europe's largest defence contractors to meet future air-defence requirements. Its direct shareholders include the French and Italian subsidiaries of MBDA and Thales, while BAE Systems and Matra BAE Dynamics are also involved in its programmes. These world-leading aerospace and missile companies have joined their efforts to design, develop and manufacture the most modern air-defence systems in the world, in a range of versions optimized for naval, ground-launched or anti-tactical ballistic missile missions.

EUROSAM's development program was originally funded by the French and Italian defence ministries, later joined by Britain's Ministry of Defence for the development of a naval area-defence variant. The company has already been selected by the Royal Saudi Arabian Navy to supply the main weapon systems of its latest F3000S air-defence frigates, and additional export sales are being negotiated to other countries.

EUROSAM's concept of a family of systems is intended to satisfy multiple operational requirements. These systems have been designed for both naval and ground-launched applications. The only major differences stem from the environment in which the system operates. The modules have been designed for flexibility to perform short and medium range missions as well for ground as for naval applications. Integration is facilitated by always being based on the same architecture, a fire control unit using multifunction phased array radar, a vertical launcher to reduce the reaction time in all directions, and a terminal active homing missile equipped with a lateral thrust system to achieve direct impact or insignificant miss distance.

Eurosam's air defence systems are based on a modular architecture, with specific modules or "building blocks" which can be combined to precisely tailor each system to the customer's specific requirements.

A basic system consists of a multi-function radar, a command and control post with Mara computers and Magics operator consoles, and a vertical launch system. But additional sub-systems can also be added as required to optimize the basic system's capabilities for specific missions, such as naval extended area defence or anti- ballistic missile defence.

The new Sea Viper air defence missile system recently demonstrated its ability to protect air, land and sea forces during a second, successful test firing. The missile system was successfully test-fired from the 12,000 tonne trials barge Longbow, near the Ile du Levant off the French coast. The Longbow barge has a full replica of the air defence equipment the new Type 45 destroyers will carry, including long-range and missile directing radars, a combat control centre and missiles in their vertical launcher silos. Sea Viper is a highly sophisticated system that has been designed to allow the new Type 45 Destroyer to protect forces, both at sea and over land, against attack by enemy aircraft, as well as defending the fleet against anti-ship missiles approaching from any direction and at supersonic speeds.

New French Base in the Gulf

BY CLAUDE ARPI

A SMALL REVOLUTION IS HAPPENING in the French defense establishment: Paris will soon open an inter-service base outside France, in Abu Dhabi in the United Arab Emirates (UAE).

Though it is not official yet, President Sarkozy plans to inaugurate the new complex during his State visit to the Emirates on May 27. The President may also participate in an international seminar on marine security planned during the preceding days in Abu Dhabi; several Gulf Heads of State may be present.

The information is kept under wraps as tough negotiations are still on with the UAE to purchase French nuclear power plants and Rafale fighter planes.

A year ago, the French Ministry of Defense published a White Paper. An interesting aspect was the change of direction in French defense strategy. Paris had started looking eastward; a communiqué of the French Defense Ministry stated: "Regarding our capacities to prevent conflicts and to intervene, the White Paper recommends concentrating on a priority geographical axis, going from the Atlantic and Mediterranean regions, to the Persian Gulf and the Indian Ocean. This axis corresponds to zones where the risks involving the strategic interests of France and Europe are the most serious. The axis allows taking into account the growing importance of Asia for International security and contributes to our presence and our cooperation in this direction [of the Gulf] from the Indian Ocean. Furthermore, France will retain its capacity of prevention and action on the Western and Eastern parts of the African continent, as well as in the Sahelian strip, mainly to fight terrorism and terrorist acts. France will radically convert the present system of defense agreements and military cooperation to evolve towards a partnership between Europe and Africa as well as cooperation in the field of defense and security which favours the rise of African capacities to maintain peace [in the region]."

This is a radical shift from Paris' traditional African strategy.

The opening of a base in the Gulf is rather unexpected at a time when the country is facing severe budgetary restrictions due to the global financial crisis. Let us not forget that the French budgetary deficit will cross 5.6 percent of the GDP in 2009, the highest ever.

The opening of a base in the Gulf is rather unexpected at a time when the country is facing severe budgetary restrictions due to the global financial crisis.

It is certainly one of the reasons why the President is not keen to publicize the opening of a new base in the Gulf.

The inter-service complex will have a strength of 450 tri-service personnel; 30 percent will be allowed to bring their families. Since 1995, a strategic partnership exists with the UAE, but previous French Presidents preferred to concentrate on Africa.

A recent article in *Le Monde* points out: "France and the Emirates insist on the fact that this new military set up is not against anybody", in other words, not against Iran whose activities greatly worry the Gulf countries. A diplomat told *Le Monde*: "The stakes are huge in the region". The Emirates are obviously an important 'energy' factor in a globalized economy; for its part, the UAE does not want to depend entirely on the United States for its security.

In a time of crisis, strategy is not the only motivation, business is also important. In fact, business and strategy are two sides of the same coin.

Claude Arpi writes regularly on Tibet, China, India and Indo-French relations in *The Pioneer*, the *New Indian Express*, *rediff.com* and other Indian and French publications. He is the author of *Tibet: The Lost Frontier* and his forthcoming book is *The Negotiations That Never Were*.
claudearpi@gmail.com

DEFENCE & TECHNOLOGY MONITOR

Abu Dhabi has already purchased nearly 400 Leclerc tanks, the main battle tank (MBT) built by Nexter[1].

Paris and Abu Dhabi have other negotiations in the pipeline: one is for two nuclear EPR reactors[2] and perhaps more importantly, the UAE would like to replace its Mirage fleet by Rafale fighter planes. Will President Sarkozy sign the deal for 63 Rafale as he arrives in Abu Dhabi? It is not certain: the Emirates would like Paris to take back 60 Mirages before agreeing to sign.

In today's world, Business is Strategy and Strategy is Business. In the long term, the base can become a productive investment for Paris.

For the time being, the new installations will officially be a support base under the command of the 'Alindien'.[3]

According to *Le Monde,* the nearby base in Al-Dhafra[4] could accommodate two refueling planes, KC-135,[5] which are presently based in Manas (Kirghizstan). The Bishkek government has asked for the return of its base.

Another advantage for the French Army is that Abu Dhabi could be a training centre for desert environment.

One year back, when we asked Mr. Jerome Bonnafont, the French Ambassador to India about the White Paper's implications for India, he had told us: "If you look at the analysis of threats in the White Paper you will see that the stability of the Indian Ocean is one of our important concerns. Cooperation with India is therefore naturally part of our strategy...Regarding the equipment, the White Paper says that we need a better equipped army with higher technological equipment. This will therefore enhance our offers for similar equipment to the countries with whom we are collaborating".

The new base is hence part of a strategy for Paris. It could certainly become a window of French technology and know-how in the Gulf (and perhaps even not further east). In today's world, Business is Strategy and Strategy is Business. In the long term, the base can become a productive investment for Paris.

Notes

1 In production since 1991, the Leclerc tank entered French service in 1992 replacing the AMX 30. The French Army has a total of 406 Leclercs.

2 The EPR is a third generation pressurized water reactor designed and developed mainly by Areva and Electricité de France (EDF). It is called the European Pressurized Reactor; the internationalized name of this reactor is Evolutionary Power Reactor.

3 In the French Navy, the 'Alindien' is the Admiral responsible for the maritime zone of the Indian Ocean, extending from the Red Sea and Africa in the west to the Philippines and Vietnam in the east. It includes countries of the Gulf as well as South Africa, India, Australia and Singapore.

4 Al Dhafra Air Base, located approximately twenty miles south of Abu Dhabi is a military installation hosting UAE, United States and French forces.

5 KC-135 Stratotanker is an aerial refueling tanker aircraft.

The New Great Game

BY COL HARJEET SINGH

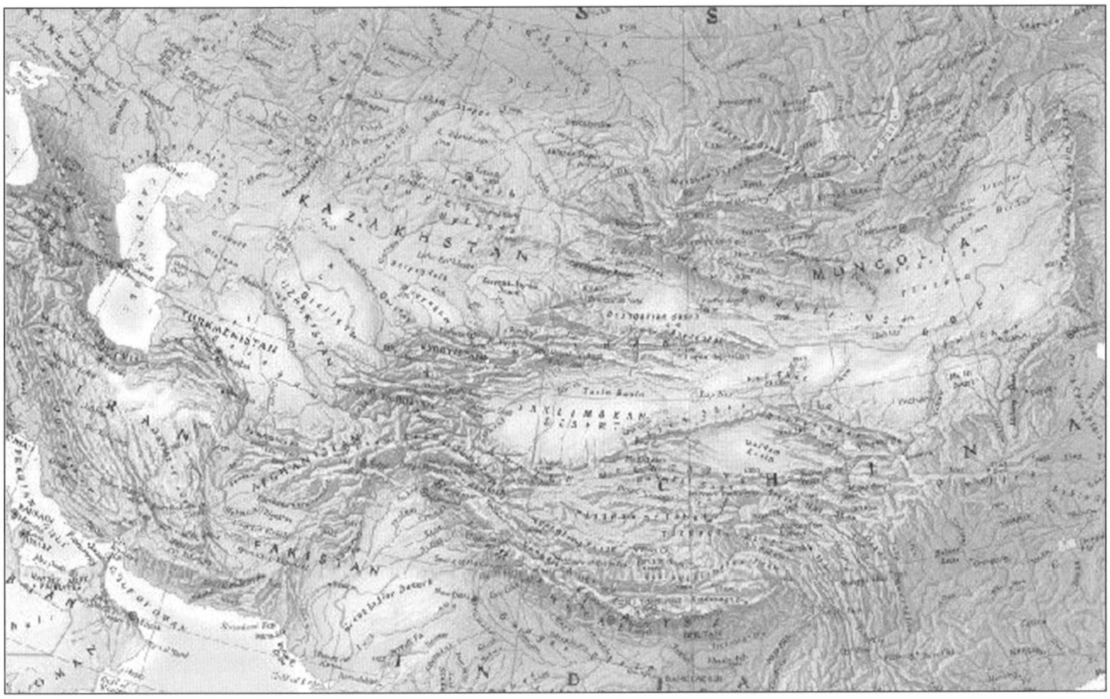

Map 1: Central Asia

Historical Background

THE "GREAT GAME" WAS A TERM PREVALENT IN THE 19TH CENTURY, FOR THE STRATEGIC rivalry and conflict between the British Empire and the Russian Empire for supremacy in Central Asia. It represented the international struggle to build a stable and secure Asian rimland from the Persian Gulf on the west to India. It aimed at securing a barrier between global economies and the networks of communication and defence linked by the sea, on the one hand, and power based in the Asian heartland on the other.

Today, the Great Game is alive again. However, it has mutated into a different dynamics with varied combinations and permutations as the actors and goals have changed with time. Specifically, the number of actors has increased, and the game is not entirely confined to the goal of security and stability of the Indian subcontinent as the geospatial centre of the Asian rimland. The availability of energy has become a larger issue. While geography remains constant there are now an increased number of factors impacting the Game, making it less predictable.

The term "The Great Game" is usually attributed to Arthur Conolly, an intelligence officer of the British East India Company's 6th Bengal Light Cavalry, though it was romanticized by Rudyard Kipling.[1] From the British perspective, the Russian Empire's expansion into Central Asia threatened to destroy the "jewel in the crown" of the British Empire, India. As the Tsar's troops began to subdue one Khanate after another, the British feared that Afghanistan would become a staging post for a Russian invasion of India.

The British were all too aware that all invasions into India, throughout history, were through Afghanistan and the Northwest Frontier. With that in mind, in 1838 they launched the First Anglo-

Col Harjeet Singh
colharjeetsingh@gmail.com

Afghan War and attempted to impose a puppet regime under Shah Shuja. The regime was short lived and the first British venture into Afghanistan ended in disaster. After the annexation of the Punjab in 1849, the British Empire extended up to the Hindu Kush mountains and Afghanistan was seen as a buffer state. The Russians continued to advance steadily southward towards Afghanistan and by 1865 Tashkent had been formally annexed.

In order to secure their interests Britain launched the Second Anglo-Afghan War in 1878, when their mission was turned back from Kabul. In retaliation a force of 40,000 men was sent across the border. The second war was almost as disastrous as the first for the British, and by 1881, they again pulled out of Kabul.

The Third Anglo-Afghan War of 1919 was precipitated by the assassination of the then ruler Habibullah Khan. His son and successor Amanullah declared full independence and attacked British India's northern frontier. Although little was gained militarily, the stalemate was resolved with the Rawalpindi Agreement of 1919 when Afghanistan became an independent state.

With the end of the Second World War and the beginning of the Cold War, the United States displaced Britain as the global power, asserting its influence in the Middle East in pursuit of oil, containment of the Soviet Union, and access to other resources. This period is sometimes referred to as "The New Great Game", and the term became an analogy or framework in the military, security, and diplomatic communities for events involving India, Pakistan, Afghanistan, and, more recently, the post-Soviet republics of Central Asia.

The Soviet war in Afghanistan was a nine-year conflict involving Soviet Union forces supporting the Marxist People's Democratic Party of Afghanistan government against the mujahideen resistance. The latter group found support from a variety of sources including the United States, Saudi Arabia, Pakistan and other Muslim nations in the context of the Cold War. This conflict was concurrent to the 1979 Iranian Revolution and the Iran–Iraq War. The Soviet war in Afghanistan began on 27 December 1979 and ended on 15 February 1989.

India's relations with Central Asia are influenced to a major degree by the actions of Russia, China, Iran, Pakistan and the US. India has lost valuable time in creating viable leverages and lacks bandwidth to use the hard power approach in pursuing its national interests in the region.

The latest war in Afghanistan began on 7 October 2001 when the United States (US) launched a military operation in response to the 11 September 2001 airline attacks. The stated purpose was to capture Osama bin Laden, destroy Al-Qaeda, and remove the Taliban regime. The US stated that, as policy, it would not distinguish between Al-Qaeda and nations that harbor them. There are now two military operations in Afghanistan, which seek to establish control over the country. Operation Enduring Freedom is a US combat operation involving some coalition partners and currently operating primarily in the eastern and southern parts of the country along the Pakistan border. The second operation is the International Security Assistance Force (ISAF), initially established by the UN Security Council at the end of December 2001 to secure Kabul and its surroundings. NATO assumed control of the ISAF in 2003 and operations are still ongoing.

The Problem of Asia

Alfred Mahan, a US Navy officer and president of the US Naval War College, best known for his *Influence of Sea Power upon History* series of books, analyzed the geopolitical structure of world politics at the dawn of the 20th century. He divided the continent of Asia into three zones: [2]

- A northern zone, located above the 40th parallel, characterized by its cold climate, and dominated by land power;
- The "Debatable and Debated" zone, located between the 40th and 30th parallels, characterized by a temperate climate; and,
- A southern zone, located below the 30th parallel, characterized by its hot climate, and dominated by sea power.

The Debated and Debatable zone, contained two peninsulas on either end (Asia Minor and Korea), the Isthmus of Suez, Palestine, Syria, Mesopotamia, two countries marked by their mountain ranges

(Persia and Afghanistan), the Pamir Mountains, the Tibetan Himalayas, the Yangtze Valley, and Japan. Within it, there were no strong states capable of withstanding outside influence or even maintaining stability within their own borders. So whereas the political situations to the north and south were relatively stable and determined, the middle remained "debatable and debated ground."

North of the 40th parallel, the vast expanse of Asia was dominated by the Russian Empire. Russia possessed a central position on the continent, and a wedge-shaped projection into Central Asia, bounded by the Caucasus mountains and Caspian Sea on one side and the mountains of Afghanistan and Western China on the other side. To prevent Russian expansionism and predominance on the Asian continent, Mahan opined that pressure on Asia's flanks could be the only viable strategy pursued by sea powers.

Areas south of the 30th parallel were dominated by the sea powers – Britain, the US, Germany and Japan. To Mahan, the possession of India by Britain was of key strategic importance, as India was best suited to exert balancing pressure against Russia in Central Asia. Britain's predominance in Egypt, China, Australia, and the Cape of Good Hope was also considered important. The strategy of the sea powers, according to Mahan, ought to be to deny Russia the benefits of commerce from the sea. He noted that both the Dardanelles and Baltic straits could be closed by a hostile power, thereby denying Russia access to the sea. This would reinforce Russia's expansionism in order to obtain wealth or warm water ports. The natural geographic targets for Russian expansionism in search of access to the sea would therefore be the Chinese seaboard, the Persian Gulf, and Asia Minor.

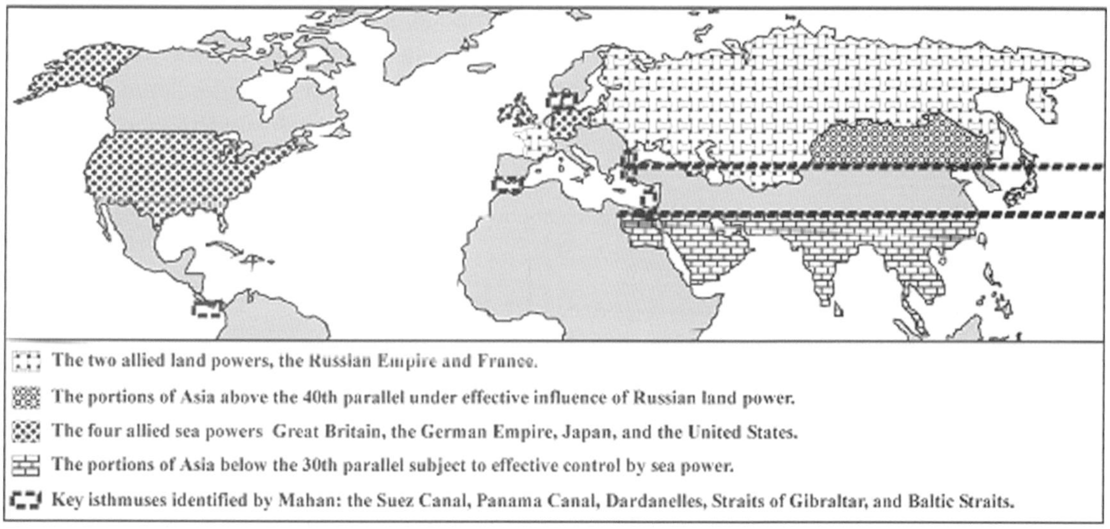

Map 2: The world as divided by Mahan

The British continued with their obsession about the Great Game till their withdrawal from India. Sir Olaf Caroe organized the Viceroy's Support Group (VSG) in 1942 in his capacity as Foreign Secretary in Britain's Government of India. It worked on the premise that the security of the Asian rimland from the Persian Gulf to Indochina "*is one complete strategical problem.*" The security of the Gulf was bound up with the security of the Indian subcontinent which in turn depended on Burma and Indochina. A stable subcontinent formed the fulcrum in the system. Its fragmentation would leave the wings isolated and the balance broken. The notion of a continuous Great Game that would survive the withdrawal of British rule in India transfixed the VSG's work.[3]

According to Olaf Caroe, the Soviet invasion of Afghanistan in 1979 was a predictable (and predicted) "after-effect" of India's partition in 1947. By creating two mutually antagonistic successor states in India and Pakistan, the partition effectively turned the subcontinent's power potential in on itself. For nearly a century, power based on a stable subcontinent had provided a counterpoise to Russia that had allowed the emergence of a viable Afghan state. The fragmentation of the counterpoise on the subcontinent allowed the Russians to calculate their interests and options in 1979 very differently than their predecessors had in 1838, 1878, and 1919. The continued hostility of India and Pakistan thus weighed heavily against the reconstruction of security and stability in Afghanistan.

The latter thus reemerged as a base area and seedbed it had once formed for forces of regional instability and terrorism.

Zbigniew Brzezinski, a former US National Security adviser, advocated a 21st century version of the Great Game after the implosion of the Soviet Union.[4] He cast Eurasia as the playing field upon which the world's fate is determined. As the US emerged as the world's sole superpower, he delineated its global strategy to maintain its exceptional position in the world. Central to his analysis was the exercise of power on the Eurasian landmass, which is home to the greatest part of the globe's population, natural resources, and economic activity. He animadverted that Central Asia is the "grand chessboard" on which US supremacy will be ratified and challenged in the years to come. The problem was to manage the conflicts and relationships in Europe, Asia, and the Middle East so that no rival superpower could rise to threaten US interests. Popular media have referred to the current conflict between international forces and Taliban forces in Afghanistan as a New Great Game. Its arena has expanded to include Central Asia, as the vantage of power has shifted to this region.

The New Great Game has different contours as the number of players has increased. Its dynamics has two mutually exclusive features – Islamic fundamentalism and the search for energy sources. These forces are moving in two opposite directions – the former from south to north (with a complementary move in the east-west direction) and the latter from north to south. The players also have different goals.

Central Asia Redux

Geographical contiguity, racial and religious affinity and long established trade have provided a strong basis for fraternization amongst the people of Central Asia. In early history it was defined by the Great Silk Road, along which trade was carried out between China and Europe. With development of trade by sea this vast region lost its prominence. With its incorporation into the Soviet Union, it faded into near-oblivion.

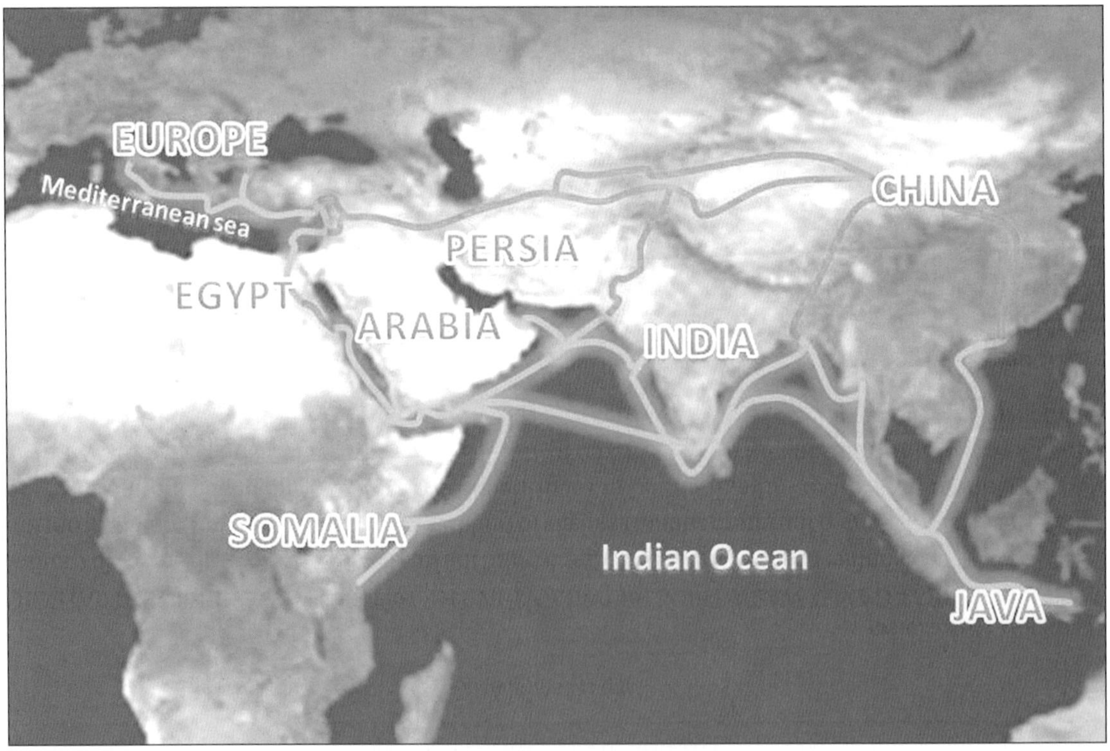

Map 3: The Silk Route and Sea Trade Routes

The Central Asia region consists of five independent republics, which came into political entities after the break up of the former Soviet Union. Kazakhstan, by far the largest state in terms of territory, (at 2,727, 300 square kilometres, it is larger than Europe) and is politically perhaps the most stable. It is the largest land-locked country in the world, with a population density of less than 6 per square kilometre. It also has the largest economy in Central Asia, with a range of natural resources (including oil and gas), a large agricultural sector and a number of oil and gas pipelines running through the country. It shares a border of over 7,000 kilometres with the Russian Federation.

Uzbekistan, south of Kazakhstan and lying in the centre of the region, has the largest population in Central Asia. It is seeking to develop its mineral and oil resources, but still depends heavily on cotton cultivation and the old Soviet-era centralized command economy. Politically it is one of the most authoritarian regimes in Central Asia, and it is its religious centre.

Turkmenistan, west of Uzbekistan and sharing a border with Iran, is rich in oil and gas. It remains an autocratic state. There are concerns about border security due to the ongoing problems with drug trafficking. Political and economic reform in Turkmenistan has been minimal since independence.

Kyrgyzstan is a mountainous state bordering China. It has some mineral resources (including gold), hydroelectric power and mixed agriculture, but little oil or gas resources.

Tajikistan is the poorest of the Soviet Union successor states. It suffered a five-year civil war almost immediately after independence (1992–1997), has limited mineral resources and is highly indebted. It does have hydroelectric power potential and its border with Afghanistan means it may benefit from development efforts there. Tajikistan has taken credible steps toward reform and all major participants in past fighting are now sharing power in parliament. This includes the only legal Islamic political party in all of Central Asia, which is also represented in President Rahmonov's government.

While all five states have undergone some economic and political reform since independence, most are still led by former Communist Party or economic figures and power remains resolutely in the hands of a few. Corruption is a problem throughout the region and this is compounded by the illegal narcotics trade: many states lie on transit routes for narcotics from Afghanistan. Energy is a key sector, especially in Kazakhstan.

These countries have long been at the crossroads of world history. So they are again today. Poor and rapidly growing populations, with intra-ethnic or intra-tribal diversities, still lacking in economic opportunity and feeling a sense of injustice are potentially susceptible to the call of violent extremism, particularly when legitimate avenues of dissent are foreclosed. A legacy of authoritarianism, as well as endemic corruption, continue to hamper the development of public institutions, good governance and the rule of law. Terrorism is one such challenge.

Map 4: Central Asia Today

The Islamic Movement of Uzbekistan and other extremist groups, including The Islamic Jihad Group, continue to pose a threat to security and stability. Retrograde regimes in Uzbekistan and Turkmenistan hold their peoples back, and detract from regional cooperation and development. Kazakhstan is the best example of the region's potential economic dynamism, as it moves to take its place among the world's top energy-producing nations. In Kyrgyzstan, civil society is gradually finding new political space to assemble freely and call for reform.

The 'New Great Game' in the region revolves around control over energy resources, economic competition, spread of Islamic radicalism and military posturing. The main players of this game are the US, Russia and China and the peripheral players include Iran, Turkey, Pakistan and India.[5]

The Energy Paradigm

Central Asia's importance on the international stage stems primarily from its energy resources. Many of the issues affecting the region are being played out through the energy sector, not least the competition for strategic influence. Perhaps less immediately or globally significant, but of considerable regional importance, is hydroelectric potential. Kyrgyzstan hopes to be able to develop an export-oriented hydroelectric power industry to substitute income from gold production, as its gold reserves are being depleted.

Russia perceives the region in terms of a 'southern security belt,' the domination of which is imperative for hedging the mainland against all forms of threats. Russia seeks to retain monopoly over the region's energy resources. China looks at the region as a Eurasian bridge through which trade can be expanded to West Asia and Europe. More significantly, the hydrocarbon reserves of the region are vital for energy starved China. The US and the European Union (EU) interests revolve around diversification of energy supply, promotion of democracy, fight against Islamic radicalism, proliferation security initiatives and counter drug trafficking.

> The New Great Game has different contours as the number of players has increased. Its dynamics has two mutually exclusive features – Islamic fundamentalism and the search for energy sources. These forces are moving in two opposite directions – the former from south to north (with a complementary move in the east-west direction) and the latter from north to south.

Central Asia has enormous quantities of undeveloped oil resources, including some 6.6 trillion cubic metres of natural gas, waiting to be exploited. The Central Asian countries contain about 4percent of the world's hydrocarbon reserves. The economies of three major countries are energy export driven (Turkmenistan - 83percent, Kazakhstan - 65 percent and Uzbekistan - 10 percent).[6] For Central Asian energy to reach Europe, it has to either transit through Russian territory or through the South Caucasus to Turkey and onwards to European markets. Construction of viable pipeline routes to Europe bypassing Russian territory would effectively break the current Russian monopoly on supply of natural gas to Europe. Routes to the South are the shortest and economically viable but are currently unfeasible due to the unstable situation in Afghanistan. Direct overland routes without passing through a third country are only feasible to Russia and China thus giving them an inherent advantage.

Today, the only existing export routes from the area lead through Russia. Investors in Caspian oil and gas are interested in building alternative pipelines to Turkey and Europe, and especially to the rapidly growing Asian markets. India, Iran, Russia, and Israel, are working on a plan to supply oil and gas to south and Southeast Asia through India but instability in Afghanistan is "posing a great threat to this effort. Afghanistan lies squarely between Turkmenistan, home to the world's third-largest natural gas reserves, and the lucrative markets of the Indian subcontinent, China and Japan. A memorandum of understanding has been signed to build a 900-mile natural gas pipeline from Turkmenistan to Pakistan via Afghanistan, but the ongoing war and absence of a stable government in Afghanistan have prevented the project from going forward. Today, its geographical position as a potential transit route for oil and natural gas pipelines, makes Afghanistan an extremely important piece of the global strategy by energy magnates to obtain control over energy resources. Controlling the transport route is controlling the product.

Russia remains an important economic partner to all five Central Asian states, and still holds a monopolist or near-monopolist position in the export of Turkmen and Kazakh oil and gas reserves, given its control over the pipeline system that runs through its territory. The EU and the US remain convinced that this threatens the security of these states (and, more importantly, the security of Europe's gas supply).[7]

The Islamic Radicalism Paradigm

In each of the Central Asian countries a strange and officially imposed dichotomy between "official" and "unofficial" Islam has appeared. Official Islam refers to religious institutions under the control of the state authorities. Unofficial Islam includes all other Muslims, especially those who believe that Islam cannot be controlled by state power. They are accused of being extremists.

The Central Asian countries have been struggling to contain religious extremism since the collapse of the Soviet Union. Islam began flourishing throughout Central Asia in the last years of Soviet rule, due to a relaxation of state management of culture and religion. Uzbekistan, the region's historic seat of Islamic learning, developed the most vibrant religious life in the region, ranging from a revival of Hanafi teachings (the dominant school of Islamic law in Central Asia) to the spread of more radical (locally termed "Wahhabist") forms of Islam. The Uzbek government began cracking down on the latter in the mid-1990s, fearing that religious ferment could contribute to the breakdown of secular political institutions (as it was doing in neighbouring Tajikistan during its civil war). While many radical Islamists have fought in Tajikistan and Afghanistan, other groups began to spread their ideology.

The Central Asian countries have been struggling to contain religious extremism since the collapse of the Soviet Union. Islam began flourishing throughout Central Asia in the last years of Soviet rule, due to a relaxation of state management of culture and religion.

Central Asia lacks a tradition of religious fanaticism but the potential of religious extremism spreading to the region is real. The Ferghana Valley, spreading across eastern Uzbekistan, Kyrgyzstan and Tajikistan, is a political fulcrum around which much of the region now moves. The most densely populated area in the region – with roughly 25 percent of the population of the region, it is in the throes of ethno-religious tensions. The regimes, mistaking the genuine desire of the people to explore their identity, have taken numerous steps to curb political Islam. It is in this milieu that the most orthodox Wahhabi strain of Islam is gaining acceptability. The main Islamic movements are:

- **Islamic Movement of Uzbekistan (IMU).** The IMU, renamed as the 'Islamic Party of Turkistan', professes creation of an Islamic state in the whole of Central Asia and Xinjiang. Its cadres have developed close links with drug cartels and arms smugglers who act as their main source of funds. It is being funded by Al Qaeda and has close links with ISI.[8]
- **Hizb ut Tehrir(HUT).** It is a secretive transnational Wahhabi fundamentalist organisation, with an avowed aim of uniting Central Asia into an Islamic Caliphate. It is involved in large scale subversive activities, religious indoctrination and renders support to hardline Islamic militant organisations.
- **Uihgurs.** Approximately 300,000 Uighurs live in Central Asia and have links with the Eastern Turkistan Islamic Movement (ETIM). The Uighurs represent a constant source of concern for China; they reject Chinese rule, and their separatist tendencies have often translated into militant resistance to Beijing. Uighur efforts have some financial and material support in Kyrgyzstan and Kazakhstan.

Increasing attacks on Russians and their continuing exodus from Tajikistan became important factors in determining Russia's active policy in this region. Senior Russian leaders in the government and military openly voiced their concern over the security of Russian minorities and vowed to discharge their responsibilities on this account.

The question of what does or does not pose a threat to security can be very subjective. Some extreme members of HUT advocate the use of force to advance their goals. The majority, however, is focused on using peaceful means to spread its message, a message that is by definition seditious as it seeks to undermine the secular nature of the state. The EU and the US do not always see eye to eye with their Central Asian, Chinese or Russian colleagues over what constitutes religious extremism, or what constitutes an appropriate response.

Impact of the NATO campaign in Afghanistan

After the first phase of the war in Afghanistan ended with the overthrow of the Taliban in 2001, Washington's limited agenda in the region was to press the Pakistani military to go after al Qaeda. Meanwhile, the US largely ignored the broader insurgency in the region, which remained marginal until 2005. This suited the Pakistani military's strategy, which is to retain the Taliban as a potential source of pressure on Afghanistan. 84 percent of the materiel for US forces in Afghanistan goes through Pakistan, and the Inter Services Intelligence (ISI) remains nearly the sole source of intelligence about international terrorist acts prepared by Al Qaeda and its affiliates in Pakistan.[9]

More fundamentally, the concept of "pressuring" Pakistan is flawed. No state can be successfully pressured into acts it considers suicidal. The Pakistani security establishment believes that it faces both a US-Indian-Afghan alliance and a separate Iranian-Russian alliance, each aimed at undermining Pakistani influence in Afghanistan and even dismembering the Pakistani state.[10]

Pakistan's military, which makes and implements the country's national security policies, shares a commitment to a vision of Pakistan as the homeland for South Asian Muslims and, therefore, to the incorporation of Kashmir into Pakistan. It considers Afghanistan as within Pakistan's security perimeter. Moreover, Pakistan does not have border agreements with either India, into which Islamabad contests the incorporation of Kashmir, or Afghanistan, which has never explicitly recognized the Durand Line, which separates the two countries, as an interstate border.[11] That border is more than a line. The frontier between Pakistan and Afghanistan was structured as part of the defence of British India. On the Pakistani side of the Durand Line, the British and their Pakistani successors turned the difficulty of governing the tribes to their advantage by establishing Federally Administered Tribal Areas (FATA). Within the FATA, the tribes, not the government, are responsible for security. The area has traditionally been kept under-developed and over-armed as a barrier against invaders.

The concept of "pressuring" Pakistan is flawed. No state can be successfully pressured into acts it considers suicidal. The Pakistani security establishment believes that it faces both a US-Indian-Afghan alliance and a separate Iranian-Russian alliance, each aimed at undermining Pakistani influence in Afghanistan and even dismembering the Pakistani state.

India has reestablished its consulates in Afghan cities, including some near the Pakistani border. India has genuine consular interests there (Hindu and Sikh populations, commercial travel, aid programmes). India has also, in cooperation with Iran, completed a highway linking Afghanistan's ring road (which connects its major cities) to Iranian ports on the Persian Gulf, potentially eliminating Afghanistan's dependence on Pakistan for access to the sea and marginalizing Pakistan's new Arabian Sea port of Gwadar, which was built with Chinese aid.

There is no more a political solution in Afghanistan alone than there is a military solution in Afghanistan alone. Unless the decision-makers in Pakistan decide to make stabilizing the Afghan government a higher priority than countering the percieved Indian threat, the insurgency conducted from bases in Pakistan will continue. Pakistan's strategic goals in Afghanistan place Pakistan at odds not just with Afghanistan and India; and with US objectives in the region, but with the entire international community. There is no multilateral framework for confronting this challenge. NATO, whose troops in Afghanistan are daily losing their lives to Pakistan-based insurgents, has no Pakistan policy. The UN Security Council has hardly discussed Pakistan's role in Afghanistan, even though three of the permanent members (France, the United Kingdom, and the US) have troops in Afghanistan, the other two have their own agendas. China, Pakistan's largest investor, is poised to become the largest investor in Afghanistan as well, with a $3.5 billion stake in the Aynak copper mine, south of Kabul.

The illegal drugs trade

Central Asia is a key region for the trafficking of illegal drugs from Afghanistan. Tajikistan was the "bottleneck for drugs trafficking to the north" particularly before 11 September 2001.[12] European, US and UN programmes have increased interdiction rates and, with better controls, drugs are now passing from Afghanistan across other Central Asian countries and Iran.

A substantial amount of drug money was actually used to jump-start certain sectors of the economy in Tajikistan, and it undoubtedly helped support the revival of the home construction industry and the service sector. The illegal drugs trade also seems to have helped ordinary Kyrgyz in southern Kyrgyzstan keep afloat, providing income to small traders who would otherwise have no livelihood. However, drug-based organized crime has overshadowed many forms of legal business, as drug barons have sought to become legitimate businessmen by buying up large amounts of commercial property. This has contributed to the general instability of political life.[13]

By contrast, in both Turkmenistan and Uzbekistan the drug trade seems to be more managed by government, which reaps financial rent from the trade. Consequently, the governments maintain a hold over organized crime.

Conclusion

With the constriction of strategic space in Central Asia, the US is now enlarging its strategic space in South Asia. One view is that the US could achieve its goal of transforming Afghanistan through establishment of a Greater Central Asia Partnership for Cooperation and Development.[14]

There appears to be a move in the US establishment to reorient the Central Asian region through trade towards the Indian Ocean.[15]. Among the many projects to help improve transportation in the region, a US-funded bridge has opened over the Pyanj River, between Tajikistan (Badakshan) and Afghanistan (Kunduz). Likewise, China seeks transformation of Gwadar into a major energy hub and plans to expand the Karakoram overland bridge to China. Conscious of its centrality as a frontline state, Pakistan would continue to leverage this factor to gain maximum favours and balance its relations with the two countries. Both the countries need Pakistan as a transit corridor. How the two countries jockey for the influence in Pakistan would add a new dimension to the 'Great Game' in the extended strategic space.

> According to Olaf Caroe, the Soviet invasion of Afghanistan in 1979 was a predictable (and predicted) "after-effect" of India's partition in 1947. By creating two mutually antagonistic successor states in India and Pakistan, the partition effectively turned the subcontinent's power potential in on itself. For nearly a century, power based on a stable subcontinent had provided a counterpoise to Russia that had allowed the emergence of a viable Afghan state.

India's relations with Central Asia are influenced to a major degree by the actions of Russia, China, Iran, Pakistan and the US. India has lost valuable time in creating viable leverages and lacks bandwidth to use the hard power approach in pursuing its national interests in the region. India, however continues to enjoy goodwill of the people and its soft power vis-à-vis other players has considerable appeal. Therefore, a soft power approach and a subtle alignment with Russia, which is a vector in the region, will pay good dividends. Iran and Afghanistan provide a gateway to Central Asia and a buffer against Wahhabi radicalism. Strategic relations with these two countries are India's imperative need.

The 'New Great Game' of the 21st Century in the region revolves around control over energy resources, economic competition, fight against international terrorism, regime change, fight against Islamic fundamentalism and military diplomacy amongst the US, Russia and China. The 'Great Game' is likely to have a significant impact on the balance of power in entire Eurasia and great power rivalry may extend to South Asia where the US and China will jockey for influence. From India's strategic security perspective, Central Asia's geo-strategic importance as a bridge cum buffer and as an alternate source of energy would remain. India needs to show ingenuity in gaining land access to CAR and explore new avenues for transportation of energy from the region. India's overarching policy should be to seek convergence of geostrategic interests with the legitimate aspirations of the people of Central Asia and prevent the rise of religious fundamentalism.

Notes

1 See Peter Hopkirk, *The Great Game: The Struggle for Empire in Central Asia,* Kodansha International, 1992, p 565.

2 See Alfred Thayer Mahan, *The Problem of Asia: Its Effect upon International Politics,* (Edison, New Jersey, Transaction Publishers; Revised edition 2003), p 179.

3 See Peter John Brobst, *The Future of the Great Game: Sir Olaf Caroe, India's Independence, and the Defense of Asia* (Akron: The University of Akron Press, 2005).

4 See Zbigniew Brzezinski, *The Grand Chessboard: American Primacy And Its Geostrategic Imperatives*, (Basic Books, 1998), p 240.

5 Nirmala Joshi, *Central Asia the Great Game Replayed: An Indian Perspective,* New Delhi, New Century Publications, 2003; Introductory remarks.

6 Akram Esanov, Martin Raiser and Willem Buiter. *Nature's Blessing or Nature's Curse: The Political Economy Of Transition In Resource-Based Economies.* European Bank for Reconstruction and Development (Available from http://www.nber.org/~wbuiter/curse.pdf; Internet; accessed 28 Jul 2008).

7 The European Commission estimates that the EU's dependence on natural gas imports will increase from 57percent to 84percent by 2030 (European Commission, no date, Gas: Security of Gas Supply, at <ec.europa.eu/energy/gas/sos/index_en.htm>). This has prompted a great deal of nervousness among European governments about the security of their energy supply and the desire among some in European circles to diversify the EU's sources of energy and means of transport.

8 Roy Meena Singh, *Pakistan's Strategy in Central Asia*, Strategic Analysis, Institute of Defence Studies (IDSA)and Analysis, Volume 30,Number 4, IDSA New Delhi, October-December 2006, pp 808-818.

9 Barnett R. Rubin and Ahmed Rashid, *From Great Game to Grand Bargain: Ending Chaos in Afghanistan and Pakistan,* Foreign Affairs, November/December 2008.

10 *Ibid.*

11 *Ibid.*

12 UN Office for Drug Control and Crime Prevention, 2000, Global Drug Report 2000, Oxford, Oxford University Press, p. 8.

13 Nine states were at 142nd place (out of 163) on Transparency International's Corruption Perceptions Index of 2006. Three of these were in Central Asia: Kyrgyzstan, Tajikistan and Turkmenistan.

14 Frederick S Starr, "A Partnership for Central Asia", Foreign Affairs , July/August, 2005, p165.

15 Joshua Kucera, "Washington Seeks to Steer Central Asian States Towards South Asian Allies", http://www/eurasianet.org/departments/insight/articles/eav042806_pr.shtml, 20 June 2006.

Pipeline Politics

BY ROHIT SINGH

The Great Oil Shortage

ONE HAS HEARD OF THE GREAT depression that has struck the world on at least two occasions, once in the early 20th century, and the other one we are going through, currently. While the current crisis took everyone by surprise and unprepared, countries world over, are anticipating and bracing for the 'Great Oil Shortage' that is going to hit the world, sometime in the middle of the century. Those who are forewarned and forearmed will tide the crisis, those who do not will collapse and almost, certainly, vanish from the map of the earth, at least as a sovereign entity. Countries may survive, either through accessing and conserving oil or may resort to alternative means of energy. It is safe to predict that the current and future geopolitics will figure in the energy great game, currently being played out in the Central Asia Region, Caucasus and the Middle East the US led GWOT in Afghanistan arguably, being an intrinsic part of an endeavour to be at a place that is going to matter in the decades to come and, that place is the Central Asian Region and Afghanistan, with Russia and China, in and around it.

Where is the Oil?

60 percent of the world's oil reserves lie in the Gulf with Saudi Arabia holding reserves of around 260 billion barrels. Iraq at 112 billion barrels is second, and Iran has the third largest reserves. These three, together, account for one fourth of the world's oil. The recently formed Central Asian Republics of Kazakhstan, Azerbaijan, Turkmenistan and Kyrgyzstan, account for 1540 billion barrels of oil and 6-9 trillion cubic meters of natural gas. The United States is cleverly conserving its oil reserves, well under ground, locked within resource rich Alaska, bracing for the looming crisis. Russia has considerable reserves of oil which has majorly contributed to its current economic resurgence. Other sources will be Africa, South America and Canada.

Consumption and Dwindling Supply

The supply of oil has gradually dwindled and is now at a stage where it is unable to keep pace with world demand. The world, today, consumes six barrels of oil for each new barrel that is discovered. The proven oil reserves are approximately one trillion barrels. New discoveries are far and few in between. Expectation of oil reserves under the Arctic and Atlantic shelf, melting under the onslaught of global warming, will lend to a race among countries to stake their claims. The world consumption of oil is 76 million barrels a day, likely to spiral to 119 million barrels per day. As against this demand, world oil production will peak at 80 million barrels per day by 2020 and then gradually decline to 40-60 million barrels per day by 2040-2050. In 2004 India's oil imports went up by 11 percent and that of China by 33 percent, exacting its toll on production operators, pipelines, refineries and shipping lines. Both these countries are expected to consume more than one-fifth of the global demand.

The 'Great Oil Shortage' is going to hit the world, sometime in the middle of the century. Those who are forewarned and forearmed will tide the crisis, those who do not will collapse and almost, certainly, vanish from the map of the earth.

Indian Consumption

At present India's requirement is two million barrels per day, but by 2025 this will quadruple, compounded by the fact that it has less then one percent of the world's reserves. 70 percent of India's crude is imported and all of it comes by sea. It is expected to be the largest importer of oil by 2050 and its oil consumption is expected to rise to 150 million tons by 2020. India's gas requirement by 2024 is said to be 125 billion cubic meters. Of this 52 BCM will be available locally and balance 75 BCM will be imported.

Rohit Singh is a Research Assistant at the Center for Land Warfare Studies (CLAWS)
rohitz.singh86@gmail.com

Oil as Source of Present Veiled and Future Conflict

The 1991 Gulf war was dictated more by considerations of protecting the oil resources of Kuwait and Saudi Arabia rather than any other concerns. US led invasion of Iraq in 2003 too had the same aim, as Iraq, besides having huge oil reserves, also, dominated the oil routes in this region. Among other reasons, the US intervention in Afghanistan is with an eye to gaining access to the new sources of oil in the Central Asian Region.

Search for WMD in Iraq was just a ruse, and the witch hunt for Osama Bin Laden in Afghanistan, has only led to the creation of more jihadis and has divided the world on religious lines as never before. Apart from 'war against terror', it is quite obvious that the US presence in Afghanistan has as much to do with securing the country so that safe transit routes for the oil and gas supplies of the region, can be established. Also, the US is attempting to carve a geopolitical role in an area where China and Russia exercise great infulence.

War and Oil

Availability, holding and transportation of oil has proved to be a decisive factor in the outcome of all wars. Rommel's Africa Korps was grounded because the much needed oil could not be transported across the Mediterranean to reach him in time. Patton's decisive thrust in the winter of 1944 cold not see the light of day because of shortage of oil. Gulf War I did not start till adequate reserves of oil were built up. In 2003, the US Army thrust on Iraq was held up for three days on the outskirts of Baghdad. India, painstakingly built up its oil reserves before embarking on the liberation of Bangladesh.

Oil fields as War Target

Oil moves the Army. But the oil fields are the target of those armies which are not in possession of one. Strategic Forces/Special Forces aim to capture oil depots and fields in fact for subsequent use by its armies. The Caucasian oil fields were a prime strategic target for German invasion of Russia during the Second World War. The terrorists in Iraq, Chechnya and Afghanistan target the pipelines and depots in a sustained manner.

Energy Security in the Indian Context

India faces daunting challenges in meeting its energy needs. The key challenges are:-

- *Exploration.* Search and tap domestic coal, gas and oil reserves. No major oil fields have been discovered in the country since the Bombay High fields in the late 1960s. Gas discoveries are more promising with the discovery of gas fields in the Krishna-Godavri basin and the Bay of Bengal.
- *Uranium.* Low concentration of uranium in India and the poor quality of uranium ores, imply that India will be dependent on imported uranium in the medium term before its three stage nuclear program fructifies and the country is able to tap its vast thorium reserves.
- *Alternative Sources of Energy.* R&D in alternate sources of energy like ground and solar energy to make it commercially viable and in a position to replace hydrocarbons to a significant level.

India's Energy Security Strategy

To meet the energy security challenges facing the country India has adopted a multi-pronged approach.

- *Diversification of imported oil.* India depends on Saudi Arabia, Nigeria, Iran and Kuwait for 60 percent of its oil imports. It is dependent on the Middle East for almost two-thirds of its oil imports for reasons of geography and cost.
- *Purchase of Exploration Blocks.* Indian oil companies have purchased exploration blocks in oilfields in a range of countries from Libya, Sudan, Iran to Myanmar and Russia.
- *Strategic Reserve.* The 2004 Government decision to establish petroleum reserve of 15 days consumption has been recommended to be increased to 90 days.
- *Refining Capacity.* The investments in oil refineries in Jamnagar have resulted in India emerging as the energy outsourcing hub. Jamnagar already boasts of the world's third largest oil refinery and is set to emerge as the largest when Reliance Petroleum Ltd begins its operations.
- *Natural Gas Pipelines under consideration.* Consumption of natural gas is set to increase exponentially. India has the option to import gas through pipelines from neighbouring states or import liquefied natural gas through long term contracts. A pipeline traversing through several countries entails complex contractual framework and has an important

bearing on geopolitics. India is keen to acquire gas from Iran, Bangladesh and Myanmar. The following pipeline proposals have been mooted :

- Oman-India deep water Pipeline (PPL).
- Iran-Pakistan-India (IPI) PPL.
- Turkmenistan-Afghanistan-Pakistan-India (TAPI) PPL.
- Qatar-Pakistan-India PPL.
- Myanmar-Bangladesh-India (MBI) PPL.

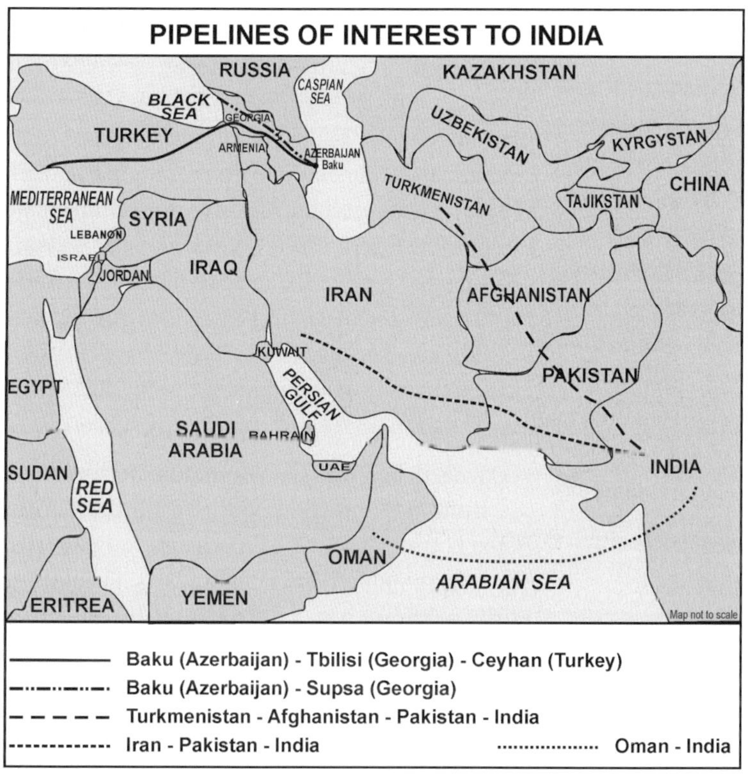

Politics in above Pipe Lines

Gas/Oil pipelines on the land route from the Persian Gulf region or Central Asian region need to traverse Pakistani territory before reaching India. It is believed that energy pipelines such as IPI and TAPI can effectively end the economic partition of the subcontinent, and give each country a stake in the other's economy. A pipeline to India through Pakistan will lower the cost of gas for Pakistan, as well as provide it transit fee. However, the current tensions between US-Iran , and Pakistan-India, have complicated the IPI pipeline. TAPI Pipeline which has the US backing is held up for improvement in the Afghan situation. Due to Dhaka's unwillingness to provide passage for Myanmar's gas to India, feasibility studies are on for a longer and more expensive pipeline that bypasses Bangladesh, altogether. However, with a new Government in place in Bangladesh, it is well nigh possible that the MBI pipeline may still fructify. The IPI may well turn into Iran-Pakistan-China pipeline due to ongoing tensions, and Chinese pressure and interest in making it a Iran-Pak-China pipeline. Also, Iran's policy for seeking a uniform price for its gas imports represents a reversion from past policies. This linkage is expected to increase the cost of Iranian gas by 80-90 percent offering India a consolidated price at Pak-India border. It is also insisting on negotiation of gas price one year prior to actual supply of gas. Keeping the above factors, and geopolitical tensions in mind India could also turn to :

- Baku-Ceyhan pipeline linking Azerbaijan and Turkey via Georgia.
- Baku-Supsa pipeline through Georgia and terminating at the Black Sea port of Supsa.
- Tengiz oil field to Novorossiysk port passing through Russia.
- Proposed Iran's Caspian pipeline which envisages laying a pipeline along the Caspian sea bed.
- Kazakhstan-China oil pipeline could be extended to India.
- Siberia-China pipeline could be extended to India.
- Central Asia-Afghanistan (newly constructed Zarang-Delaram) route to Chabahar port of Iran-Persian Gulf.

It is important, here, to dwell on, at least, two of the above feasible pipelines, i.e. the Baku-Ceyhan and the Kazakh-China pipeline.

Baku-Tbilisi-Ceyhan PPL

A 1,768 kms long crude oil pipeline, connects Baku, capital of Azerbaijan, Tbilisi, capital of Georgia and Ceyhan a port on the south-eastern Mediterranean coast of Turkey, the second largest pipeline in the world after Druzhba. The oil first pumped from Baku on 10 May 2005 reached Ceyhan on May 28, 2006. The Caspian Sea lies above one of the world's largest groups of oil and gas fields. As the Caspian Sea is landlocked, transporting oil to western markets is complicated. During the Soviet era, all PPLs transportation routes from the Caspian went through Russia. The collapse of the USSR initiated a search for new routes. Route as above proposed by Turkey, and accepted by Georgia and Azerbaijan, was found to be a viable one bypassing the dominating influence of Russia in the North and Iran in the South. It even bypassed Armenia which was a shorter route. Armenia and Azerbaijan have strained relations.

- *The Politics.* The south Caucasus – a Russian backyard is being exploited by the USA to leverage a control over its oil potential, and thus, implicitly encouraging the countries that form the region to break from Russian influence. Therein lies the signinficance of the BTC pipeline – a symbol of independence from Russia in the north and Iran in the South. The US browbeating Iran on its proposed nuclearization is albeit with an eye towards the Caucasian oil fields. The PPL independent of Russia, encouraged Georgian enclave of south Ossetia to break free of Russian control, riding as it were, a false sense of security imbibed from US interests. That Russia reacted decisively in physically quelling the rebellion signaled Russian's correct assessment of the US interventions in this regard.

Analysts have proposed that Indian strategic petroleum reserve should also encompass a regional facility in cooperation with Nepal, Bhutan, Pakistan and Bangladesh. This would not only tie the economies of these smaller countries with India but also confirm Indian centrality in South Asia.

- *The Economics.* The US and European nations believe that the BTC will ease its dependence on the Middle East. But skeptics opine that the BTC will meet only one percent of global demand in the first phase. Be that as it may, it still is a protection of some assured supply from an alternative source, free of Middle Eastern and Russian threats of breaking off supply and its hegemony. One-third of European energy needs is met by Russia. The PPL has given a tremendous boost to Azerbaijan's economy (its GDP hitting a record of 35%). Substantial transit fees accruing to Georgia and Turkey will give a huge stimulus to their economies, too. Apart from the cost India, by choosing this PPL can steer clear of troubled waters of Pakistan and Iran.

The Kazakh–China Oil PPL

There is a massive three stage PPL project linking Kazakhstan to western China. By doing so, it became the first major export pipeline (ahead of BTC) from land locked CAR, not to transit through Russia. In 2008 China recived six million tonnes of oil through this PPL which was a 26 percent increase over the previous year. Once all the stages of the project are complete, China is expeceted to recieve 20 million tonnes, i.e. 2020. China's booming economy stands to get a great stimulus from this pipeline. Another pipeline will link this with the one from Caspian sea transiting through west Kazakhstan. Development in Xinjiang province of west China is set to see a dramatic change. The significance of the Kazakhstan strides in its oil pipeline is lost on no one, particularly Russia, as it sees its hand grip over the oil tap and its interest loosen considerably. Kazakhstan is also in talks to tap the BTC PPL for a Mediterranean route. If India latches on to this PPL, or the one through Kazakhstan–Western China it will be a great boon. However, it has to contend with US seeing its leverage over India vis-a-vis China and Russia, loosen.

Strategic Course for India for the Energy Great Game

Building strategic relations with the Central Asian countries and the Caucasus along with the West Asian states to include Iran, Iraq, Kazakhstan and Turkmenistan is of critical importance. Myanmar, too, will be a key energy ally of the country. While focus has also been in obtaining oil rights in Syria (50 : 50) partnership between ONGC and Chinese company, Sudan, Sakhalin and Vietnam, these will require greater naval strategic reach and ability to secure these sea routes. Thus, the SAARC and Central Asian regions (along with support from Iran and Afghanistan) are of great importance to the country for oil security, and should dictate our strategic and diplomatic focus.

Choke Points

In case India goes in for sea routes of transit, then it must also factor in the Choke Points, *en route.* Choke points are narrow channels along widely used global routes. They are a critical part of global energy security due to the high volume of oil traded through their narrow straits.

- *Strait of Hormuz.* Connects Persian Gulf with the Gulf of Oman and Arabian Sea. Is the worlds most important oil choke point due to its daily outflow of 16.5–17 million barrels, roughly 40 percent of all seaborne traded oil.

- *Strait of Malacca.* Located between Indonesia-Malaysia and Singapore, links the India Ocean to the South China Sea and Pacific Ocean. Is the shortest sea route between Persian Gulf supplies to China, Japan, Indonesian and South Korea. Is the key chokepoint in Asia with an estimated 15 million bbl/ day flow.

The Way Forward

Analysts have proposed that Indian strategic petroleum reserve should also encompass a regional facility in cooperation with Nepal, Bhutan, Pakistan and Bangladesh. This would not only tie the economies of these smaller countries with India but also confirm Indian centrality in South Asia. However, in the present context with the levels of suspicion, between these countries, this is unlikely to happen. Again on Apr 06, the US had put forth the proposal for an electricity grid stretching from Central to South Asia. This power grid was to be fed by gas and oil from Kazakhstan and Turkmenistan and hydropower from Tajikistan and Kyrgyzstan to supply Afghanistan, Pakistan and India. Such a move would expand India's influence in Central Asia.

India has also proposed the formulation of an Asian Gas Grid, which would expand the IPI gas pipeline to southern China. Such a move reduces US's geopolitical influence in the region. This can also be seen in the light of the proposal to include China in IPI and TAPI pipelines, with or without Indian participation. Another strong proposal for consideration is to extend the Siberia-China gas pipeline to India. India could look at swap alternatives that would allow China to access India's oil and gas in Sakhalin in eastern Russia in exchange for gas deposits at Xinjiang in to western China.

Though longer and more expensive, the Baku-Ceyhan pipeline free of geopolitical tensions, maybe a good option. The other reasonable option could be CAR-Afghan (Zaranj)-*Chabahar* (Iran) pipeline, under the present circumstances. However, it could run into jeopardy due to adverse changes in Afghanistan. The Indo-US Nuclear deal will be able to provide assured supply of Uranium for India's nuclear power plants, but can also be seen as a step to wean away India from growing Russian influence through energy. The straits of Hormuz and Malacca are the strategic choke points to ensure smooth supplies of oil and gas to India. India's maritime capability needs to be geared to meet this challenge.

Conclusion

In its critical phase of economic consolidation, India will have to depend on oil, notwithstanding the advantage accruing out of the recently concluded Nuclear energy deal with the US. Keeping the geopolitical dynamics in mind, India will have to seriously consider the sea transit route either or both through the Persian Gulf and Red sea for its oil pipelines. It will need to work on Myanmar and Bangladesh, and Russia and China, to allow pipelines through these corridors, as well. For the land routes through Pakistan, it may have to adopt a wait and watch policy for relations to stabilize. But with China pressurizing Iran and Pakistan, to expedite the pipeline with or without India, it may be a case of missed opportunity.

Needless to say, if India goes in for the sea routes for its pipelines, the importance of a modern blue water Navy cannot be underscored, especially in light of the recent forays by Chinese warships in the Arabian Sea. The 'Great Energy Game' must form a key strategic driving force in the decades to come. However, the growing competition over scarce energy resources is not necessarily destabilizing. A disruption of supplies anywhere would translate into higher prices everywhere. Therefore, every consuming state is equally vulnerable to the effect of such shocks. As such, all states have a stake in avoiding conflict.

> A disruption of supplies anywhere would translate into higher prices everywhere. Theretore, every consuming state is equally vulnerable to the effect of such shocks.

Competition over energy resources can actually be beneficial by developing new markets and providing advanced new exploration and exploitation techniques, which ultimately contribute to increased energy supplies. Revolution in energy technologies (super conductivity, solar energy and electric energies), may profoundly change the dynamics of global energy security. Alternative energy may reduce demand on hydro-carbon fuels and minimize the risks of confrontation on this issue, considerably. The Central Asian Region has emerged as the new frontier for oil and gas exploration. China is moving aggressively to spread its influence in the region. The recent moves by the US to connect Central Asia to SE Asia through gas and electricity grids would benefit India by opening up new sources of energy and also increasing Indian influence in the region.

Strategic Implications of Dalai Lama's Flight to India

BY CALUDE ARPI

FIFTY YEARS AGO, ON MARCH 10, 1959, the population of the Tibetan capital revolted against the Chinese Communist presence on the Roof of the World. A few days later, the Dalai Lama, the temporal and spiritual leader of the Tibetan people left his native land, taking the direction of India.

An aspect of this event is rarely debated in India: the strategic angle, though it has serious implications for the country, probably at par with the Partition of the subcontinent 12 years earlier. The flight of the Tibetan leader meant that a second front opened for the already stretched Indian defence forces. Indirectly (some say directly), this triggered the war with China three years later.

Let us recollect the facts.

On October 7, 1950, 40,000 troops of the People's Liberation Army (PLA) led by Lui Bocheng, the one-eyed General and his Political Commissar, Deng Xiaoping, crossed the Yangtze river and smashed the weak Tibetan defences.

Less than a year later in Beijing, some Tibetan delegates signed a '17-Point Agreement for the Peaceful Liberation of Tibet' (the Dalai Lama later asserted that it was signed 'under duress').

For the first time in their history, the Tibetan people had accepted China's suzerainty. Article 1 said: "The Tibetan people shall return to the big family of the Motherland." The declared objective of the Agreement was to 'drive out the imperialist aggressive force from Tibet' and to 'liberate' the Roof of the World.

The Indian leaders should have asked, "But who are these 'imperialist aggressive forces' at our door?" Was it for India who had a few hundred jawans posted in Gyantse till 1954? The tragedy is that Delhi never realized that it was indeed targeted.

The Dalai Lama arrives in India (West Kameng district of NEFA)

Claude Arpi writes regularly on Tibet, China, India and Indo-French relations in *The Pioneer*, the *New Indian Express*, *rediff.com* and other Indian and French publications. He is the author of *Tibet: The Lost Frontier* and his forthcoming book is *The Negotiations That Never Were*.
claudearpi@gmail.com

Another article of the 17-Point Agreement said: "Tibetan troops shall be reorganized step by step into the PLA and become a part of the national defence forces of the People's Republic of China (PRC)." It meant that the few-thousand strong Tibetan Army was to be disbanded and merged into the PLA. This would be implemented during the following years.

Further a Military Area Headquarters (HQ) was created on the Tibetan plateau: "In order to ensure the implementation of this agreement, the Chinese People's Government (CPG) shall set up a Military and Administrative Committee and a Military Area HQ in Tibet and apart from the personnel sent there, the CPG shall absorb as many local Tibetan personnel as possible to take part in the work. Local Tibetan personnel taking part in the Military and Administrative Committee may include patriotic elements from the local government of Tibet, various districts and various principal monasteries."

'Patriotic elements' was an ominous term.

At the time of the Agreement, the Chinese government promised that the status of the Dalai Lama would not be changed and unwanted reforms would not be imposed. "The Local Government of Tibet should carry out reforms of its own accord", said one article.

Apart from the merger of the Tibetan Army into the PLA, none of the promises made in the 17-Point Agreement were kept.

On September 9, 1951, several thousand Communist troops entered the Tibetan capital under the command of General Wang Qimei. Soon

Tibetan Army with their flag before being disbanded by the PLA

Members of Volunteer Freedom Fighters Force (also known as Khampa guerilla)

20,000 troops began to occupy the most strategic points on the Tibetan Plateau. A year later, the first surveys to build a new road on the Aksai Chin were conducted; Xinjiang and Tibet needed to be connected.

The first years following the 'liberation', the Dalai Lama tried his best to 'cohabit' with the Chinese, but the situation rapidly worsened.

Fifty years later, one can say that as long as the Tibetan issue is not resolved, it is doubtful if any serious progress can be made on the Sino-Indian border, which for millennia had been the Tibeto-Indian border.

His presence in Tibet restrained the Communist leaders to a certain extent, at least militarily. It is only after his departure that the aggressiveness towards India took new heights.

During this period, for the first time in Tibet's 2000-year history, the local population experienced famine. Tibet was not able to feed its own people and the Communist troops in addition.

The situation reached a climax in early 1959. The last straw was the invitation by the commandant of the Chinese forces in Lhasa to the young Dalai Lama for a theatrical performance inside the Chinese camp. A strange condition was specified: he should come without his body guards' escort.

On March 10, the population of Lhasa surrounded the Dalai Lama's palace to prevent him from attending the performance. The stalemate continued for a few days and finally during the night of March 17, the young Tibetan leader secretly fled his palace for India.

For the following days, the world remained in

the dark about the happenings on the Roof of the World.

On March 28, Xinhua issued a communiqué in Beijing giving the Chinese version of the uprising: "The Tibetan Local Government and the upper-strata reactionary clique colluded with imperialism-assembled rebellious bandits and launched armed attacks against the PLA." It added that the valiant units of the PLA stationed in Tibet had completely smashed the rebellious bandits.

Nehru, the eulogist of an eternal friendship between India and China, was deeply hurt by the

Uprising on March 10, 1959

tone used by Beijing. During a debate in the Parliament, he said that the *Xinhua* statement was written in a 'cold-war language': "To say that a number of 'upper strata reactionaries' in Tibet were solely responsible for this appears to be an extraordinary simplification of a complicated situation."

At the end of March, Xinhua issued a communiqué: "For a long time the Tibet Local

Members of Volunteer Freedom Fighters Force with their flag

General Zhang Jingwu, Representing the Central Committe of the CCP arrives in Tibet (1951)

Government and the upper strata reactionary clique have plotted rebellion in collaboration with imperialists and reactionaries outside the country. For quite some time they have assembled rebellious bandits and connived at their ravages, destruction of communications, plunder of merchants and travelers, rape, and arson, and murder in various parts of Tibet, thereby inflicting suffering on the people."

Dalai Lama and party crossing a frozen river on their way to India

Behind this jargon, Beijing's intentions were clear: to take full control of the Tibetan plateau. Conveniently, they put the blame on the Dalai Lama's Cabinet Ministers (often referred as the 'Dalai's clique'): "By March 10, most of the Kalons [ministers] and the upper strata reactionary clique in Tibet had joined the rebels. They put the Dalai Lama under duress, tore up the 17-article [Point] Agreement, openly betrayed the motherland and undermined unification of the country."

Interestingly, the unarmed Tibetan crowd surrounding the Norbulinka Palace was accused to have attacked the PLA: "They launched an all-out attack on the People's Liberation Army stationed

Members of Volunteer Freedom Fighters Force

in Lhasa on the night of March 19. Their crime could not be more heinous."

The Army was given the order to defend the 'motherland': "In order to protect the unification of the motherland and national unity and to relieve the people of the Tibet region from misery and suffering, our army is ordered to take punitive action against and put down the rebellion."

On March 21, though the whereabouts of the young Lama were still unknown, the Chinese began to shell the Norbulingka palace; thousands of men, women and children camping in the vicinity were slaughtered. The Dalai Lama's bodyguard regiment was disarmed and publicly machine-gunned. According to the Tibetan government in exile, over 86,000 Tibetans in

September 1951 – PLA enters Lhasa

Central Tibet were killed by the Chinese during this period. The rebellious bandits had been smashed.

The Dalai Lama finally crossed into India on March 31, 1959.

He was immediately granted asylum by Nehru's government.

With the departure of the Dalai Lama, the People's Liberation Army could finally take control of the entire Tibetan plateau.

The consequences did not take long to appear.

Members of Volunteer Freedom Fighters Force in Lhuntse Dzong near the Indian border (NEFA)

On August 27, the PLA crossed the McMahon line and ventured onto Indian territory in an area called Longju in NEFA. As they had done several times in the Aksai Chin or the central sector and before Delhi could react, the Chinese accused the Indian troops of trespassing into Chinese territory.

The Ministory of External Affairs (MEA) had to send a strong note to Beijing on 5 September 1959: "The Chinese deliberately fired on our forward picket killing one person on the spot and seriously wounding another. Later the Chinese detachment opened fire on the main outpost at Longju at 03.00 on 26th August and over-ran the surrounding area. Our personnel had to fire back in self defence. The Government of India emphatically protest against this unprovoked firing on a static post within Indian territory."

Today, whether one considers China or Pakistan as India's enemy No 1, the fact remains that Delhi has two frontiers to defend and not one anymore. The consequences of the 1959 events are incalculable.

The quibbling continued during the following years and despite the visit of Zhou Enlai, the Chinese Premier to India in April 1960–during which he proposed to exchange NEFA against Akai

The Khampas fighters escorted the Dalai Lama to India

Chin–the situation continued to deteriorate.

In October 1962, the first Chinese troops entered India through the same West Kameng Division of NEFA that the Dalai Lama's party had used to escape. The Chinese have always been fond of symbols and signs.

The departure of the Dalai Lama from the Roof of the World is certainly the watershed of Sino-Indian strategic relations. As long as the Tibetan leader was physically in Tibet and his 'local' government in function, certain limits vis-à-vis India could not be crossed.

By the end of March 1959, Zhou Enlai on behalf of the State Council (Cabinet of Ministers) dissolved the Dalai Lama's government: "The Tibet Local Government is dissolved and the Preparatory Committee for the Tibet Autonomous Region shall exercise the functions and powers of the Tibet Local Government. During the time that the Dalai Lama, Chairman of the Preparatory Committee for the Tibet Autonomous Region, is under duress by the rebels, Panchen [Lama], Vice-Chairman of the Preparatory Committee will act as Chairman." The chief Tibetan collaborator Ngabo Ngawang Jigme was nominated as a member of the Standing Committee and Secretary General of the Preparatory Committee. At the same time 'eighteen traitorous elements', meaning the Dalai Lama's senior officials were "...relieved of their posts as members of the Preparatory Committee for the Tibet Autonomous Region and of all their other posts and are to be punished individually under the law." They were replaced by Chinese Party members and a few Tibetan puppets.

The destiny of Tibet was thereafter in the hands of the Chinese Communist Party; India had a new neighbor.

Fifty years later, one can say that as long as the Tibetan issue is not resolved, it is doubtful if any serious progress can be made on the Sino-Indian border, which for millennia had been the Tibeto-Indian border.

The Tibetan leader crossed the border at Khenzimane on March 31, 1959, thereafter the Chinese were the lone masters of the Roof of the World; the age-old buffer area between the two Asian giants had been gobbled up.

Today, whether one considers China or Pakistan as India's enemy No 1, the fact remains that Delhi has two frontiers to defend and not one anymore. The consequences of the 1959 events are incalculable.

Khampa body guards

China's Emerging Cyberwar Doctrine

BY BRIG GURMEET KANWAL

"CHINESE CYBER SPIES HACK INDIAN embassy in US," screamed a bold headline splashed across the front page of a leading national daily on March 30, 2009.[1] Based on a research brief issued by the Toronto-based Munk Centre for International Studies, the news report stated: "A vast electronic spying operation from China has infiltrated computers and stolen documents from hundreds of government and private offices around the world, including those of the Indian embassy in the US..." It was reported that the operation "was being controlled from computers based almost exclusively in China." Several other Indian newspapers carried similar reports.

Earlier it had been reported that the Chinese army uses more than 10,000 "cyber warriors" with degrees in information technology to maintain an e-vigil on China's borders: "With a vast pool of IT-trained officers in place, China's border vigil is turning electronic. At its long border with 14 countries, including India, the Chinese soldiers now swipe cards and work on laptops as they monitor the border with great efficiency with electronic sentinels functioning 24 hours a day along the sea and land boundaries while sentries work with IC cards and other sophisticated equipment. The use of electronic devices has enhanced the army's ability to deal with emergencies quickly and efficiently..."[2] While information about the People's Liberation Army's (PLA) cyber warriors have begun to appear in the public domain only recently, PLA watchers across the world have known for long about China's well conceived doctrine on information operations and cyberwar. China's cyberwar doctrine is designed to level the playing field in a future war with better equipped Western armed forces that rely on Revolution in Military Affairs (RMA) technologies and enjoy immense superiority in terms of weapons platforms and intelligence, surveillance and reconnaissance (ISR) and command and control networks.

Informationization

Early in the first decade of the new century, the Central Military Commission (CMC) called for a detailed study of the concept of people's war under conditions of informationization. Describing the new concept, Ka Po Ng, an associate professor at Aichi Bunkyo University, Japan, has written:[3] "...what the PLA is prepared to fight is a people's war in the form of a 'local war under high-tech conditions' with increasing attention to the application of information technology." Since then China has spent a lot of time and effort in assessing the implications of information technology and knowledge-based warfare on the modern battlefield and to applying the lessons to its own war concepts.

> China's cyberwar doctrine is designed to level the playing field in a future war with better equipped Western armed forces.

The PLA expects to fight the next war under conditions of what it calls "informationization" or "informationalization".[4] In the White Paper on National Defence issued in 2004, informationization was explained only in general terms, but bears repeating: "To adapt itself to the changes both in the international strategic situation and the national security environment and rise to the challenges presented by the RMA worldwide, China adheres to the military strategy of active defense and works to speed up the RMA with Chinese characteristics:[5]

- **To take the road of composite and leapfrog development.** Going with the tide of the world's military development and moving along the direction of informationalization in the process of modernization, the People's Liberation Army (PLA) shall gradually achieve the transition from mechanization and semi-mechanization to informationalization. Based

Brig Gurmeet Kanwal
Director, Centre for Land Warfare Studies, New Delhi

on China's national conditions and the PLA's own conditions, the PLA persists in taking mechanization as the foundation to promote informationalization, and informationalization as the driving force to bring forward mechanization. The PLA will promote coordinated development of firepower, mobility and information capability, enhance the development of its operational strength with priority given to the Navy, Air Force and Second Artillery Force, and strengthen its comprehensive deterrence and warfighting capabilities.

- **To build a strong military by means of science and technology.** The PLA works to improve its combat capabilities by taking advantage of scientific and technological advances and aims at building qualitative efficiency instead of a mere quantitative scale, and transforming the military from a manpower-intensive one to a technology-intensive one. Implementing the Strategic Project for Talented People, the PLA focuses on training a new type of high-caliber military personnel.

China's new doctrine and the strategy and tactics associated with it have been influenced by the lessons of Gulf War I in 1991 and the Iraq War of 2003, both of which have been extensively studied by Chinese scholars.

- **To deepen the reform of the armed forces.** Based on the transformation of modern warfare and the requirements of the socialist market economy, the PLA seeks to achieve development and breakthroughs in the process of reform and innovation. The PLA develops its military theories in an innovative spirit, and explores the laws of building the army and conducting operations under the condition of informationalization.
- **To step up preparations for military struggle.** The PLA takes as its objective to win local wars under the conditions of informationalization and gives priority to developing weaponry and equipment, to building joint operational capabilities, and to making full preparations in the battlefields.

PLA analysts have called the ongoing RMA an "informationized military revolution".[6] It emerges that informationization "clearly relates to the PLA's ability to adopt information technologies to command, intelligence, training and weapon systems. This would include broad investment in new automatic command systems linked by fibre-optic Internet, satellite and new high-frequency digital radio systems. The PLA can also contest the information battle space with its new space-based, airborne, naval and ground-based surveillance and intelligence gathering systems and its new anti-satellite, anti-radar, electronic warfare and information warfare systems. There is increasing 'information content' for new PLA weapons as it moves to link new space, airborne and ELINT sensors to missile, air, naval and ground-based 'shooters' to enable all its services to better use new precision-strike weapons."[7] According to the 2004 White Paper, "In its modernization drive, the PLA takes informationalization as its orientation and strategic focus." The PLA has adopted what it calls a "double historical mission" and a "leapfrog development strategy" – accelerating military informationization while undergoing mechanization.[8]

Basic PLA Doctrine of Local Wars under Hi-tech Conditions

Underpinning the new professionalism of the PLA is the basic doctrine of "active defence" (*jiji fangyu*) that seeks to conduct "people's war under modern conditions" (better understood as "local wars under hi-tech conditions" – *gaojishu tiaojian xia de jubu zhanzheng*). The 'active defence' doctrine calls for integrated, deep strikes – a concentration of superior firepower that is to be utilized to destroy the opponent's retaliatory capabilities through pre-emptive strikes employing long-range artillery, short-range ballistic missiles (SRBMs) and precision guided munitions. The new doctrine and the strategy and tactics associated with it have been influenced by the lessons of Gulf War I in 1991 and the Iraq War of 2003, both of which have been extensively studied by Chinese scholars. The doctrine requires the creation of a capability to project force across China's borders through rapid deployment, conventional SRBMs and cruise missiles, information warfare, electronic warfare, precision-guided munitions, night fighting capabilities and other advanced military technologies. Beijing has defined the following five likely limited war scenarios: Military conflict with neighbouring countries in a limited region; military conflict on territorial waters; undeclared air attack by enemy countries; territorial defence in a limited military operation; and, punitive offensive with a minor incursion into a neighbouring country.

Information Operations – Acupuncture Warfare

The denial of information, strategic deception and the achievement of psychological surprise have for long been an integral part of Chinese military doctrine. The Chinese find information warfare (IW) extremely attractive as they view it as an asymmetric tool that will enable them to overcome their relative backwardness in military hardware. The Chinese are devoting considerable time and energy to perfecting the techniques of IW to target the rapidly modernizing Western armed forces that are becoming increasingly more dependent on the software that runs computer networks and modern communications. In Chinese thinking, IW presents a level playing field for projecting power and prevailing upon the adversary in future wars. However, it has not been possible to ascertain from open public sources whether IW is fully integrated with the doctrine of people's war under modern conditions or if it is still treated as a separate but complementary pattern of war (zhanzheng xingtai). There is also some confusion created by the use of the term informationized warfare (xinxihua zhanzheng) instead of IW (xinxi zhanzheng).[9] However, there is no ambiguity in the manner in which the Chinese view information operations:[10]

- Intelligence operations, which include intelligence reconnaissance and protection.
- Command and control operations to disrupt enemy information flow and weaken his C2 capability while protecting one's own.
- Electronic warfare by seizing the electromagnetic initiative through electronic attack, electronic protection and electronic warfare support.
- Targeting enemy computer systems and networks to damage and destroy critical machines and networks and the data stored on them.
- Physical destruction of enemy sources like information infrastructure such as C4ISR through the application of firepower.

The Chinese call their pursuit of information warfare and other hi-tech means to counter the overwhelmingly superior conventional military capabilities of the Western Alliance "acupuncture warfare", a term that first surfaced in a 1997 PLA National Defence University publication entitled "On Commanding Warfighting under High-Tech Conditions".[11] Acupuncture warfare (also called "paralysis warfare"[12]) was described as "Paralysing the enemy by attacking the weak link of his command, control, communications and information as if hitting his acupuncture point in *kung fu* combat." Acupuncture warfare is a form of asymmetrical warfare dating back to the teachings of Sun Tzu, China's pre-eminent military strategist from the 5th century BC. For quite some time now the PLA has been simulating computer virus attacks in its military exercises.

According to a US Congressional Research Service report entitled "Cyberwarfare", authored by Steve Hildreth, China is developing a strategic information warfare unit called "Net Force" to neutralize the military capabilities of technologically superior adversaries.[13] This new information warfare unit will "wage combat through computer networks to manipulate enemy information systems spanning spare parts deliveries to fire control and guidance systems." The PLA's research into the theoretical aspects of information warfare is fairly advanced and it is well on its way to developing a coordinated and integrated information warfare doctrine.

Chong-Pin Lee, Vice Chairman of Taiwan's Mainland Affairs Council, says Beijing is re-directing its emphasis away from nuclear deterrence to this new asymmetrical strategy and its "overarching purpose is to deter the United States from intervening around China's peripheries and to seize Taiwan with minimum bloodshed and destruction."[14] In another five to 10 years China will develop depth and sophistication in its understanding and handling of information warfare techniques and information operations. With Indian society becoming increasingly dependent on automated data processing and vast computer networks, India will also become extremely vulnerable to such information warfare techniques. The fact that it can be practiced from virtually any place on the earth even during peacetime makes acupuncture warfare even more diabolical. India can ill-afford to ignore this new challenge to its security.

The Chinese call their pursuit of information warfare and other hi-tech means to counter the overwhelmingly superior conventional military capabilities of the Western Alliance "acupuncture warfare", a term that first surfaced in a 1997 PLA National Defence University publication.

Defence analysts Timperlake and Triplett have written that economic, political and social systems are essentially unprotected against Chinese information warfare attack. In their view, China has adopted a comprehensive strategy to further its information warfare plans:[15] Information warfare has the support of the top PLA brass; the PLA's best strategists and defence scientists have had extensive open discussions about information warfare; the PLA is conducting military exercises in information warfare; it is expanding its already strong signals intelligence (SIGINT) capability in Cuba; and, the PLA is buying the hardware necessary. As supercomputers require huge capital investments, a strong political and financial commitment is implied. The Chinese are recruiting scientists and technicians and are building related weapons such as high-powered microwave weapons.

The PLA is acutely conscious of its continuing relative backwardness in information technologies. To prepare itself for a conflict with an RMA-ready opponent, China's military thinkers recommend that China must:[16] Close the information gap; network all forces; attack the enemy's C3I to paralyze it; use directed energy weapons; and computer viruses. Physical measures include the use of submarine-launched munitions; anti-satellite weapons; forces to prevent a logistics build-up; and special operations raids. Timothy Thomas, of the Foreign Military Studies Office at Fort Leavenworth, has written about a 1999 "network battle" fought between Chinese and American "hackers after the US bombed the Chinese embassy in Belgrade".[17]

China's military thinkers recommend that China must: Close the information gap; network all forces; attack the enemy's C3I to paralyze it; use directed energy weapons; and computer viruses.

Cyberwarfare

Developing cyberwarfare capabilities is seen is presenting a level playing field in an otherwise David versus Goliath scenario as Chinese hardware is no match for the weapons technology fielded today by the US and its allies. Recent cyber attacks directed against Taiwan and the US are indicative of the efforts to develop new techniques, viruses and logic bombs. Information warfare will be crucial in the opening phases of a war aimed at the re-unification of Taiwan or a border conflict with India as it will be important to knock out the adversary's communications infrastructure by cyber as well as physical means. A private army of young civilian hackers on whom the state can bank during crises is being developed for this purpose besides the employment of regular PLA personnel.[18] China is known to have called on its citizens to join this national endeavour and, in about a decade, the world can expect to be confronted with over a million "laptop warriors" who will use China's rapidly expanding broadband networks to disrupt and even subvert military and civilian computer networks the world over from the safety and comfort of their homes.

Compared with China's historically reactive stance of luring the enemy in deep and destroying him through strategic defence, the present doctrine is essentially pro-active and seeks to take the battle into enemy territory. It also strives to achieve surprise in a pro-active manner that is demonstrated by new "quick-strike" tactics. The aim is to catch the enemy unprepared in order to inflict substantial damage on strategic targets and disrupt logistics to gain psychological ascendancy. While the land frontier is expected to continue to generate some local tensions, the CMC has identified space and the oceans as the new areas where future conflict might take place.

The Chinese have rejected the doctrine of deterrence as, in their view, it is associated with imperialism, amounts to military blackmail, glorifies the use of force and would be an empty threat if not substantiated by tangible power.[19] The "active defence" doctrine also calls for integrated deep strikes a concentration of superior firepower that is to be utilized to destroy the opponent's retaliatory capabilities by employing long-range artillery, short-range ballistic missiles (SRBMs) and precision guided munitions. The doctrine emphasizes the effective use of advanced equipment wielded by elite units, with a focus on joint operations. The overall aim in this "limited war under hi-tech conditions" doctrine is to cause heavy attrition and disrupt the enemy's combat forces and logistics so as to bring about a negotiated end to the conflict or dictate terms if possible.

India should adopt an inter-ministerial, inter-departmental, inter-Services, multi-agency approach to dealing with emerging cyber warfare threats and must develop appropriate responses. A nodal agency must be nominated to spearhead India's cyberwar effort. The armed forces must be part of this effort from the very beginning so that emerging tactics, techniques and procedures can be incorporated into doctrine and training. The strategy must be defensive to guard India's vulnerable assets, such as military command and control networks and civilian infrastructure dependent on the use of cyber space, as well as offensive to disrupt the adversary's C4I2SR and develop leverages that can be exploited at the appropriate time. With some of the finest software brains in the world available to India, it should not prove to be an insurmountable challenge. This is too important a field to allow the traditional Indian approach digging heads into the sand while waiting for the threat to go away to hold sway and react only when the enemy has reached Panipat and is knocking on the gates of Delhi. In this case, the nothingness of cyberspace connects Beijing and hundreds of other Chinese cities directly with Delhi and Mumbai, and Kolkata, and Chennai, and Bangalore and Hyderabad...

Notes

1 "Chinese Cyber Spies Hack Indian Embassy in US", *Times of India*, March 30, 2009.

2 Saibal Dasgupta, "China Keeps E-vigil on its Borders", *Times of India*, June 13, 2007.

3 Ka Po Ng, *Interpreting China's Military Power: Doctrine Makes Readiness"* (Abingdon, Oxon: Frank Cass, 2005), p. 21.

4 Western governments and analysts are using both the terms "informationisation" and "informationalisation" inter-changeably. It has not been possible to get an exact equivalent to the corresponding Chinese phrase from an authoritative source. From the point of view of language aesthetics and phonetics, the term informationisation is preferred here. It is also to be noted that the Chinese themselves now increasingly prefer the term informationisation in their writings.

5 *China's National Defence in 2004,* White Paper on national defence published by the Govt of the People's Republic of China.

6 Zhou Fangyin, "The Impact of Information Revolution upon Military Affairs and Security", *Contemporary International Relations,* 7 (2001), p. 28.

7 "China's Military Power: An Assessment from Open Sources", Testimony of Richard D. Fisher, Jr., International Assessment and Strategy Centre, before the Armed Services Committee of the US House of Representatives, July 27, 2005; www.strategycenter.net.

8 Ka Po Ng, *Interpreting China's Military Power: Doctrine Makes Readiness"* (Abingdon, Oxon: Frank Cass, 2005), p. 109.

9 Ibid.

10 Ibid.

11 Barbara Opall-Rome, "PLA Pursues Acupuncture Warfare", *Defense News*, Springfield, Virginia (USA), March 1, 1999.

12 "According to the Taiwanese Ministry of National Defence, China is shifting from deterrence-based strategy to pre-emptive strike strategy... 'Paralysis warfare features web-based information warfare, saturation ballistic missile attacks, joint precision strikes and seizure of the enemy's capital city by special operation units... Such tactics will become major options for the Chinese military in its choice of modes of modes of attack..." Srikanth Kondapalli, *A Great Leap Forward Modernization: China's Armed Forces in 2003",* Centre for China Studies, National Chengchi University, Taiwan, 2005, p. 27, cited from Brian Hsu, "China Developing 'Paralysis Warfare", Taipei Times, October 8, 2003, FBIS-CHI-2003-1008, October 10, 2003.

13 Jason Sherman, "Report: China Developing Force to Tackle Information Warfare", *Defense News,* November 27, 2000.

14 Robert Karniol, "Power to the People", *Jane's Defence Weekly,* Surrey (UK), July 12, 2000.

15 Edward Timperlake and William C. Triplott III, *Red Dragon Rising: Communist China's Military Threat to America* (Washington, D.C.: Regnery Publishing, Inc., 1999).

16 J.S. Bajwa, *Modernisation of the PLA: Gauging its Latent Future Potential,* (New Delhi, Lancer Publishers, 2002), p. 216. (Cited from Michael Pillsbury, "PLA Capabilities in the 21st Century: How does China Assess its Future Security Needs?" Article in Larry M. Wortzel, ed. *The Chinese Armed Forces in the 21st Century, pp 113-114.*

17 Greg Keizer, "China Develops Cyberwar First Strike Strategy: Viruses could Attack Overseas Computers", Computerworld.com, May 30, 2007, http://www.pcadvisor.co.uk/news/index.cfm?newsid=9527

18 Mac William Bishop, China's Cyberwarriors, *Foreign Policy, September/October 2006,* http://www.foreignpolicy.com/story/cms.php?story_id=3553

19 Colonel Narendra Singh, "Chinese Armed Forces", *USI Journal*, New Delhi, October-December 1998, pp. 587-608.

Post Elections Scenario
national security strategy

BY MAJ GEN GD BAKSHI

A DEMOCRACY RENEWS AND reinvents itself every five years when elections are held to change or renew the mandates to govern. Only a Democratic dispensation therefore can reinvent itself and change strategic directions, if needed, in a non-linear fashion. That is what the world's strongest democracy in the United States has just done. The Obama administration represents a non-linear change of direction from its predecessing regime. At the time of writing, the world's largest democracy with an electorate of over 670 million is now going to the hustings. It provides an opportunity to take stock and reinvent itself and effect broad strategic changes in direction, wherever needed.

> Above all it must be remembered "If you do not have a strategy of your own, you will soon become a part of someone else's strategy". This is a pitfall that India must consciously seek to avoid. A great state in the Bismarckian context in Europe was characterized by this one litmus test – it was able to decide on its own whether it would engage in war or not. It did not look over its shoulders for clearances or nods from any other nation.

The next administration in New Delhi will therefore have to begin the redefinition and reappraisal process at the outset of its term and set the compass for the next decadal cycle. There is a dire need in the Indian context for long term overviews and a non-partisan consensus on security and foreign policy issues. Such a consensus did exist in the initial decades after Independence. However, ever since the 1990s, the growth of identity based politics has brought about a sharp polarization in the Indian polity. This has had an adverse impact on policy formulation and adoption of long term vision and overviews. In this sphere India presents a sharp contrast to China. Chinese security policies span a significant long term horizon and are characterized by an impressive level of consensus and continuity. To be effective, Indian policy formulation will have to generate these long term perspectives/overviews and strive for consensus and continuity in the core areas. It could make a good beginning by articulating and putting in the open domain its national security strategy. India today faces tremendous challenges from the natural and social environment. However, Arnold Toynbee assures us that great civilizations in the past, have only arisen in response to such great challenges.

Evaluation of Indian Grand Strategic Practice

The post Independence era was characterized by Nehruvian idealism and an exaggerated emphasis on Soft Power as opposed to a Realist or a Hard Power based approach. However, the policy of non-alignment initially served India very well and enabled it to get the best of both the blocs. Its neutral stance conferred on it a Soft Power advantage almost at par with Swiss neutrality in Europe during the World Wars. This enabled India to play an activist role in international diplomacy which was far in excess of its Hard Power capabilities. Unfortunately India's military adversaries subscribed entirely to a Realist and Hard Power approach. Pakistan's strategic competition with India led it to align itself with extra-regional balancers to overcome India's natural advantage of size and resources. Membership of SEATO and CENTO alliances gave Pakistan a tremendous military windfall. Pakistan in fact acquired a substantial military edge over India in key weapon systems like main battle tanks (MBT), fighter aircraft and artillery. The leadership of Communist China had emerged from a ruthless civil war and Japanese atrocities during the Second World War. They had a very Realist, Hard Power approach based on realpolitik. They had little patience with India's perceived notions of a Soft Power based approach to an exaggerated role in international affairs.

The 1962 Sino-Indian War was just a tactical engagement in which India suffered a traumatic and uncalled for humiliation. This battle is hardly remembered in China. However it had a very disproportionate impact on the Indian national psyche. It resulted in the tragic demise of Pandit Nehru and India's Soft Power based approach to foreign policy. For a decade India had been underfunding its defense and deliberately marginalizing and downgrading its armed forces. A decade of severe neglect of Hard Power capabilities caused India a major loss of prestige. This ended the pacific Nehruvian approach. India was forced to expand and modernize its Armed Forces. Pakistan watched this process with trepidation. It saw its local military edge fast eroding and cynically decided to press it home while it lasted. Zulfikar Ali Bhutto aligned Pakistan very closely with China. He convinced Ayub Khan that 1965 was Pakistan's last chance to grab Kashmir by force. In Aug-Sep 1965 Pakistan gambled and lost. The Indian leadership under Lal Bahadur Shastri displayed the political will and resolve to transfer the war to Pakistan's territory. Even though the Indian Armed Forces had been caught half way in their modernization and expansion process and were in a great state of flux and transition, they gave a reasonably good account of themselves. Pakistan was forced to recoil from Kashmir and its First Armoured Division was destroyed at Khem Kharan. In the final analysis, the 1965 War was an inconclusive stalemate.

The Onset of Hard Realism. The onset of hard realism in the Indian foreign policy approach can be traced to the Indira Gandhi era. She had learnt her lessons from her father's tragic over-reliance on Soft Power and a persoanlized diplomacy approach to national security. Indira Gandhi turned to the Soviet Union to balance the China-Pakistan alliance. The Soviet Union heavily subsidized India's military build up. The Indian military leadership had learnt a great deal in the 1965 War when it was able to graduate from the tactical level to the level of Operational Art. By 1971, when the next major challenge came up with Pakistan's genocidal crack down in Bangladesh, India was ready. As 10 million refugees were driven into India, India's new political leadership took the bold and courageous decision to react in a forceful and decisive manner. The armed forces asked for time to prepare fully and mount operations in winter when risks of Chinese intervention would be minimized. The political leadership accepted this professional advice. 1971 was India's finest hour. India decisively defeated Pakistan and for the first time after World War II, created a new nation state with the force of arms. Pakistan was cut in two and over 93,000 POWs were taken in a classic tri-service campaign. India had deliberatly restructured the security scenario in South Asia to establish its unquestionable pre-eminence as a major regional power. In 1974 India carried out a peaceful nuclear explosion and ushered in what Paul Bracken calls, the "Second Nuclear Age, at the global level."

Erosion of the Post-1971 Gains. Unfortunately, thereafter the Indian nation-state seemed to enter a phase of geopolitical decline. The Soviet Invasion of Afghanistan made Pakistan once more a frontline state. For renting out its territory for the CIA's Afghan Jihad, it received huge amounts of military and economic aid. To prevent Soviet retaliation, China built Pakistan up into a clandestine nuclear and missile power with a degree of proliferation support that is simply unprecedented in global history. The USA conveniently looked the other way, as it seemed to serve the ends of the Afghan Jihad. Economic difficulties caused the Soviet Union to withdraw from Afghanistan in 1989. However before leaving it had stabilized that state and recreated its Army and Security Service (Khad). This state held out against the Mujahideen for three years till Gorbachov unexpectedly pulled out the economic plug.

Consequences of the Soviet Economic Collapse. The Soviet Union collapsed economically in 1990. The Indian economy was also on the verge of collapse in that year. India was seen as being on the losing side in the Cold War. The Afghan Jihad had given the Pakistani Military-ISI Complex a strident air of triumphalism. In 1990 China had tested Pakistan's nuclear weapon at Lop Nor. The same year Pakistan launched its Proxy War in J&K. The Soviet withdrawal had freed its XI and XII Corps from the Afghan front. In 1989 Pakistan had carried out its Zarbe Momein Exercise to advertise its post-Afghanistan conventional military parity with India. This would deter India from reacting to its Proxy War. The nuclear capability achieved with Chinese help emboldened Pakistan to launch a concerted

Asymmetric War (the war of a thousand cuts) to bleed India to death. The degree of triumphalism in Islamabad was amazing. The Pakistani ISI Generals were now talking of a new Islamic Caliphate centered in Islamabad. The Americans seem to have gifted it the over-lordship of Afghanistan and Central Asia as the spoils of the Afghan Jihad. Pakistan's Military – ISI complex felt that it had single handedly defeated a super power and that it could use the same asymmetric war prescription to bring a regional power like India to its knees.

The Grand Strategy of Economic Reconstruction. In 1990 India deliberately made a grand strategic choice. In an era when the geo-economic theory ruled the roost it had little choice. India liberalized and opened up its economy. China had done the same 13 years earlier in 1978 and reaped an economic windfall. China was now focusing on its economic modernization and consciously adopted the strategy of seeking a "peaceful periphery" to pursue its economic modernization, unhindered. India's capital military stock of Soviet tanks, fighters and Naval ships was in need of replacement. This military modernization was postponed in favour of economic reconstruction. India therefore decided to react to Pakistan's proxy war in a purely defensive manner and on its own territory. The economic managers of our reconstruction in fact were keen to enforce the World Bank prescription to downsize our Army. Low Intensity Conflict however needed boots on the ground. As the Americans were to learn later in Iraq, downsizing could be highly detrimental to such operations. India in fact was forced to raise six divisions worth of Rashtriya Rifles for countering the proxy war in Kashmir.

Paradigm Shift: South Asia Goes Nuclear. The most significant paradigm shift in the South Asian Security Architecture occurred in 1998 with the overt nuclearization of India and Pakistan. It radically transformed the geopolitical landscape. The Indian leadership finally displayed the will to power and braved US and world economic sanctions to go nuclear. It is this single step that underlined India's status as a major economic and military power. The economic sanctions brought the Pakistani economy to the brink of complete collapse. It was left with just US $ 1 billion in its forex kitty. The Indian political elite felt that in consonance with Kenneth Waltz's theories, nuclear capabilities would prove to be a stabilizing factor in South Asia because they would make war simply too costly to contemplate. The Indian leadership therefore felt that war in South Asia was no longer a viable option. Hence it made a high profile bid for peace with Pakistan through its Lahore Bus Journey and a Back Channel (Track II) initiative between the representatives of both the PMOs.

Pak Hubris in Kargil. The strident post-Afghanistan air of triumphalism in Islamabad had reached a shrill crescendo after the Chagai Nuclear Tests. (Even as the civilian establishment in Pakistan was engaged in peace parleys with India, the Pak military decided to press home the logic of nuclear and conventional symmetry with India by making a bold bid to wrest Kashmir diplomatically by engineering a crisis that would paint J&K as an explosive nuclear flashpoint.) The world could then be forced to pressurize India to part with Kashmir simply to avoid the outbreak of nuclear war. It was a most irresponsible and hair brained strategy. The Pak military had pegged the South Asian nuclear threshold at an absurdly low level. It had imagined a single rung escalation ladder that would prove to be highly untenable. India was stupefied by the bizarre turn of events. Once it recovered from its complete strategic and tactical surprise however, its response was fairly matured and restrained but creative and nuanced. Since operations to retake the Kargil heights were bound to be slow and tortuous, it decided to avoid coming under diplomatic time pressure by confining its military reaction to their own side of the LoC. This removed the locus standi for any international intervention and pressure for an early ceasefire.

Shock and Awe in Kargil. India now carried out a partial military mobilization. It employed its Air Force and deployed its Navy. It concentrated two Mountain Divisions to launch frontal attacks on the enemy held heights in Kargil. This led to a brutal and slogging match of attrition. However, India massed effects (instead of troops) by massing a 100 guns to support each battalion attack and throwing in its air force. This stunned the NLI defenders and created local "shock and awe". The Indian Infantry led by spirited young officers then bloodily ejected the Pakistani intruders from peak after peak. Pakistan was forced to sue for peace. This led to the overthrow of Nawaz Sharif.

The Penalty of Not Crossing the LoC. Though India gained tremendous diplomatic leverage by not crossing the LoC and established its credentials as a mature and responsible nuclear power, its failure to cross the LoC sent a very wrong message to the Pakistani Generals. Though India's strong response cured them of their new found nuclear hubris, India's failure to cross the LoC convinced them that their conventional military parity with India had deterred it from any trans-LoC or trans-IB response options. This needlessly seemed to cast the LoC in stone and the precedent severely constrained Indian responses in any future conflict. Peter Lavoy writes that by the time of Op Parakram, 95 percent of the weight of deterrence in Pakistani thinking had shifted from nuclear deterrence to conventional deterrence. Pakistan felt that the Zarbe Momein Offensive-Defense format had completely succeeded in deterring any Indian trans-LoC/IB response in Kargil and would equally work in any future conflict also.

Op Parakram. This resulted in an intensification of the Pakistani proxy war in J&K. India responded by raising troop densities and raised three more RR Divisions post Kargil. 9/11 brought yet another paradigm shift in the security scenario. Once again Pakistan became a frontline state, was economically revived and militarily strengthened by the Americans. Pakistan upped the ante by spreading its jihad from J&K to the rest of India. It now attacked iconic targets like the J&K State Assembly and finally the Indian Parliament itself. This led to great outrage in India. The Indian State now carried out a complete mobilization of its armed forces for a major conflict. Possibly the intention initially was for a limited J&K centric conflict. However, the Indian ground forces mobilization took nearly a month. The NDA Government meanwhile came under intense American diplomatic pressure. The Americans ostensibly pressurised Gen Parvez Musharraf to give assurances of not permitting his territory to be used by terrorists. India relented and turned its massive deployment into a coercive exercise. In the absence of any live action, this coercive diplomacy exercise rapidly lost its traction and credibility. A second flash point came after the Kaluchak massacre. However India did not engage in any actual combat. Once more it failed to cross the LoC or IB. The "all or nothing" format of the Op Parakram deployment magnified the stakes and severely constrained the political options. This only added to the decision dilemma. India ended up doing nothing and quietly stood down its armies after a 10 month long standoff. Between an all out conventional offensive or nothing, there were many steps in the escalation ladder that could have fired very credible "shots across the bow". There were air-power centric options that were far more flexible and precise as compared to a land war. The massive mobilization had initially shaken up Pakistan but India's failure to undertake even limited combat convinced the Pakistanis that their conventional deterrence had worked in a fool proof manner. Given the conventional military parity between India and Pakistan, India, they felt, simply had no viable military response options to Pakistan's sub- conventional provocations. Op Parakram therefore highlighted the urgent need to generate a visible conventional military edge over Pakistan that would generate credible response options to its proxy war provocations.

The UPA Watch. The 2004 elections led to the installation of the Congress led UPA alliance to power in New Delhi. At the grand strategic level, the UPA came to the determination that India was living in a totally uni- polar world order dominated by America. Multi-polarity still appeared to be a distant formulation. India now consciously decided to graduate from a policy of "omni-directional engagement" to seeking a close strategic partnership with the USA. It found the Bush administration to be highly supportive of India's regional and global power aspirations and keen to build up India as a counter weight to China in Asia. In the National Security Doctrine 2002, President Bush had spoken in terms of a strategic regime in which the USA and India had complementary interests in ensuring stability and security of the sea lanes in the region and promote a larger concept of strategic community in Asia . This policy saw promotion of American interests through a wider balance of power between Japan, China and India. The USA tried to enroll India into a concert of democracies formed by the USA-Japan-India-Australia quadilateral. The UPA administration had invested major political capital in the nuclear deal and the 123 Agreement with the USA that would end India's technological quarantine and the post nuclear sanctions. This resulted in a fierce and acrimonious debate within the country that led to a keenly contested vote of confidence. The opposition felt that India was aligning itself far too closely with the USA at the cost of its time tested relations with Russia, which was still the primary source of high tech arms for India. Too close an embrace with the USA it was felt was painting India into a corner in

Asia - with Russia, China and Iran increasingly adopting strident anti-American postures. Was the world still as uni-polar as the UPAs Grand Strategy seemed to assume as its anchor premise? The world had changed very much since 1990. Some felt it had transited from a purely uni-polar to an asymmetric uni-polar configuration where even though there was no global peer competitor to US military power, countries like Russia and China could successfully challenge it in their own regional spheres of influence. The Russian invasion of Georgia clearly vindicated this assessment.

Though the Nuclear Deal had removed technology sanctions and enabled India to buy Uranium from Kazakhstan and Reactors from Russia and France, detractors felt that there had been hidden costs. Critics felt that relations with Russia had become frosty and major arms deals were turning acrimonious as a result. They complained that India was virtually compelled to distance itself from Iran (which had been its strategic ally in the struggle against Pakistan's Taliban in Afghanistan). About 21.1 percent of India's energy imports are sourced from Iran. China gained a great deal of traction in Iran at the cost of India. China signed a massive US $70 billion deal for the development of the Yadavaran oil field in Iran. It has signed a deal for the supply of some 350 million metric tons of LNG from Iran for the next 25 years. This deal is worth over a US $100 billion. Iran-China trade now has crossed US $20 billion annually and China is the second highest exporter to Iran. In contrast, five Indian energy deals signed earlier with Iran failed to fructify. America itself has now made peace overtures to Iran which leave India in a self painted corner.

Despite its booming economy why is it taking so long for India to translate this into a clear asymmetric edge over Pakistan in terms of conventional military capabilities? The lack of a clear and credible edge was so apparent during Op Parakram. Why did it have to be the same six years later when Mumbai happened? There is an urgent need to radically overhaul our decision making system for weapons acquisition.

To support the American led GWOT, India was "encouraged" to improve relations with Pakistan. The UPA Government accordingly made a highly determined and concerted bid to improve relations. It absolved Pakistan of the responsibility for terrorist attacks in India by labeling it equally a victim of terror. Concerted back channel diplomacy had reportedly almost finalized a deal over J&K by 2007. However, the Musharraff regime itself went into a tailspin and the deal could not be sealed officially. History now seemed to repeat itself. Like in the run up to Kargil, even as a concerted Track II effort to secure a peace deal was ongoing, the ISI launched a virtual sub-conventional assault on the undefended cities of India. The ISI found the troop density too high in J&K and the fence quite effective. It realized that it had lost the proxy war in J&K. it changed tack and employed local Tanzeems like the IM with local narratives to spread the jihad to the rest of India. These Tanzeems used commercially available chemicals to fabricate multiple IEDs and caused mass casualty actions in Jaipur, Hyderabad, Ahmadabad, New Delhi and Guwahati. The intention seemed not only to sabotage the Track II Peace negotiations but provoke India to a point where it would react militarily. This would possibly give the Pak Army an excuse to call off the War on Terror in FATA and NWFP and regain its lost popularity with the masses by raising the bogey of India. When these failed to provoke the desired response it staged a virtual assault from the sea on India's financial capital of Mumbai. This led to intense public outrage in India. There were strident demands for a military response but the Indian Government exercised extraordinary restraint in the face of such horrendous casualties. It was however compelled to put the peace process on-hold. It relied heavily upon the USA to put diplomatic pressure on Pakistan.

The Mumbai operation was fairly botched up (even by the terrorists). One operative was captured alive and lot of tell-tale evidence was left behind. Shrill war hysteria was Pakistan's initial response. Its armed forces seemed to be spoiling for a fight and the Taliban and Al Qaida pledged support with an alacrity that was surprising. Finding a flat denial untenable - Pak made a clever part admission of guilt by acknowledging the role of its non-state actors. The whole charade has now been drowned out by the political crisis in Pakistan. After a decent pause, Mumbai may well be repeated in other parts of India. Deterring such attacks should be India's primary national security concern. The most agonizing question is systemic. Despite its booming economy why is it taking so long for India to translate this into a clear asymmetric edge over Pakistan in terms of conventional military capabilities? The lack of a clear and credible edge was so apparent during Op Parakram. Why did it have to be the same six years later when Mumbai happened? There is an urgent need to radically overhaul our decision making system for weapons acquisition. The fielding of dominant war fighting capabilities alone can deter the Military-ISI complex in Pakistan from its sub-conventional provocations and adventurism.

Anchor Premise: Strategic Alliance with USA

Though the Bush presidency was a particularly good period for Indo-US relations, the Obama Administration seems to have knocked out the anchor premise for the change in the Indian grand strategy. So far, the new administration has been rather lukewarm towards India. The global financial crisis dominates its concerns and it has made it plain that to overcome this crisis it needs China's cooperation. Secretary of State Hillary Clinton's first major visit was to China and Japan.

That unfortunately knocks the bottom out of the concept of a "Concert of Democracies" and the quadrilateral of USA, Japan, India and Australia to contain the power of a rising China. The Obama administration has also held out the olive branch to Iran. All this has destroyed the very anchor premise of India's much hyped grand strategy of seeking a significant strategic convergence with the USA, directed towards the containment of China. The Bush presidency was on its last legs and a Republican win could not have been made the central premise of a long-term shift in policy perspective. After all it was President Obama who as senator had moved the killer amendments to stop the 123 Nuclear Deal. All this possibly highlights the need to revert to a policy of "omni-directional engagement" and a possible need to repair relations with Russia and Iran and reduce the hype about the containment of China and deal first with the immediate threat from Pakistan. Israel has proved to be a very reliable source of cutting edge military technology and this relationship should be strengthened further.

A Multi-Polar Matrix. The global financial meltdown has made multi-polarity inevitable. If anything it has hastened its onset. Multi-polar world orders were in place before both the World Wars. These were characterized by rapid shifts in alignments and re-alignments. The CIA has identified India as the key Swing State in the 21st century. A swing state enhances its potential energy by remaining stationary and deferring major strategic choices till the time the ambiguities have been resolved and the trajectories of other major state actors have become apparent. As a major state India must be highly Indo-centric in its outlook and give primacy to its own national interests. It must consciously draw up a national security strategy to preserve and promote these interests. Above all it must be remembered, "If you do not have a strategy of your own, you will soon become a part of someone else's strategy". This is a pitfall that India must consciously seek to avoid. A great state in the Bismarckian context in Europe was characterized by this one litmus test – it was able to decide on its own whether it would engage in war or not. It did not look over its shoulders for clearances or nods from any other nation.

The global financial meltdown has made multi-polarity inevitable. If anything it has hastened its onset. Multi-polar world orders were in place before both the World Wars. These were characterized by rapid shifts in alignments and re-alignments. The CIA has identified India as the key Swing State in the 21st century.

Broad Contours of an Indian National Security Strategy

- **Global Security Architecture**. The key determination that India has to make is what kind of a global security architecture is likely to emerge in the coming decades? Which will be the key poles of power and what will be the dynamics of their interaction? The world is definitely headed for a multi-polar or polycentric global order. Though the USA continues to be the lone super power with global reach, Iraq and Afghanistan have highlighted the limits of its power. India and the US share a great deal in terms of a commitment to democratic values and a liberal and market oriented economic outlook. People to people relations have always been excellent and significant progress in improving relations was made during the Bush presidency. However, the new administration in Washington seems to have marginalized India from its concerns and knocked the bottom out of the UPA government's anchor premise for bringing about a major strategic re-orientation. Classical non-alignment (in a more Hard

Power oriented avtar) may serve Indian interests much better in the decade ahead.

- **India's Three Front Dilemma.** From the 1990s onwards, India (like China) sought a peaceful periphery to complete its economic reconstruction and modernization. However China had a 13 years head-start. It has now shifted gears to a major military modernization drive that is proceeding apace at an accelerated rate. The creation of significant military capacities could in itself provide the temptation for their use. Besides, security planners base their calculations on an analysis of capabilities and not of intent. Military capacities take decades to build. Intentions can change overnight. India is in an uncomfortable two front scenario with China to its north and Pakistan to its west. Chinese strategy hinges upon building up the Pakistani nuclear and conventional military capabilities to a level that will keep India permanently locked into the sub-continent. No other country in the world has provided this degree of proliferation support to another as China has to Pakistan. China is definitely following a concerted policy of the containment of India with Pakistan as a key component of this containment architecture. Pakistan's strategy in turn is premised upon creating a nuclear and conventional military parity with India that can allow it to proceed apace with its sub-conventional assault to bleed India to death through a war of a thousand cuts. Internal security therefore is fast becoming India's third major front. The key elements of an Indian national security strategy therefore must ensure that India tackles these three fronts sequentially and not concurrently. Allowing these threats to coalesce and impinge cumulatively would lead to a civilisational disaster. There is an urgent need therefore to plan in a proactive manner and define "national time lines" and event horizons so that we deal with these threats sequentially and not all together.

A self respecting state cannot afford to act like a sponge that absorbs casualties for others. American and Chinese arms are giving the Pakistani state the military parity that it needs to proceed unchecked with its war of a thousand cuts. India can no longer afford not to articulate and underline its serious security concerns vis-a-vis this state. The fiction that it poses no threat has become highly implausible after Mumbai.

The Immediate Threat from Pakistan

Mumbai underlined the most pressing and immediate threat to India's security and well-being that emanates from Pakistan. The country presents a curious paradox. It is on the verge of economic and systemic collapse. Yet it is a NWS that by holding a pistol to its own head (and threatening to collapse) blackmails the world into doing its bidding. It has suckered its patrons not only to keep its bankrupt economy afloat, but pay indefinitely for its military and nuclear competition with India. Even as it faces economic and systemic collapse, Pakistan is trying to impose a regime of its choice in Kabul and persuade the US to pressurize India into making major concessions in J&K. It seeks to win diplomatically what it failed to secure through its proxy war. Out-gunned in Kashmir it has simply spread the war to the undefended cities of India.

The humiliation of Mumbai served to highlight the fact that the time for a second restructuring of sub-continental security may fast be approaching. India's sole option is to create conventional force asymmetries vis-a-vis Pakistan that generate credible military response options to its unending Sub-conventional assaults. A defensive-defense approach would no longer be cost effective or viable in the face of such an asymmetric war. India has to urgently manage the threat from Pakistan - either diplomatically, economically or by military means, before the threat from the North becomes menacing. The long overdue recapitalization of its key military stock has to be done in a manner that generates force asymmetries in the here and now. These alone will serve to deter the slaughter of its citizens.

A self respecting state cannot afford to act like a sponge that absorbs casualties for others. American and Chinese arms are giving the Pakistani state the military parity that it needs to proceed unchecked with its war of a thousand cuts. India can no longer afford not to articulate and underline its serious security concerns vis-a-vis this state. The fiction that it poses no threat has become highly implausible after Mumbai. Like Taiwan is an obstacle to China's quest for global power status, Pakistan is ensuring that it becomes a serious impediment to India's economic growth and regional/global power aspirations.

It interprets its manifest destiny in terms of limiting, constraining and confining India to its immediate neighborhood. India, unfortunately, can no longer ignore Pakistan. It will have to deal with it in a comprehensive manner before the threat from the North becomes unmanageable in tandem. The first and foremost requirement for the next Indian administration would be to field dominant war fighting capabilities in the realm of conventional military force in the most urgent time frame possible. This alone will serve to deter Pakistan by creating credible and plausible response options.

The Long Term Threat from China

It is not essential that India and China should become natural adversaries in Asia. However, they will perforce have to compete for scarce resources. The benefits of cooperation are manifest but the threat of the competition taking an adversarial turn cannot be dismissed lightly. There is an unfortunate dichotomy between Chinese rhetoric and practice. Though the rhetoric is peaceful and reasonable, China in practice is following a deliberate strategic policy of the military containment of India through a highly adventurist Military-ISI complex in Pakistan. India therefore needs a hedging strategy that safeguards its vital interests. It needs to create military capacities that dissuade and deter a rising China from adventurism and unprovoked aggression either directly or through Pakistan. India needs to monitor and respond to the growth in Chinese military capabilities. Intent can change overnight. China has affected a paradigm shift in its logistical capabilities in Tibet. Its grand strategy seeks to bypass the choke point of the Malacca Straits. It has obtained major naval footholds on the Makran and Myanmar coasts and influence in Bangladesh, Sri Lanka and Nepal . It has hemmed in India by its string of pearls strategy. However, what hurts Indian security the most is China's overwhelming military and nuclear proliferation support to Pakistan. It is this alone which emboldens Pakistan to sustain its violent asymmetric assault against India. This is now reaching levels that are clearly unacceptable. China will have to restrain its protégé if it sincerely desires peace.

Afghanistan. Afghanistan has always held the key to Indian security. India has been content so far to let Pakistan marginalize it from this strategic region. It can no longer afford its continual marginalization from this region. The war-like tribes on the Afghan-Pak border have been militarized to an alarming level. The proliferation of small arms has been unprecedented in scope and scale and threatens to erode the very foundations of the nation-states, Afghanistan and Pakistan. Pakistan cannot be given the free hand it is seeking in ordering the shape of events in Kabul. The implications for Indian security are enormous and cannot be minimized. India can downplay them only at its own peril. Pakistan is counting upon American military exhaustion to install the moderate Taliban in Kabul and regain its strategic depth.

There is an unfortunate dichotomy between Chinese rhetoric and practice. Though the rhetoric is peaceful and reasonable, China in practice is following a deliberate strategic policy of the military containment of India.

Internal Security. Demographically India will have the most youthful population in the world by 2026. The most significant long term challenge to Indian security is educating and skilling this population for productive employment. By 2026 India will have the largest Recruitable Male Population (RMP) in the world. A failure to generate adequate employment can pose a dangerous threat to Internal security. Left Wing Extremism is its major manifestation. It has to be contained before it acquires insurmountable proportions and invites foreign support and abetment. It is an insurgency and will ultimately demand a military response. Nowhere in the world has the police ever quelled an insurgency. Para militarizing our police is not a cost effective or viable option. It will take too much time and resources and will not work ultimately. Coupled with this is the asymmetric warfare threat posed by Pak sponsored jihadi Tanzeems. Identity based politics has a dangerous destabilization potential that must be checked at the earliest. The project of fashioning a singular dominant pan-Indian identity that began with the freedom struggle has to be urgently revived.

In sum then, a democracy has this singular advantage – it can periodically reinvent itself. A parliamentary election is precisely the time to take stock and if needed reorient our policy perspective. The next administration in New Delhi would do well to enunciate a declaratory national security strategy at the very outset of its term.

Refrences

1. Gen VP Malik, *'Kargil From Surprise to Victory.'* Harper Collins Publishers. India. New Delhi 2006

2. The Kargil Review Committee Report *'From Surprise to Reckoning'* Sage Publications, New Delhi 2000.
3. Robert. G. Wirsing *'Kashmir in the Shadow of War : Regional Rivalries in a Nuclear Age,'* ME Sharpe Armank. New York. London. 2003.
4. Lt. Gen. VK Sood and Prawin Sawhney. *'Op Parakram : The War Unfinished,'* Vision Books, New Delhi, 2003.
5. Jaswant Singh *' A Call to Honour : In Service of Emergent India,' '* Rupa & Co. New Delhi, 2006.
6. Gen. Pervez Musharaff *'In the Line of Fire : A Memoir,'* Free Press (Simon & Schuster) New York, 2006.
7. Gaurav C Sawant *'Dateline Kargil'* ABC Publishers, Delhi.
8. Amrinder Singh *'A Ridge Too Far'* Vikas Publishers, New Delhi.
9. S. Kalayana Raman *' Operations Parakram :An Indian Exercise in Coercive Diplomacy'* Strategic Analysis. Vol. 26 No 4 Oct-Dec 2002.
10. Michael Kreepon and Chris Gagne *' Nuclear Risk Reduction In South Asia'* Henery Stimson Centre. Indian edition by Vision India ,Delhi 2003.
11. George Perkovich *' India's Nuclear Bomb : The Impact of Global Proliferation'* University of California Press. 1999.
12. Gen. K. Sundarjee *'Blind Men of Hindostan: India-Pakistan Nuclear War'* VBSPD Publishers. New Delhi. 1993.
13. Lt Gen VR Raghavan *' India's Need for Strategic Balance : Security in the Post Cold War World'* Delhi Policy Group. New Delhi 1996.
14. Draft Report of National Security Advisory Board on the Indian Nuclear Doctrine, 17 Aug. 1999 (Unclassified) (www. Indian embasy.org/policy/ CTBT/ nuclear-doctrine. Aug 17, 1999.html)
15. Hennery D. Sokolski (ed) *'Pakistan's Nuclear Future: Worries Beyond War'* Strategic Studies Institute. US Army. Jan 2008. (http./www. Strategic Studies Institute.army.mil/)
16. Dr. E. Shridharan *'The India-Pakistan Nuclear Relationship: Theories of Deterrence and International Relations'* Routledge. Talyas & Frances Group. London. New York. Delhi, 2007.
17. Moed Yusuf *'India's Cold Start Doctrine : Explaining Pakistan's Stance'* Presentation at US Naval Post Graduates School Seminar. Montery. California, 28 Apr. 2004.
18. Stephen P. Cohen *'The Indian Army'* Brookings Institution Press, Washinton.
19. Ibid. *'Emerging Power India'* Brookings Institution Press, Washington. 2007.
20. Ross Babbage and Sandy Gordon *'India's Strategic Future: Regional State or Global Power'* Oxford University Press.
21. Shiya Nawaj *'Cross Swords: Pakistan its Army and Wars Within'* Oxford Press. Oxford, 2008.
22. B. Raman *' The Kao boys of R&AW: Down Memory Lane'* Lancers New Delhi. 2007.
23. Ashley J. Tellis *'Stability in South Asia '* Rand Arroyo Centre. Report prepared for the US Army.
24. A Chibber *'National Security Doctrine : An Indian Imperative'* Lancers. New Delhi. 1990.
25. Annual Report to Congress *' Military Power of the Peoples Republic of China 2008'* Office of the US Secretary of Defense.
26. John E. Peters, James Dickens et al *' War and Escalation in South Asia'* Rand Corporation Report (prepared for US Air Force) Santa Monica, USA.
27. C. Christine Fair *'The Counter Terror Coalitions; Cooperation with Pakistan and India'* Rand Project Report (prepared for US Air Force) Santa Monica, USA. 2004.
28. Barnett R. Rubin *'The Fragmentation of Afghanistan: State Formation and Collapse in the International System"* Yale University Press. New Haven and London. 1995.
29. Gen S. Roychowdhry *"Officially at Peace"* Rupa and Co. New Delhi
30. Antonio Giustozzi *"Koran, Kalashnikov and Laptop: The Neo-Taliban insurgency in Afghanistan"* Foundation Books. New Delhi 2007 (Indian Edition)

Does India have National Security?

BY LT GEN HC DUTTA

PAKISTAN HAS BEEN A VOLATILE AND turbulent neighbor to India. Since partition, India has had to resort to war on three occasions - 1947, 1965, 1971 plus two sizeable conflicts in Rann of Katchh in 1965 and Kargil in 1999, apart from series of skirmishes in Siachen Glacier area in 1985,1987 and 1995. In between it has been bedeviled by unremitting depredation of various kinds, ranging from infiltrations to hijacking to instigating of insurgencies in Kashmir and Punjab, attacks on Indian parliament and Indian embassy in Kabul. In addition, there has been a spate of bomb blasts in Indian cities. The latest horror has been an audacious commando type raid on Mumbai on Nov 26, 2008 which has lead to public outcry against failure of the government to protect its people and property. There is widespread doubt as to whether India has national security.

How do we define national security? One formulation is that "A country can be said to have security if it does not have to avoid war when its national interests are threatened or violated". In other words, a country should have the option (capacity and will) to retaliate when provoked or hurt. Option of armed retaliation or resort to war is bound by restrictions or ground rules. First: It is a mistake to start something that you cannot finish. Examples: Indian mobilization (operation Prakaram) consequent to Pak inspired attack on Indian parliament which resulted in an eyeball to eyeball confrontation lasting nine months with India looking for a face saver to disengage. Similarly, Pak abortive misadventure in Kargil in 1999,which only earned it international ignominy, embarrassment and unnecessary casualties. This dictum assumes overriding imperative if both countries have nuclear weapons. It is perhaps this reason which has forced India to shy-off war or war-like options after the Mumbai carnage. Second: Do not act tougher than you are. India suffered a humiliating defeat in 1962 because it miscalculated its strength vis-à-vis China. Third: In modern times, it is not possible to take significantly decisive action unless the attacking country has firm support of a veto wielding super power. India could not have undertaken operations in Bangladesh in 1971 if it did not have support of the USSR. However, these are but examples of limitations to national security, i.e., when lack of capacity inhibits a country from exercise of its sovereignty to fully safeguard or further its interests.

The operative concept then is "national interests". Of course, there is no such thing as absolute security or unfettered freedom - even a sole super power in a unipolar world has limitations as was brought home to President Bush. So, while setting its goals, a nation has to sift through its many interests so as to narrow them down to basic interests or goals which will then be held sacrosanct and to protect which the country will be prepared to go to war. The goals should be achievable, reasonable, and in consonance with norms of international morality and norms of civilized behavior. The goals of the Indian Republic are manifestly just and unexceptionable, and the national ethos is peaceful, almost bordering on pacifism. Contrary to propaganda of its detractors, India has no hegemonistic or imperialistic designs. After defeating the Pak Army in East Pakistan, India withdrew unconditionally after Bangladesh gained its independence. It maintains open borders with Nepal and soft borders with Bangladesh. It has not arrogated to itself a moral right to foist democracy and secularism or social philosophy on its neighbouring countries. It is a true example of a pluralistic, multi-ethnic and secular society. So much so that it is often perceived as a soft state with porous borders though history has shown that though slow to anger, it has shown the capacity to take resolute action when attacked.

Pakistan, on the contrary, has been the initiator,

Lt Gen HC Dutta,
former GOC-in-C
Central Command.
harishdutta@pacbell.net

taking the first step in all the wars on the sub-continent. The Indo-Pak war of 1947 commenced as an Indian reaction to Pak Tribal raiders supported by elements of regular army in Kashmir. The 1965 war was started by the launch of Pak infiltrators into Kashmir (operation Gibraltar). 1971 war was started by Pak preemptive air strikes in Punjab as well as its crack-down on civil population in East Bengal which resulted in mass exodus of Hindus into India. The Kargil operations were triggered by Pak aggression in Kashmir across the "Line of Actual Control" in violation of the Simla Agreement of 1972.

In practical terms, national security means territorial integrity, freedom for economic development, protection against demographic aggression and freedom to pursue its chosen social and political philosophy. These goals have to be adjudged in the context of likely threats. Territorial integrity or defense of the borders is the 'sine qua non' of national security. India has not fared badly in this respect barring loss of parts of Kashmir to Pakistan and areas in North and North East to China.

However, future portents are worrisome since along all its land borders, India is surrounded by countries inimical or unfriendly. There is 3310 km of 'live' border with Pakistan extending from Rann of Kachh to Rajasthan to West Punjab and then along the entire LoC in Kashmir. The hostility and capacity of Pakistan has vastly enhanced. India's common border with China runs to 3440 Km from Ladakh to Arunachal is fully aligned with Pakistan and has never disguised its unfriendliness to India. True, it has not actively intervened in any Indo-Pak conflict so far, but its menacing military power has to be taken into account. In between, there is a stretch of 1751 km of border with Nepal which has assumed critical proportions after the Maoist victory and burgeoning influence of China. There is Bangladesh to the east with which India shares 4096 km of an uneasy border. Recent electoral success of Sheikh Hasina notwithstanding, Pak influence and its export of Jihadist Islam to Bangladesh have taken firm root. In sum, the perils of a multi-front war combined with a festering Kashmir and an unstable Bangladesh, add up to a strategic nightmare.

> With respect to defense of borders, except for loss of chunks of territory in Kashmir and against China, Indian Armed Forces have performed exceedingly well for integrity of the "core issues". India has successfully beaten off numerous Pak offensives in Kashmir, Siachen Glacier, and Kargil and helped Bangladesh gain its independence – a good report card by all standards.

Seaward, the Indian Navy has to guard more than 7000 kms of coastline which again has become potentially troublesome with the recent foray of the Chinese Navy into the Indian Ocean and availability of Gwadar naval port in Baluchistan which was developed by help from China. Protection of ports of Mumbai and Kolkata, important hubs of commerce, along with another 20 major ports and 200 minor ports, constitute areas of vulnerability. The recent raid on Mumbai used the sea route which may well be replicated increasingly in the future. India's expanding maritime trade hence security of sea lanes becomes important. Security of air envelope above both land frontiers and maritime borders is a major responsibility of Indian Air Force, all the more critical in the age of high performance aircraft, deadly munitions and nuclear-tipped long range missiles. Indeed, the old concepts of geographical borders have changed. Now the borders are everywhere, even thousands of miles in the hinterland. Hence, there is need for round-the-clock radar coverage.

Indian defense forces have also to ensure safety of vulnerable points of high value deep inside the country such as civil airports, oil installations, nuclear power plants, centers of critical research and above all, the seat of central government and parliament buildings in Delhi. As seen in the last few decades, external threat has morphed into a new face of war such as, infiltration, instigation of insurgency, terrorist attacks as also deep raids and bomb blasts in cities inside the country. Besides, the nuclear dimension has all but rendered full scale conventional war unlikely. Whatever be the case, a country has to maintain an elaborate security apparatus comprising requisite force levels of army, navy and air force forces supported by an integrated support structure of paramilitary forces, armed police, et al. No wonder, outlay on defense accounts for a sizeable chunk of the national budget. Force levels needs must be commensurate with the enhanced capacity of Pakistan and China. The specifics of augmentation of Pak and Chinese defense forces is a function of professional assessment and intelligence but it will be prudent to assume that in the next encounter, India will find itself confronted with a vastly enhanced Pak military machine and a powerful Chinese naval presence in the Indian Ocean.

With respect to defense of borders, except for

loss of chunks of territory in Kashmir and against China, Indian Armed Forces have performed exceedingly well for integrity of the "core issues". India has successfully beaten off numerous Pak offensives in Kashmir, Siachen Glacier, and Kargil and helped Bangladesh gain its independence – a good report card by all standards. In comparison, the Pak Army for all its braggadocio and vaunted prowess, has never won a war. However, they have shown awesome expertise for instigating insurgencies in Afghanistan, India and Kashmir. Lately their chief "export" has been terrorism and message of radical Islam – Pakistan is the acknowledged epicenter of global terrorism. Against this threat, the Indian defense apparatus has been found wanting and Indian record for combating external as well as internal threat of this kind has been dismal.

India has been at the receiving end of unending terrorist attacks and bomb blasts showing little capacity for prevention, adequate response or retaliation except for issuing demarches, scoring doubtful scoring points and appeals to world community. To make matters worse, Pakistan has perhaps been successful, albeit to a limited extent, in infecting Indian Muslims as seen in suspected hand of home-grown jihadis in bomb blasts in Mumbai. Insurgency in Kashmir is raging undiminished, the main reason being Pak aid and abetment and infusion of terrorists. India has unwisely left the situation to fester without taking timely action against terrorist training camps in Pak held Kashmir. Now the situation has vastly deteriorated by Taliban successes in Pakistan which has brought them practically to India's doorstep. India has to address this problem with courage and determination, lest it has to pay a heavy price later. India has to be prepared to face terrorist attacks of greater sophistication and ferocity everywhere in the country. Indeed, one cannot rule out a nuclear blackmail by a Taliban/Al Qaida smuggled bomb overland or through an Indian port. The picture is also unsatisfactory regarding internal threats by Naxals, Maoists and such like fringe elements.

Traditionally, countries are concerned with developments in their neighbouring states for reading portents of threats arising thereof. USA formulated the "Monroe Doctrine" concerning hostile regimes or developments in Southern Americas. President Bush went further and promulgated a policy of "Preemptive Action". India is not a super power yet so it may not make such grandiose pronouncements, but it will do well to maintain a discreet watch on happenings around its periphery. It is quite unexceptionable for a country to perceive its security borders as beyond its geographical borders. There are many non-military means to influence events and policies in neighbouring countries such as economic pacts, treaties of friendship and a whole gamut of mutual cooperation. For example, India has vital interests in happenings in Pakistan, Afghanistan, Tibet, Nepal, Bhutan, Bangladesh, South Eastern China adjoining its Arunachal region, Myanmar, Sri Lanka, islands in the Indian Ocean. Such interest would inform focus of foreign policy. A case in point is the loss of Indian influence in Nepal despite centuries old history of ethnic and cultural bonds and despite the strong military links of having thousands of Gurkha soldiers in the Indian Army. The creeping shadow of China could be discerned since construction of a link road over Kodari Pass, but through neglect or misreading of situation, India lost its priceless advantage in Nepal. Similarly, India wielded significant influence in Afghanistan for ages, so but for India's inflexible tilt to Russia, USA would have seen it as a more logical ally instead of or along with Pakistan. India also surrendered its influence in Tibet by accepting Chinese suzerainty. In times of rapid developments, there is need for nimble, vigilant and creative foreign policies. In fact this has been the Pak expertise for decades and which has paid her handsome dividends. At the present juncture, the geopolitical situation in the Indian neighbourhood is extremely fluid and evolving, so India has to think "out of the box" and not be afraid to take bold decisions.

> Pakistan will undoubtedly intensify efforts to subvert the Indian Muslim community and foment religious unrest in India. By all accounts, this is the crucial frontier, indeed the soft "under-belly "of Indian security system.

Demographic or ideological threat is perhaps the most critical to pluralistic Indian polity. India is home to 150 million Muslims. Its Hindu population, though an 82 percent majority is riven into ethnic and regional diversities. There are many faiths and many tongues. In other words, an ideal breeding ground for mischief and trouble making. To make matters worse, Pakistan is pedaling a particularly virulent and fundamentalist brand of Islam. Human infiltrators and raiders are bad enough but a war of ideas or ideology is a horrendous prospect to an open society like India. Add to that, the endemic Pak hostility and resolve to "make India bleed from a thousand cuts", and it means that India is faced with prospects of increased incidence of infiltration into

India and Kashmir. Pakistan will undoubtedly intensify efforts to subvert the Indian Muslim community and foment religious unrest in India. By all accounts, this is the crucial frontier, indeed the soft "under-belly "of the Indian security system.

Pakistan's ISI has shown uncanny ability for instigating insurgencies and sedition. The shadow of the Taliban is lengthening over Pakistan as borne out by recent news about capitulation by the Zardari government to the Taliban demand for imposition of Sharia over Malakand Division and Swat. This has brought the Taliban's threat closer to India thereby posing enhanced threat of cross border infiltrations and worse, attempts to subvert our Muslim minority. Pakistan is fast becoming a Taliban state. It is perhaps too early to discern the full dimensions of this phenomenon or the direction it will ultimately take. Hopefully, Pak society itself will find this harsh division of Islam unacceptable. And hopefully it will remain a largely domestic religious reformation movement and will not become a "second-coming" of the whirlwind of militant Islam which arose out of the sands of Arabia in 7th century and flattened empires and kingdoms and cast its shadow over half the globe.

Hopefully, Pak society itself will find this harsh division of Islam unacceptable. And hopefully it will remain a largely domestic religious reformation movement and will not become a "second-coming" of the whirlwind of militant Islam which arose out of the sands of Arabia in 7th century and flattened empires and kingdoms and cast its shadow over half of the globe.

India is also extremely vulnerable with respect to its economy which is growing extremely well in marked contrast to the 'near collapse' of Pak economy. Recent terrorist raid on Mumbai, commercial capital of India, was clearly aimed at causing damage to Indian economy and India's image as a safe place for international business. Terrorist attacks of this kind are likely to intensify unless India takes strong preventive action. Pakistan lacks economic clout to compete against India in the international market but it will exploit all avenues including the system of preferential import quotas which are often determined by political considerations. Pakistan also pursues pernicious fake currency smuggling rackets through Nepal. In short India has to be vigilant with regard to Pak capacity for mischief and inimical activity. India needs a period of quiet and peace so as to be able to grow and realize the full potential of its natural resources, whereas Pak aim will be to cause disruption by warlike activity or threats thereof. Further, India would need to address issues of cyber security and defense against "hacking" for economic and industrial secrets.

The nuclear capability of India and Pakistan has introduced a new dimension into an already volatile situation. It has made Pakistan more bellicose and bold. This is a complex subject and needs detailed professional analyses. In principle, this "weapon in being" should work as a constraint to war or put a lid on size and scale of conventional war, but it also gives leeway for raids and limited military adventures, although this cuts both ways. So there is no cause for alarm or undue caution for India which can be equally bold. In the ultimate analysis, if there is a nuclear exchange between India and Pakistan, geographically smaller Pakistan has much more to lose than India with its large land mass. There is great deal of confused thinking in Indian on the nuclear issue - some thinkers are still of the view that the nuclear option by India has been a mistake. Fact of the matter is that nuclear weapon is a weapon of great power and it makes the country stronger, not weaker. Even so, Pakistan has a track record of irrational adventurism which India dare not ignore. A case in point is that the Indian declaration of "no first use" and "no use against a non-nuclear state" versus Pak assertion that if attacked by a nuclear weapon, Pakistan will immediately unleash a nuclear barrage "against India" and ask questions later! Be that as it may, it is incumbent upon India to build a credible nuclear deterrent which requires adequate number of weapons together with delivery systems of requisite ranges. In addition, an essential concomitant is an assured "second strike" capability which requires mobile launchers, hard sites or naval deployability. There is need for continuing production and design development. India also needs to build or urgently obtain AB missile capability. Alternately, at least in the initial stage, India should attempt to negotiate an assured "missile shield cover" with the USA.

In international relations, traditional view is that power flows out of the barrel of a gun. This age old truism still holds true. It is no doubt also true that power resides in the hearts of men and in the wisdom and courage of its leaders, and that it also lies in its factories, universities and engines of economic growth. However, all these need protection by military power. Actually, both are complementary. Hence, strength of a nation depends as much upon its populations or "human capital" and politico-economic systems as upon its military. A happy and secure citizenry is an important part of "natural resources" of a country. Similarly it is necessary to have a well equipped, satisfied soldiery with high morale and confidence regarding its due recognition, a fair system of pay and emoluments and "equilance" of status vis-à-vis other segments of government. In this context, recent controversies concerning the perceived denigration and erosion of status of the military (and sad spectacle of ex-servicemen observing fasts and returning their war medals to the President of India) are extremely unfortunate and must be addressed on highest priority. The defense forces have critical shortages of equipments and of officers. It must be understood that the "Jawan" is the bedrock of national strength, so anything which weakens the military will weaken the country. India has long cherished traditions of sound statecraft based on morality or "dharma", therefore people of all faiths and followings have lived in this country in harmony and prospered for centuries. Hence, it is all the more important for India to continue to project an image of a healthy polity and good governance and not present a picture of scams, wrangling politicians and divisive politics. The political system should ensure stability of government whose tenure should not be subject to vagaries of coalition politics which often mean policy decisions by compromise. Perhaps, India needs to seriously examine the presidential form of government and desirability of reducing number of national political parties.

A structured system of command and decision-making in high echelons of government is an essential requirement of statecraft in modern times when crises tend to occur very rapidly, requiring equally rapid decisions, which also need to be well-considered and made with highly professional advice. India is one the few countries which does not have a structured mechanism for including the military in the policy planning process at the highest level. There is no mechanism or a standing committee where the PM meets the service chiefs on a regular basis There is a lot of turbulence in India's neighbourhood and frequent crises situations within the country, so there is need for on-going (weekly or even daily) review at the highest level with heads of intelligence, homeland security, police as also service chiefs. Further, India does not have an overall "Chief of Defense Staff" who can render single point-integrated professional advice to government at critical policy deliberations, This is a lacuna in the military system which has been allowed to exist through prejudice or misguided thinking. In the present system, this integrated tri-service advice is the province of a politician (Defense Minister) or a bureaucrat (Cabinet Secretary). Equally, there is need to streamline decision making procedures in all ministries to avoid surrender of unexpended allocations. India has in place a fine web of institutions ensuring checks and balances, but there should be a mechanism for updating and pruning old procedures to keep abreast of times.

To conclude, does India have national security? The answer is "yes", though like the proverbial vicar's quilt, it is only good in patches. Also, it has had its ups and down. India has fought off all Pak Army attempts to capture Kashmir, it has soundly defeated the Pak Army in East Pakistan and has held on to the Siachen Glacier. It has overcome the insurgencyis Punjab. However, It has failed in Arunachal, ceding territory to China and it has not been able to resolve insurgency in Kashmir. Also, at present, India is being subjected to a spate of terrorist attacks, which the country seems to be unable to prevent or punish. The vicious raid on Mumbai in Nov 2008 has brought to light serious gaps in the security, and worse, seeming inability of the country to retaliate. However, the government is vigorously reviewing the entire security structure and inter alia, has made enhanced allocations to defense in the recent "vote on account". However, the fast changing security scenario in "Af-Pak" region is posing newer and ever greater challenges to India. Taliban is on the march. It seems fully established in Swat and Malakand, and has secured an agreement with the Zardari government. The fear is that it may be the beginning of Talibanization of the entire Pakistan, which will be bad for India and will adversely affect the situation in Kashmir. Indeed, there are troubled times ahead.

It is no doubt also true that power resides in the hearts of men and in the wisdom and courage of its leaders, and that it also lies in its factories, universities and engines of economic growth. However, all these need protection by military power.

Designer Wars and India

BY COL RAJINDER SINGH

Emerging Forms of War

BE IT MILITARY PHILOSOPHIES, SOCIAL systems, cultural ethos, political doctrines, economic concepts, business environments and cosmic theories, technology over the last fifty years has been the prime mover of change. Myths have exploded, systems have collapsed, doctrines have been turned upside down; philosophies have been questioned; theories have been replaced; concepts have fallen apart and last but not the least, even the human anatomy is under the threat of reshaping itself. The pace of change has suddenly accelerated with the beginning of the last decade of the second millennium. As it drew to a close, every known field of human activity and existence was in a state of upheaval and disorientation. The theme of the opening decade of the 21st century is to change, adapt, adjust and mount the technology-driven band-wagon of the times or perish.

> What future war are we thinking of if India loses the current war imposed on it? What good will be the army if there is no India tomorrow? In fact, deep maneuvering by the armies has been relegated to the last act of war.

All these changes have had the cascading effect on the general strategic environments as well, which in turn have affected the global balance of power and the philosophy of war. Rapid progress in 'Nano technology', space research, robotics, computers, genetic engineering, chemical, physical and biological sciences have revolutionized communications and energized the weapon systems, whose synergistic impact questioned the old form of war and war-making. Everything from philosophy to doctrines, tactics to strategy, 'battlefield-fronts' to 'battlefield-rears', combat soldiers to non-combat operators, there is a virtual shift from the old form of war. Enhanced ranges, deadly lethality and perfect accuracy characterizes the modern world arsenal. Smart ammunition, with their mid-course and terminal guidance, has made the old dud-ammunition look ridiculous. There is a fusion of the battlefield and the rear areas, leading to extended frontiers of war but as synchronized and integrated fronts.

Col Rajinder Singh has over 15 years of experience in handling insurgency in Nagaland, Assam, Punjab and J&K.
rajee749@yahoo.com

Nuclear devices, ethno-bombs and chemical agents spell as much danger to the white-collared gentlemen in the rear as to the men donning 'olive greens' on the front, implying there is no shield from their deadly effect for any one. In a given geographical area, users may suffer as much damage as the target. Consequences of a nuclear conflagration are unimaginable. The world is now getting to the view that there are no winners in a nuclear war. Theories are being advanced which speak of 'Designing of War' (DOW) at the global level and War by Other Means (WOM) at the regional and local levels. Implicit in the DOW and WOM theories of war is a fact, where war is no more seen, merely as a 'bull-fight' of the two opposing armies in the ringed arena of national borders. It is the military truism for the first few decades of the third millennium.

Also, alluded to it is a corollary that future war would no more remain the sole domain of soldiers in olive green. There are soldiers of different hue and cry who would play more vital roles than the conventional soldiers. Think of 'Smart Soldiers' (Computer boys, scientists and technicians); 'Irregular Soldiers' of private armies call them terrorists, militants, insurgents, fifth columnists – what have you; 'Cyber-Soldiers' (info-manipulators), software experts, spin doctors and media barons and defense analysts. Thus, conventional soldiers have their roles considerably reduced. This is the reason most armies of the world have been cutting their flab. The trend is towards lean and thin armies of quality for a future envisaged role rather than heavyweight armies of quantity and numbers. All this due to the changing nature and form of war.

Niche War

In the functional form, the war in the twenty first century is being viewed as a synchronized module of a 'three act stage play' rather than a hither-to-fore known 'one act play' of uniformed soldiers monkey-dancing across the borders. This 'monkey dancing' has been relegated to the last act of the synchronized module, which may or may not be necessary. Postulating his theory on the 'brain-force-wars' of the 'third wave civilization' in the twenty first century, Alvin Toffler paraphrases them as 'Niche wars' or the 'Designer Wars'. The first two acts of these Designer Wars are more important than the third act because of their low costs.

The first act is of 'Info War' – a constant diatribe against the potential adversary to show him in poor light. Information will be controlled, manipulated, twisted and distorted to show the adversary as the mother of all worldly evils – a 'rogue state' which ought to be punished. 'Cyber-soldiers and the Spin doctors' have a tailor-made role to emotionally agitate world public opinion. Electronic and print media is the stage (read battlefield) on which this phase of war is waged. Near-authentic visual clips and in-person details of gory tales of woes are planted in the media to hypnotize the targeted audience. The world will be shown what is intended to be shown. Visibly disgusting, apparently shocking and morally unbelievable episodes, spun out of the fertile but imaginative minds of Spin doctors, will rake the moral consciousness of even the alleged accused. Gulf wars in 90–91 and 2001 have demonstrated as to how public opinions will be manipulated. Use of air waves will add different dimensions to this concept of war. War will be in the drawing rooms of everyone. Gulf wars, Kargil episode–1999 and Mumbai 26/11 have amply demonstrated that war has become soap operas of television. The case of Saddam Hussein and Iraq's elusive WMD (Weapons of Mass Destruction) is very well known to all of us. This dimension of the war had become apparent during the First Gulf War in 1990. It is part of history now as to how the young daughter of the Kuwaiti ambassador to USA in 1990 was doctored to narrate to the US senate an imaginary tale of rape and molestation by Iraqi soldiers.

The second act of the Designer War module is the 'bleeding and squeezing' phase. It may follow two courses, either concurrently together or separately or even singly. The first course could follow aggressive 'Economic-War' in the form of trade embargo, choking off development funds or levying economic sanctions. The second course would be to initiate covertly a 'Bleeding War' to destabilize or even balkanize the adversary. National vulnerabilities of the adversary in the form of ethnic and racial cleavages, religious divisions, regional dissimilarities, lingual heterogeneity, economic imbalances and the cultural-chasm would be exploited to create a condition of anarchy and chaos. Separatists' movements will be encouraged. We will talk about it more in context of India, later.

The final act of the 'Designer War' is the quick 'surgical operation', using both smart-soldiers and conventional soldiers to inflict ultimate unacceptable damage to force the adversary to capitulate. This act, may or may not be enacted if 'Act-One' and 'Act-Two' have already produced the desired results. The 100 hours ground battle in the Gulf War in 90-91 was the culmination point of this nature of the 'Designer-War'. 'Act-Two' was partially enacted as 'Act-One' had produced a very favorable world opinion for a quick surgical operation. The promised mother of all battles of Saddam Hussein turned out to be a damp squib. Then, version-two of the Gulf war in 2001 showed its real impact. Also, there was no need for a low cost option of 'Act-Two' as the opposing players were the military unequal. On one side was the high-tech army of 'Third wave civilization' which was lean and efficient. On the other side was a low-tech army of Second wave-civilization which was all flab and human mass. It was brain versus brawn or quality versus quantity. The brain won, the brawn disintegrated.

> The final act of the 'Designer War' is the quick 'surgical operation', using both smart-soldiers and conventional soldiers to inflict ultimate unacceptable damage to force the adversary to capitulate. This act, may or may not be enacted if Act-One and Act-Two have already produced the desired results.

But imagine a condition if technological parity had existed between USA and Iraq, say like erstwhile Soviet Union and the USA: would the third act of the Designer War be possible? It would have been unthinkable. Pigs Bay crisis of 1961 had amply underlined this fact. Then, Soviet intervention in Afghanistan in 1979 invited only clandestine and covert opposition from USA. It dared not take direct action. In any case, it would not have been supported by the world body as it had done in case of Iraq in 2001.

Ever since the collapse of the Soviet Union the geo-strategic environments have undergone a change. As the 20th century came to a close, USA is the only 'Ring Master' in the world circus of nations. It enjoys the freedom of action which no other nation can. Therefore, except the world 'Ring-Master' no other nation enjoys the freedom of pursuing its national interests across the borders. Perhaps the votaries of hot pursuit in India ought to understand this. Arguably, in the light of the prevailing geo-strategic environments, along with the current level of technological disparities with the USA and parity at the regional level, nations cannot think in terms of launching surgical operations against their adversaries. The only nation, who has some semblance of a near-technological and weapon-system parity to defy USA, is China. But then think-tanks in USA have been keeping themselves occupied to deliver 'a-la-Soviet' on China. In short, military and technological parity prevents opposing nations from going all out as per the old and classic concept of war. Kargil-99 and Mumbai-26/11, despite the rhetorical noise of our leaders, demonstrated as to why we are constrained to take all out action against Pak-sponsored terrorists.

It would be apparent now that the Designer War aims at graduated escalation of conflict. Though each act of the module is aimed at virtual capitulation of the likely adversary, yet the real capitulation will come through second or third act. Thus, in all situations, the introductory act is a pre-requisite, where the main weapon is the world media and the battlefield is the living room of every home equipped with television.

But in most cases, either the second or the third act may be omitted. The omission or non-omission is subject to the non-availability of time to wage a protracted 'Bleeding War'; degree of success achieved in the introductory act and finally the existing technological parity or disparity. If there was near parity in the technological quality of available weapon systems, then the third act definitely will not be enacted. In such a case, the Designer war may be kept limited only to the Bleeding war phase. If there was total disparity, the Bleeding War phase may only be partially enacted or totally omitted. Also, the success of the introductory act is directly related to the third condition of technological parity or disparity.

In the age of manifold lethality of nuclear weapons, the last thing the world wants to see is a world wide nuclear conflagration, where there will be no winners. All the same, the basic reasons behind NPT (Non-proliferation Treaty) or the CTBT (Comprehensive Test Ban-Treaty) is not to rid the world of such deadly arsenal of mass-destruction but to allow 'Nuclear-Haves' a clear monopoly and a basic edge in the Designer War of the future. Albeit unsaid, implicit in these treaties is a clumsy attempt to keep the world uni-polar and prevent it from becoming multi-polar.

The theorists of the Designer War in USA had clearly foreseen its implications in the mid-eighties and set upon to fool the world through NPT and START (Strategic Arms Reductions Talks). They insisted on Non-proliferation, but not on total destruction or total disarmament. In any case, in the world of today, to talk of total destruction and total disarmament of WMD is a misnomer. We must know that the knowledge and expertise to produce these weapons exists and will be safe-deposited. Therefore, what is the guarantee that they can not be assembled again even if total disarmament was carried out?

All the same, in a way, the availability of nuclear weapons have made the wars of active and naked-aggression, as in the case of Hitler's war, a totally redundant phenomenon. Come what may, nuclear weapons have come to stabilize outward peace in the world. Clandestinely and covertly, nation after nation, yearn for this capability to reduce the threat of naked aggression. If they do not, they will be subjected to a similar humiliation as did Iraq of Saddam Hussein. Whether the five nations of the Nuclear Club – accept or do not accept the nuclear-status of the new member, it is immaterial. The fact remains they would have a proportionate deterrence to discourage naked aggression. Thus, as the 'Nuclear-Haves-Club' enlarges itself, 'Active and direct wars' will be replaced by 'Bleeding Wars', where there will be no monkey-dancing across the borders but a sole thrust will be on exploiting sensitive vulnerabilities deep inside the enemy territory. 'Fronts' and 'Rears' of the battlefield, as known to mankind, will soon disappear.

The condition of 'ugly-peace' or 'ugly-stability' brought about by proliferating nuclear weapons, will make 'Bleeding War' the only tool of Clausewitz's concept of war as the other extension of political ambition of a nation. Bleeding War is going to be the order of the day in the first and second or even third decade of the twenty first century. Nations after nations are going to fall prey for it. Emphasis will shift to war by other means or WOM and Bleeding Wars will be the results. Internal vulnerabilities of nations will provide adequate spark for ignition by interested adversaries and become the battleground of this new war.

'Nuclearised' South Asia and Impact of WOM on India

Let us not see Mumbai-26/11 in isolation. It is closely linked to the war India has been fighting for the past 20 years, whether In Kashmir, Assam, Punjab, Northeast, or even Maharashtra, Andhra, Karnataka and Gujarat. The serial blasts in New Delhi, Ahmadabad, Bangalore, Kanpur, Jaipur and Guwahati in 2008, were glimpses of the war India fights unabated since the rehearsal of exercise "Zarb-e-Momin" (strike of the pure) by the Pakistan Army. The aim of this war was to take the war into enemy territory to create a strategic depth for Pakistan. The actual rehearsal and exercise was the third part of the Designer War or WOM General Zia-Ul-Haque had envisioned. Its second part was to "bleed india through thousand cuts" and balkanize it. It is this part which was launched by Pakistan with the "azadi movement" in Kashmir and Punjab in 1989-90. In the mid nineties, it extended it to North East and Assam. It has now made in-roads in UP, Tamil Nadu, Karnataka, Maharashtra and Gujarat.

For a while, let us flash back to the years 1990-92 in India. Punjab was in flames; Assam was in turmoil; Manipur, Nagaland and Tripura were burning; J&K had begun to generate heat; Mumbai and Maharashtra were exploding under the weight of serial blasts; UP was being torn apart by communal riots and Tamil Nadu had begun to feel the tremors. Do not forget about the Naxlite movement in Andhra Pradesh. Now turn to the present times. In the year 2009, fires in Punjab have not yet been fully doused. Assam continues to be rocked by ULFA and Bodo extremists. Do not discount ISI-backed Muslim militant organizations in Assam; Manipur, Nagaland and Tripura have not been cured of separatist fever. Add to it UPVA (United People's Volunteer of Arunachal) and ULFA (United Liberation Volunteers of Arunachal Pradesh) movements in Arunachal Pradesh; MELTA (Meghalya Liberation Tigers) and MULA (Meghalya United Liberation Association) organizations of Meghalya and HPC (Hammer People's Convention) rising aspirations in Mizoram, you get a rather gloomy picture of the entire North East.

Further west while, one finds the Gorkhaland issue waiting to erupt again, at the same time, West Bengal will soon have another headache from Malda and its surrounding areas where demand for a separate state is raising its head. Moving west of it, you find UP, Bihar, Orissa, Chattisgarh and Jharkhand witnessing rampant growth of left wing extremists, equipped with sophisticated weapons. In the north J&K threatens to become a painful brain-tumor for India. No cure seems to be in sight. Its pain extends to Himachal Pradesh. Gujarat and Maharashtra, as always, sit on a communal powder keg, which can be anytime ignited by ISI operatives. Its shock waves can always travel unhindered to Gujarat, Madhya Pradesh and Rajasthan. Rise of Al-Umma type of organizations in Tamil Nadu is another major concern. Notwithstanding the recent reverses, the LTTE bases could still pose problems. In Andhra Pradesh, the Naxalite movement of People's War Group (PWG) continues to be a painful ulcer in the abdomen. And now, the long-drowned voices of Telengana are now again being heard. Karnataka and Kerala have their own problems of communal disharmony. Thus, in the year 2009, the body-politic of 'Mother India' presents a gory tale. The internal wounds of India make it a fit case for an external virus to enter its body politic and enlarge its wounds. India is in the thick of a bleeding war, aided and abetted both from inside and outside. Merely blaming the external virus will not help in the matter. What India needs to do is to apply the balm on internal wounds and at the same time immunize itself from the external virus.

> India is in the thick of a bleeding war, aided and abetted both from inside and outside. Merely blaming the external virus will not help in the matter. What India needs to do is to apply balm on internal wounds and at the same time immunize itself from external virus.

The irony is, in India, people still do not realize that they have been at war for the last 18 to 20 years. It is because we have not yet grasped the nuances of WOM and the Bleeding War. The Indian mind-set continues to see war as monkey-dancing across the borders. We called the Kargil Conflict of 1999 as 'war-like-situation' and not war. We call Mumbai 26/11 as an act of terrorism. They came by sea with a well planned objective of paralyzing the financial capital of India, nay India. They held India to ransom for 60 hours. Pray, what was it, if not war.

Still, our definition of war is partaken from the model of the Bangladesh war of 1971. No wonder, while India has been bleeding form head to toe for the past one/two decades, we have been dismissing it as insurgency, terrorism, sponsored violence or even as 'war-like-situation.' Some people are as naïve as to describe the situation in various states as law and order problems. While others, who are endowed with more clearvision, go to the extent of calling it a proxy-war. No one seems to accept, nay, not even Generals and Colonels that India has been involved in an active war, for the last 20 years. Perhaps, the nation awaits a clarion call from the ramparts of the Red Fort by the Prime Minister of India to formally tell the nation that it was at war. Such is the degree of thought-bankruptcy and mind-stagnation in India that we fail to clearly read the writing on the wall..

Defense services and military analysts in India are primarily responsible for this mind-set of the people. They are the people who have been telling the nation that there was insurgency in Kashmir, a war-like-situation in Kargil, militancy in Assam and Punjab and law and order problems in Tamil Nadu and Maharashtra. Matters are further complicated by the army, when it tells the nation that it should not be overly used for handling or tackling of militancy, terrorism and other so called law and order problems. And what is the reason? It feels that its prolonged deployment in internal security operations would hamper its preparations for their primary role. Pray, what is its primary role, if not to safeguard the sanctity and integrity of the nation? Do we think that the army is only there to watch the borders against external aggression?

This is where the basic flaw lies because the army too thinks modern war is all about a drama on the borders. This is the reason when most military-men shout at the top of their voice and vociferously plead to spare the army from such jobs as internal security (IS) duties and allow it to prepare for a future war. What future war are we thinking of if India loses the current war imposed on it? What good will be the army if there is no India tomorrow? In fact, deep maneuvering by the armies has not only been relegated to the last act of the war but sophistication in the weapon system, in terms of lethality, enhanced ranges and accuracy, has made it an insignificant act of war.

Therefore, this much ado about nothing of the future war, fails to tickle the mind. It is this lop-sided thinking of the military minds which has disallowed the nation to understand the WOM and the Bleeding War it has been fighting. Consequently, we have looked at the internal situation in India in a compartmentalized and an isolated manner. Time has come when it must be viewed in a holistic and integrated manner to understand the intricacies of Bleeding War and WOM. The concept of 'unity in diversity' of pluralistic nations like India serve as a testing laboratory for the exponents of the 'Designer War' to refine their doctrines.

India will soon eclipse if it does not fight the Bleeding War with clear vision and proper understanding of this emerging military philosophy of war. National security is not only in terms of ensuring geographical integrity of borders from external dangers but it is also preserving the social stability, political unity and economical sanctity of its interests. And the modern war encompasses all these four fronts. This is what we need to understand. 'War by Other Means' or WOM does aim at disturbing social stability, political unity and economical sanctity.

Prepare for the Next Great War

BY BHARAT VERMA

The Security Environment

TODAY, INDIA IS RINGED BY TURBULENT states - Pakistan (land boundary with India 3,310 kms in the northwest), Nepal (land boundary with India 1,751 kms in the north), Bangladesh (land boundary with India 4,095 kms in the southeast) and Myanmar (land boundary with India 1,463 kms in the northeast). Turbulence has percolated through India's porous borders in the form of arms and narcotics to finance insurgents, militants, terrorists and religious fundamentalists.

India remains Pakistan's primary target and operating ground for Islamic fundamentalists and terrorist groups who infiltrate through Jammu & Kashmir (J&K), Nepal and Bangladesh and carry out anti-Indian activities with impunity.

Nepal is vulnerable to China's influence. Its extremists have linkages with the People's War Group (PWG) in India. In its bid to expand its influence, the PWG has carved a corridor ringing the states of Andhra Pradesh-Madhya Pradesh-Chhattisgarh-Orissa-West Bengal-Jharkhand-Bihar.

This endless internal turbulence in India is also inter-linked with external factors. To the North, India shares a 3,440 km long border with China, which can pose the entire spectrum of conventional, nuclear and missile threats. It can also influence and use as proxy India's neighbors to weigh India down in every possible way.

In short, India's 14,058 km long land frontier is impacted by a perpetually hostile or semi-hostile environment. Indian security stands threatened by demographic assault, arms and drug smuggling, and the safe havens that the insurgents have in India. Fundamentalist-religious groups in Bangladesh under Pakistani tutelage, West Asian finance and China's patronage have synergized sufficiently to add to India's security headache.

The grim reality is that the unending turbulence will continue to afflict our land and sea frontiers and airspace.

The Indian Temperament

By nature, the average Indian is highly individualistic and an entrepreneur. In every endeavor, his calculation is simply based on, "What's in it for me?" He does not have the time or the inclination to actively get involved with the intricacies of the nation's security.

This kind of entrepreneurial society requires a steel frame of military, naval and air power to ensure that India's accommodative temperament and societal characteristic of gentleness remains protected from the turbulent violence that assaults the values of our democratic polity.

India's Armed Forces

On attaining Independence in 1947, India inherited possibly the best instrument of war in Asia — a fine battle-ready military machine with a formidable reputation of winning wars in distant lands. Britain had employed it skillfully for over a century to sustain her empire and treasured it as the jewel in its crown.

It is sad that 60 years after Independence, the stability of India still depends directly on the stability of the Indian Army. Field Marshal Wavell who was India's British Viceroy in 1946, was prophetic when he said "... the stability of the Indian Army may perhaps be a deciding factor in the future of India."

In the years after Independence, India's Army has been unendingly deployed for internal policing tasks to cope with the complex security situation. This deployment has kept the Union of India physically intact. But it is sad that 60 years after Independence, the stability of India still depends directly on the stability of the Indian Army. Field Marshal Wavell who was India's British Viceroy in 1946, was prophetic when he said "... the stability of the Indian Army may perhaps be a deciding factor in the future of India."

Making India's Armed Forces Younger

For a number of reasons, and despite considerable efforts, the Armed Forces remain short of the manpower they need. It is imperative that this manpower shortage be removed speedily before the system buckles under the ageing profile of its leadership. There is only one viable strategy to attract the kind of talent that is needed and that is to assure military personnel of assured lateral induction into the para-military and police forces, the intelligence services and the civil administration.

Unfortunately, a consensus has not been achieved that "Lateral Induction" is the best way to attract India's young but savvy population to the tough profession of arms, where risk-to-life is an everyday affair.

Major benefits will accrue from Lateral Induction. First, the transfer of highly disciplined, trained and skilled manpower to the civil set-up will contribute towards the creation of a 'discipline culture' in the country. Second, the superior training standards of lateral inductees will aid civil and para-military forces in combating terrorism and internal violence.

Unfortunately, a consensus has not been achieved that "Lateral Induction" is the best way to attract India's young but savvy population to the tough profession of arms, where risk-to-life is an everyday affair.

However, placing a large segment of a young Army on the land borders cannot entirely ensure the security of India. There are two aspects to it.

First, if a football team defends only its half of the field, it is certain that an adversary determined to create mischief, short of going to war, will create opportunities for its irregular forces (jihadis) to score goals through infiltration, smuggling and creeping invasions. The hostile environment that impacts India's long frontiers requires that the role of military power to defend strategic frontiers must be firmly embedded in India's foreign policy.

The second aspect is the need for political will to project the power of the Armed Forces beyond the Indian subcontinent to secure the sea-lanes for external trade and ensure the security of imported energy supplies.

India's Place in Asia

India's geo-strategic location with its 7,500 km long peninsular coastline jutting into the Indian Ocean makes India a continental, as well as a maritime power.

India impacts directly on East, West and Central Asia. As a rising economic power dependent almost entirely on foreign energy supplies, a time may come when India has to project its military power to protect and preserve the energy resources from Central Asia, West Asia, and Africa. For India, with its pacifist temperament, this may sound imperial. But without a ruthless winning attitude, India's multi-religious and multi-cultural society cannot survive endless undermining by disaffected elements.

The world has already recognized that with its democratic institutions, its liberal philosophy and its unique strategic location, India's influence will extend beyond South Asia and directly affect Asia's well being.

Dovetailing Foreign-Economic-Military Objectives

A nation's foreign policy is dependent primarily on the strength of its economic and military power. The ability and the will to wield military power ruthlessly, to defend and advance national interests, when combined with the capacity and resolve to create wealth, constitute the proven route for every aspirant seeking recognition as an eminent power.

India has the potential and the prerequisites of becoming a great power within the next few decades, provided it can dovetail its foreign, economic and military objectives and mainstream its military power.

The crucial question is whether India will be a surrogate power or be a 'great power'?

Ostensibly, our national objectives are to have a peaceful neighborhood. What should be the strategy to achieve it? Statements like "...stable and secure neighbors are in India's interest" are well meant. The fundamental question however is – "Will India's neighbors ever be stable and secure?" Appeasement of neighbors cannot constitute a strategy for any country.

India's larger objective in Asia is to emerge as a geo-economic hub that can integrate and influence its extended neighborhood through mutually beneficial economic linkages and military relationships. As a benevolent power that has no external territorial interests, India is uniquely located — geographically and culturally to play this role effectively. India's free media can be intelligently harnessed to further these national objectives and develop the complementarities that influence Asia.

To attain eminence in Asia, India needs to move simultaneously on three axes. These are India–West Asia, India–Southeast Asia and India–Central Asia. Of these, the critical one is the India-Afghanistan-Iran-Russia axis. Today, Russia is reacting firmly to intruders into its neighborhood. Her economic and military resurgence presents an opportunity for a relationship which would lend stability to the region.

Moreover, as the second largest consumer of oil and gas in Asia, the assurance of uninterrupted energy supplies is a vital factor in India's security calculus. By 2010, a substantial amount of oil and gas will be sourced from Central Asia. This resource-rich region will succumb to fundamentalist-religious Talibanisation if India and like-minded countries do not pre-empt it. In such an eventuality, American oil corporations will be expelled, particularly with the Chinese gaining ground and occupying positions that could dictate the future agenda in Central Asia. It is therefore time for American capitalists to join hands with their Indian counterparts in joint ventures.

Create Mutually Beneficial International Alliances

India's 'near abroad' is under unprecedented turmoil. Pakistan is almost split into two states. The Pakistan Army controls one part and the other it ceded to radical Islam. The Pakistan Army appears to be under retreat. In Bangladesh the war between Pakistan backed radical Islam threatens to undermine the present regime. Maoists in Nepal look up to China. Beijing successfully out-maneuvered New Delhi's influence in the latter's backyard. These regimes being authoritarian in one way or the other have more in common amongst themselves than a multi-cultural democratic India.

They are also technology deficit regressive states. Therefore, to preserve its values, India needs to create an international alliance with like minded technologically surplus 'far abroad' to out-maneuver the inimical intentions of the 'near abroad'. The international community including Russia in the near future, will be compelled to wage the next Great War against the forces of radical Islam threatening the world at large. As the core of jihad is located in a state wielding nuclear weapons, the evolving scenario appears to be more threatening than witnessed during Nazi Germany. New Delhi's support in the looming next Great War will be a critical element for swift victory for democracies and others.

> As a rising economic power dependent almost entirely on foreign energy supplies, a time may come when India has to project its military power to protect and preserve the energy resources from Central Asia, West Asia, and Africa.

India's strategy must be to strengthen existing friendly relationships, while decisively cementing mutually advantageous new relationships in the favorable geo-political scenario now emerging.

Civil Disobedience Movement by Tibetans Continues

1

THE CIVIL DISOBEDIENCE MOVEMENT LAUNCHED BY THE TIBETANS LIVING IN THE KARDZE AREA of the Sichuan province continues. Local Tibetan farmers have been refusing to cultivate their land in protest against the alleged Chinese suppression of the Tibetans. It has been reported by reliable sources that the Chinese authorities have warned the protesting farmers that if they do not resume farming by April 11, 2009, their land will be confiscated by the State. Despite the warning, they continue to be defiant.

The Qinghai province, where His Holiness the Dalai Lama was born, and the Kardze area of the Sichuan province, which is the homeland of the Khampas, continue to be affected by peaceful protests by Tibetan monks, nuns, and students. Over 40 instances of peaceful protests have been reported from these areas since March 10. The Chinese security authorities have been following the same tactics in dealing with the protests - allow them to take place and arrest those involved after they have returned to their homes or monasteries.

March 28, which was observed by the Chinese as the "Emancipation of the Serfs Day" to mark the 50th anniversary of the end of the rule of His Holiness, passed off peacefully without any violent incident reported from the Tibetan-inhabited areas. Since the emancipation of the serfs by Beijing has been a popular measure with a large number of Tibetans whose parents and ancestors had served as serfs, the call for a protest by the Tibetans on that day did not receive much response from the local people.

> A problem faced by the supporters of the Dalai Lama arises from the fact that the Tibetan-inhabited areas have benefited from economic development. How does one maintain and increase the protest movement against the Chinese without jeopardising the fruits of the economic development? This is a major question confronting the anti-Chinese dissenters in the Tibetan areas.

While the protest movement by the supporters of His Holiness continues, it has failed to pick up momentum. A problem faced by the supporters of the Dalai Lama arises from the fact that the Tibetan-inhabited areas have benefited from economic development. How does one maintain and increase the protest movement against the Chinese without jeopardizing the fruits of the economic development? This is a major question confronting the anti-Chinese dissenters in the Tibetan areas.

Apart from the civil disobedience movement by the farmers of the Kardze area, another matter of concern to the Chinese arises from the recent killing of two soldiers of the People's Liberation Army (PLA) by suspected Tibetans, who have not yet been identified and arrested. On March 19, 2009, an unidentified person wearing a mask shot dead an 18-year-old PLA soldier in Chongqing and ran away with his sub-machine gun. On March 26, another soldier from the same PLA battalion was repeatedly stabbed in the residential area of the PLA unit at Leshan in the Sichuan province by an unidentified person, who managed to run away. It is not known whether the soldier survived his injuries. The Chinese are treating both the incidents as possible terrorist attacks.

The Tibetan Autonomous Region (TAR) itself remained free of incidents during March when three important and emotional (to the Tibetans) anniversaries were observed. Relieved by the absence of any violent incident in the TAR, the Chinese authorities in the TAR have announced that group tourism to the TAR will again be allowed from April 5. The Chinese authorities in Beijing have also taken a group of foreign journalists on a conducted tour of the TAR. The anti-Dalai Lama rhetoric has come down since the end of March. Significantly, *The Hindu* of Chennai, which generally disseminates only the Chinese version of the events in the TAR and censors foreign news agency reports which reflect negatively on China, has prominently carried a detailed interview with His Holiness in its issue of April 1, 2009.

B Raman
seventyone2@gmail.com

This prominence to the views of His Holiness has come at a time when the Chinese themselves through academics and others have undertaken an exercise to assess the impact of the success of their diplomatic campaign against His Holiness on his thinking regarding his own future and that of the Tibetan people. They have been gratified by the refusal of the South African Government to issue a visa to His Holiness to enable him to attend a peace conference in South Africa and by the public statement of President Nikolas Sarkozy of France that Tibet is a part of China after a meeting with President Hu Jintao in the margins of the G-20 summit in London.

The Chinese, whose confidence in Tibet was rudely shaken by the violent incidents of March-April, 2008, have regained their confidence after the success of their security agencies in preventing any repetition in March, 2009, and after the muted international reaction to the curbs imposed by them to achieve this. They are now convinced that the international community as a whole - barring sections of non-governmental opinion, particularly in the US and West Europe - has accepted the irreversibility of the ground reality of Tibet as an integral part of China. They also show fresh confidence that they would be able to deal with the continuing protests in the Qinghai province and in the Kardze area of the Sichuan province.

They are prepared to show patience and wait for the death of His Holiness and thereafter nominate their own Dalai Lama. What they are worried is that His Holiness might try to preempt this by changing the traditional process by which a successor to His Holiness is chosen. One thing is certain - if and when His Holiness dies, his successor - however chosen and by whom — may not enjoy the same reverence and loyalty from the Tibetans in China as His Holiness. The Chinese are counting on this possibility for ultimately wearing out the Tibetan resistance.

At present, the Chinese are not making an issue of the activities of His Holiness from his place of exile in India. They understand the love and reverence for His Holiness from the Indian people. If and when His Holiness dies, the Chinese attitude to the activities of the Dalai Lama's followers from Indian territory may harden. This could become a new friction point in the relations between the two countries. It is important for the Government of India to identify the various possible scenarios with regard to Tibet during the next 10 years and examine its options.

Pirates or Naval Al Qaeda or Both? 2

I HAVE BEEN IN RECEIPT OF THE FOLLOWING MESSAGE ON APRIL 8, 2009, FROM ECOTERRA INTERNATIONAL, which disseminates a periodic "Somali Marine & Coastal Monitor": "Danish owned and US-American operated MV MAERSK ALABAMA, a container ship of 14,120 gross tonnage under US-American flag with a 21 men crew of at least 20 US-American nationals, who are said to be all unarmed according to the company that owns the vessel, had been sea-jacked this morning at 07/30 on the Indian Ocean off the capital of Somalia, Mogadishu and about 280 miles (450 kilometers) south-east of Eyl, a town in the northern Puntland region of Somalia. The vessel was en route to Mombasa, Kenya, when it was attacked about 500 kilometers (310 miles) off Somalia's coast, the statement issued by Maersk Line Ltd. said. The 20 unarmed crew members fought back against the four hijackers and hours later regained control of their vessel, according to second mate Ken Quinn. Quinn, sounding harried in a terse mobile phone call to CNN, said the crew had released one of the pirates they had tied up for 12 hours. But the hijackers were refusing to return Captain Richard Phillips. "Right now, they want to hold our captain for ransom and we're trying to get him back," Quinn told the US network. "He's in the ship's lifeboat," he said, explaining the four pirates had taken the lifeboat off the Maersk Alabama and that Phillips was in touch with his crew via ship's radio. "So now we're just trying to offer them whatever we can. Food. But it's not working too good." Quinn added: "We have a coalition (vessel) that will be here in three hours. So we're just trying to hold them off for three more hours and then we'll have a warship here to help us."

The message continues: "Quinn said that all four pirates were on the lifeboat, after sinking their own boat after they seized the container vessel. Earlier, the crew took one pirate hostage, trying to swap him for their captain, but the deal went wrong, he told the American CNN news channel. Though the ship is the sixth seized within a week in the dangerous region around Africa, Cdr Jane Campbell, a spokeswoman for the US Navy's Bahrain-based 5th Fleet, said it was the first pirate attack "involving US nationals and a US-flagged vessel in recent memory." No American merchant vessel has been attacked by pirates since 1804 during the North African Barbary Wars. US President Barack Obama's chief spokesman said the White House was assessing a course of action. Press secretary Robert Gibbs told reporters that officials there were monitoring the incident closely. Said Gibbs: "Our top priority is the personal safety of the crew members on board." The White House offered no other immediate details about what actions it was considering. Pentagon spokesman Bryan Whitman said there has not yet been any communications from the pirates for ransom. But he would not go into military plans. "I'm not going to speculate on any future military actions," Whitman said, when asked what the US military may do. Whitman said there are still no US Navy ships within view of the vessel, and instead they are still "hundreds of miles away. "The nearest US Navy warship was about 300 nautical miles away at the time of the hijacking," other US-American government sources said. No action has been taken so far, a spokesman for the US military's 5th Fleet in Bahrain said first, according to CNN. "There is a task force present in the region to deter any type of piracy, but the challenge remains that the area is so big and it is hard to monitor all the time," 5th Fleet spokesman Lt Nathan Christensen said. US Army Lieutenant Colonel Elizabeth Hibner, a Pentagon spokesperson, said later on Wednesday that the US Navy destroyer Bainbridge was en route to the scene. The cargo ship is directly owned and operated by a Maersk subsidiary in Norfolk, Virginia, Maersk spokesman Michael Storgaard said. "We have very strict policies on the vessel ... crews are trained to handle these types of situations," Storgaard said from Maersk's headquarters in Copenhagen, Denmark.

The message further adds: "5th Fleet spokesman Lt. Nathan Christensen said US-flagged ships are not normally escorted by the military, unless they request it from the US Navy. The 155-metre (511-foot) vessel had been due to dock in the Kenyan port of Mombasa on April 16. The hijacked boxship is run out of the huge merchant and naval base of Norfolk by Maersk Line Ltd., a division of Denmark's A.P. Moller-Maersk Group and was carrying emergency relief to Mombasa, Kenya, when it was hijacked," said Peter Beck-Bang, spokesman for the Copenhagen-based container shipping group A.P. Moller-Maersk, but analysts wondered, since relief food is usually shipped as bulk and not by a rather expensive container-ship. Though the shipping company has had some Defense Department contracts it was said this time not to be on a Pentagon job when attacked, a governmental statement read. The high seas standoff drew an expression of concern from Hillary Clinton, the US Secretary of State, who called on the world to unite to "end the scourge of piracy".

The message clarifies that the information contained in it came from "own sources, AFP, AP, Al-Jazeera, Pentagon, White House, et al". An earlier message of April 6, 2009, from ECOTERRA INTERNATIONAL had said: "With the latest captures and releases now, still at least 17 (18 with an unnamed sole Barge which drifted ashore) foreign vessels with a total of not less than 297 crew members accounted for (of which 110 are confirmed to be Filipinos) are held in Somali waters and are monitored on our actual case-list, while several other cases of ships, which were observed off the coast of Somalia and have been reported or had reportedly disappeared without trace or information, are still being followed. Over 134 incidents (including attempted attacks, averted attacks and successful sea-jackings) have been recorded for 2008 with 49 fully documented, factual sea-jacking cases (for Somalia, including presently held ones) and the mistaken sinking of one vessel by a naval force. For 2009 the account stands at 52 averted or abandoned attacks and 14 sea-jackings on the Somali/Yemeni pirate side as well as one wrongful attack by friendly fire on the side of the naval forces. Mystery pirate mother-vessels Athena/Arena and Burum Ocean as well as not fully documented cases of absconded vessels are not listed in the sea-jack count until clarification. Several other vessels with unclear fate (also not in the actual count), who were reported missing over the last ten years in this area, are still kept on our watch-list, though in some cases it is presumed that they sunk due to bad weather or being unfit to sail. In the last four years, 22 missing ships have been traced back with different names, flags and superstructures."

Cdr Jane Campbell, a spokeswoman for the US Navy's Bahrain-based 5th Fleet, said it was the first pirate attack "involving US nationals and a US-flagged vessel in recent memory." No American merchant vessel has been attacked by pirates since 1804 during the North African Barbary Wars.

Despite the deployment of anti-piracy patrols from a number of countries including India, China and Japan, the Somali pirates continue to operate with virtual impunity and have been collecting millions of dollars in ransom money. The vast area involved, the inabilitry of the international community – due to legal and operational reasons–to undertake land-based operations against the pirates in Somalian territory and the suspected (by me) lack of co-ordination among anti-piracy patrols from different countries have come in the way of effective and deterrent action against the pirates, who are becoming more and more audacious and innovative.

A number of questions remain unanswered: Are different pirate groups operating autonomously of each other or is there a common command and control? Who are the leaders of the different pirate groups and where are they based? Apart from the pirates themselves and their leaders, are there any other beneficiaries of the ransom money? Since Al Qaeda has been very active in Somalia for over a decade, does it have any links with the pirates and is it financially benefiting from the ransom payments?

The possibility of links between Al Qaeda and at least some of the pirate groups needs to be taken seriously. Ever since 9/11, Al Qaeda has been wanting to organize a major act of maritime terrorism to disrupt word trade and movement of energy supplies. Many of these pirates–if well-trained and well-motivated by Al Qaeda–could provide a new source of oxygen to it. The time has come to treat the campaign against the Somali pirates as seriously as the campaign against Al Qaeda.